Academic research and writing

A concise introduction

Christian Decker and Rita Werner

Academic research and writing

A concise introduction

Bibliographic information of the German National Library:

The German National Library lists this publication in the German National Bibliography; detailed bibliographic information can be found on the Internet: http://dnb.ddb.de.

Bibliografische Information der Deutschen Nationalbibliothek:

Die Deutsche Nationalbibliothek verzeichnet diese Publikation in der Deutschen Nationalbibliografie; detaillierte bibliografische Daten sind im Internet über http://dnb.dnb.de abrufbar.

© 2016 iCADEMICUS GmbH, Frankfurt am Main, Germany

Herstellung/Print: BoD – Books on Demand, Norderstedt, Germany

ISBN: 978-3-9815-5861-6

Preface

This book addresses fundamental aspects and techniques of academic research and writing in order to provide the beginner and the intermediate student with a solid basis for working on essay assignments, term papers as well as undergraduate and graduate research projects.

The objective is to deliver an easily applicable, yet theoretically profound introduction into the field of academic research and writing, which can be understood without additional literature.

Applying a classroom tested instructional design, each chapter starts with an abstract and keywords followed by a structured overview explaining the chapter's context und relevance, from which learning objectives are derived. As supporting elements, examples and sample cases are used throughout the book. End of chapter questions and problems deepen the understanding of the chapter's contents.

The book forms part of an integrated educational media concept developed on the basis of our experience in working with students on academic research projects. We aim at combining the advantages of e-learning with the advantages of classic textbook formats. Accordingly, the textbook can be used either separately or in combination with complementary e-learning tutorials. E-learning and further materials are available for free at:

> https://academic-research-and-writing.org

Readers of this book may submit their constructive suggestions and expressions of opinion under the following address:

> comments@academic-research-and-writing.org

We would like to thank Stephan Beier and Dawid Patryk Szmigielski for their helpful comments and valuable advice.

Christian Decker and Rita Werner

Frankfurt am Main, March 2016

About the authors

Prof. Dr. Christian Decker

Christian Decker is a Professor of International Business at the Hamburg University of Applied Sciences. His teaching focuses on international and corporate finance as well as academic research and writing. He has specialised in didactical concepts that are grounded on competency-based education as well as educational media. His focus lies on the development and execution of course scenarios deploying e-learning, blended learning and the inverted classroom model (flipped classroom) as well as problem-based, case-based and research-based learning. Previously, he spent ten years within the corporate and investment banking division of a large German bank and worked three years as consultant and evaluator in the corporate finance department of a Big Four auditing firm. Christian Decker graduated with a degree in Business Administration from the University of Hamburg and received his doctorate in Business Economics from the University of Bremen, Institute for World Economics and International Management. He was awarded the Hamburg Teaching Award 2012 for his academic lecturing achievements and e-learning activities.

For further information please refer to: https://christiandecker.de

Rita Werner, M. A.

Rita Werner, M.A., is co-founder of iCADEMICUS, an educational media service provider. As an author and editor she writes and edits textbooks. She has specialised in different forms and applications of language and text. Furthermore, she runs Communi-cat, a company for text and marketing consulting. Her fields of expertise include strategic advisory, branding, naming, corporate and crisis communication. Previously, she spent eleven years at international advertising agencies as creative director and copywriter in Frankfurt and Hamburg. Prior to that, she was employed as a trained journalist and editor at a German newspaper and an environmental magazine. Rita Werner studied Sociology, Economics and American Literature at Goethe University, Frankfurt am Main, Germany. As a Fulbright scholar, she received a Master of Arts in Political and Social Science from the New School University, New York City, USA.

For further information please refer to: http://www.icademicus.com and http://www.communi-cat.com

Brief table of contents

Preface V
About the authors VI
Brief table of contents VII
Detailed table of contents IX
1   Foundations 1
2   Academic principles 25
3   Research logic 43
4   Research process 69
5   Identification of a topic 89
6   Sourcing of information 103
7   Elements of a research paper 131
8   Interpretation of a topic 159
9   Structuring technique 183
10   Referencing 217
11   Academic language and writing style 237
12   Argumentation 263
List of figures 289
List of tables 295
List of abbreviations 297
Bibliography 299
Keyword index 303

Detailed table of contents

Preface V
About the authors VI
Brief table of contents VII
Detailed table of contents IX
1   Foundations 1
     1.1   Context and relevance 1
         1.1.1   Context of chapter 1 1
         1.1.2   Relevance of chapter 1 2
         1.1.3   Learning objectives of chapter 1 2
     1.2   Sample cases 2
         1.2.1   Professional research 2
         1.2.2   University research 3
         1.2.3   Institutional research 3
         1.2.4   Collaborative research 3
         1.2.5   Similarities of sample cases 4
     1.3   Terminology 5
         1.3.1   Academia 5
         1.3.2   Science 6
         1.3.3   Theory 7
         1.3.4   Method, set of methods and methodology 8
     1.4   Philosophical considerations 9
         1.4.1   Truth 9
         1.4.2   Theories of truth 11
         1.4.3   Ontological positions 12
         1.4.4   Epistemic objectives 13
         1.4.5   Model 15
     1.5   Book structure 17

		1.5.1	Topic structure	17
		1.5.2	Chapter structure	18
	1.6	Summary and exercises		20
		1.6.1	Synopsis	20
		1.6.2	Questions	21
		1.6.3	Problems	22
			1.6.3.1 Science in politics	22
			1.6.3.2 Science at a party	23
			1.6.3.3 Financial research	23
			1.6.3.4 Epistemic objectives	24
			1.6.3.5 Reductive and constructive models	24
		1.6.4	Additional reading	24
2	Academic principles			25
	2.1	Context and relevance		25
		2.1.1	Context of chapter 2	25
		2.1.2	Relevance of chapter 2	26
		2.1.3	Learning objectives of chapter 2	27
	2.2	Accuracy		27
		2.2.1	Observation of applicable rules and norms	27
		2.2.2	Intersubjective comprehensibility	28
		2.2.3	Timeliness and currentness	30
		2.2.4	True and fair representation	31
	2.3	Completeness		32
		2.3.1	Qualitative completeness	32
		2.3.2	Quantitative completeness	32
	2.4	Clarity		33
		2.4.1	Clearness	33
		2.4.2	Proper composition	34
	2.5	Comparability		35
		2.5.1	Status quo of discipline	35

		2.5.2	Expectancy of deviations 35
	2.6	Materiality 36
		2.6.1	Adequate reduction of inherent complexity 36
		2.6.2	Adequate decision usefulness 37
	2.7	Summary and exercises 38
		2.7.1	Synopsis 38
		2.7.2	Questions 39
		2.7.3	Problems 40
		2.7.4	Additional reading 42
3	Research logic 43
	3.1	Context and relevance 43
		3.1.1	Context of chapter 3 43
		3.1.2	Relevance of chapter 3 44
		3.1.3	Learning objectives of chapter 3 44
	3.2	Reasoning 45
		3.2.1	Types of reasoning 45
		3.2.2	Inductive reasoning 46
		3.2.3	Deductive reasoning 47
	3.3	Syllogism 48
		3.3.1	Logical reasoning 48
		3.3.2	Modus ponens 55
		3.3.3	Modus tollens 56
	3.4	Falsification 57
		3.4.1	Falsifiability and verifiability of propositions 57
		3.4.2	Falsification with modus tollens 60
		3.4.3	Indicator and causal hypotheses 60
	3.5	Summary and exercises 64
		3.5.1	Synopsis 64
		3.5.2	Questions 65
		3.5.3	Problems 67

		3.5.3.1	Penicillin	67
		3.5.3.2	Economies of scale	67
	3.5.4	Additional reading		67

4 Research process 69

4.1 Context and relevance 69
4.1.1 Context of chapter 4 69
4.1.2 Relevance of chapter 4 70
4.1.3 Learning objectives of chapter 4 71

4.2 Research question and the research hypothesis 71
4.2.1 Differentiation of questions 71
4.2.2 Types of questions 72
4.2.3 Types of hypothesis 74
4.2.4 Depth of hypotheses 75
4.2.5 Inner logic of hypotheses 75
4.2.6 Scientific hypotheses 76
4.2.7 Interdependence of research question and hypothesis ... 77
4.2.8 Why a thesis is called a thesis 77

4.3 Research approaches and methods 78
4.3.1 Overview of approaches 78
4.3.2 Philosophical research 78
4.3.3 Developmental research 79
4.3.4 Empirical (social) research 80
4.3.5 Mixed research approaches 80

4.4 Scientific styles and structural designs 81
4.4.1 Overview of scientific styles 81
4.4.2 Theoretical solution-driven style 83
4.4.3 Empirical solution-driven style 84
4.4.4 Hypothesis-driven style 85

4.5 Summary and exercises 86
4.5.1 Synopsis 86

		4.5.2	Questions	87
		4.5.3	Problem	87
		4.5.4	Additional reading	88
5	Identification of a topic			89
	5.1	Context and relevance		89
		5.1.1	Context of chapter 5	89
		5.1.2	Relevance of chapter 5	90
		5.1.3	Learning objectives of chapter 5	90
	5.2	Candidate		91
		5.2.1	Motivation	91
		5.2.2	Qualification	91
		5.2.3	Information access	92
	5.3	Abstract and problem-based aims		92
		5.3.1	Definition	92
		5.3.2	Characteristics	93
	5.4	Process and techniques		93
		5.4.1	Idealised process	93
		5.4.2	Techniques	94
	5.5	Verbalisation		95
		5.5.1	Topic and title	95
		5.5.2	Qualitative aspects	97
		5.5.3	Examples of refining a topic	98
	5.6	Summary and exercises		100
		5.6.1	Synopsis	100
		5.6.2	Questions	100
		5.6.3	Problem	101
		5.6.4	Additional reading	101
6	Sourcing of information			103
	6.1	Context and relevance		103

		6.1.1	Context of chapter 6	103
		6.1.2	Relevance of chapter 6	104
		6.1.3	Learning objectives of chapter 6	104
	6.2	Information sources		105
		6.2.1	Literature	105
		6.2.2	Empirical data	105
	6.3	Types of literature		106
		6.3.1	Monographs and textbooks	106
		6.3.2	Articles in academic journals	108
		6.3.3	Concise dictionaries	108
		6.3.4	Edited works	108
		6.3.5	Working papers	109
		6.3.6	Conference proceedings	110
		6.3.7	White papers and green papers	110
		6.3.8	Consultation papers, technical papers, manuals	111
		6.3.9	Legal sources and documents	111
	6.4	Appraisal of references		111
		6.4.1	Citability	111
		6.4.2	Credibility	112
		6.4.3	Peer review	113
		6.4.4	Citation indices	115
		6.4.5	Journal rankings	116
		6.4.6	Grey literature	117
	6.5	Literature search		117
		6.5.1	Information access and retrieval	117
		6.5.2	Search strategies	120
		6.5.3	Thesaurus	122
		6.5.4	Search logic	123
			6.5.4.1 Truncation	123
			6.5.4.2 Boolean operations	125
			6.5.4.3 Phrase searching	126

	6.6	Summary and Exercises	127
		6.6.1 Synopsis	127
		6.6.2 Questions	128
		6.6.3 Problems	129
		6.6.3.1 Citation indices	129
		6.6.3.2 Peer review	129
		6.6.4 Additional reading	130
7	Elements of a research paper		131
	7.1	Context and relevance	131
		7.1.1 Context of chapter 7	131
		7.1.2 Relevance of chapter 7	132
		7.1.3 Learning objectives of chapter 7	133
	7.2	Structural elements and their application	133
		7.2.1 The four sections of a research paper	133
		7.2.2 Page numbering of sections	134
		7.2.3 The three types of structural elements	135
		7.2.3.1 Overview	135
		7.2.3.2 Mandatory structural elements	136
		7.2.3.3 Optional structural elements	137
		7.2.3.4 Special structural elements	138
		7.2.4 Application	139
	7.3	Description of structural elements	140
		7.3.1 Elements	140
		7.3.2 Cover page	140
		7.3.3 Abstract	141
		7.3.4 Outline	143
		7.3.5 Directories	145
		7.3.6 Main body	147
		7.3.6.1 Numbering and structuring	147
		7.3.6.2 Intermediate text	151
		7.3.6.3 Figures and tables	152

		7.3.7 Bibliography and references	152
		7.3.8 Glossary	154
		7.3.9 Appendix	155
		7.3.10 Declaration of originality	155
		7.3.11 Data carrier	155
	7.4	Summary and exercises	156
		7.4.1 Synopsis	156
		7.4.2 Questions	156
		7.4.3 Problem	157
8	Interpretation of a topic		159
	8.1	Context and relevance	159
		8.1.1 Context of chapter 8	159
		8.1.2 Relevance of chapter 8	160
		8.1.3 Learning objectives of chapter 8	160
	8.2	Interpretation technique	161
		8.2.1 Process of interpretation	161
		8.2.2 Negative interpretation	162
		8.2.3 Positive interpretation	163
		8.2.4 Decision on an aim	163
		8.2.5 Sample case "Windy decision"	164
	8.3	Abstract interpretation	166
		8.3.1 Abstract analysis of aims	166
		8.3.2 Description	167
		8.3.3 Causal connection	168
		8.3.4 Intention	169
		8.3.5 Function	171
		8.3.6 Comparison	172
	8.4	Problem-based interpretation	174
		8.4.1 Problem-based analysis of aims	174
		8.4.2 Sample case "Sinking ships"	174

		8.4.3	Sample case "Smelly shampoo"	175
		8.4.4	Sample case "Printing money"	176
		8.4.5	Sample case "Windy decision"	177
		8.4.6	Sample case "Clara Couture"	178
		8.4.7	Implications of sample cases	179
	8.5	Summary and exercises		179
		8.5.1	Synopsis	179
		8.5.2	Questions	180
		8.5.3	Problem	181
		8.5.4	Additional reading	181
9	Structuring technique			183
	9.1	Context and relevance		183
		9.1.1	Context of chapter 9	183
		9.1.2	Relevance of chapter 9	184
		9.1.3	Learning objectives of chapter 9	185
	9.2	Deductive reasoning and research problem		185
		9.2.1	From title to research question	185
		9.2.2	Deduction of major components	187
		9.2.3	Structure of a research problem	189
		9.2.4	Rules	190
	9.3	Research problem, outline and course of investigation		191
		9.3.1	Aligning research question and outline	191
		9.3.2	Structure of outline	192
		9.3.3	Aligning course of investigation and outline	193
		9.3.4	Aligning and the triangle of synchronisation	194
		9.3.5	Research method	195
	9.4	Conclusion, summary, critical acclaim and outlook		196
		9.4.1	Conclusion	196
		9.4.2	Summary	197
		9.4.3	Aligning summary and outline	198

		9.4.4 Critical acclaim	198

- 9.4.4 Critical acclaim 198
- 9.4.5 Outlook 199
- 9.5 Interpretation-based structuring 200
  - 9.5.1 Impact of interpretation on structuring 200
  - 9.5.2 Examples 202
    - 9.5.2.1 Description 202
    - 9.5.2.2 Causal connection 204
    - 9.5.2.3 Intention 205
    - 9.5.2.4 Function 206
    - 9.5.2.5 Comparison 207
- 9.6 Advanced structuring techniques 209
  - 9.6.1 IMRaD 209
  - 9.6.2 Variations 209
  - 9.6.3 Sections 210
  - 9.6.4 Hourglass model 211
- 9.7 Summary and exercises 212
  - 9.7.1 Synopsis 212
  - 9.7.2 Questions 212
  - 9.7.3 Problems 213
    - 9.7.3.1 Aligning topic, aim and research question 213
    - 9.7.3.2 Aligning aim and structure of outline 215

10 Referencing 217

- 10.1 Context and relevance 217
  - 10.1.1 Context of chapter 10 217
  - 10.1.2 Relevance of chapter 10 218
  - 10.1.3 Learning objectives of chapter 10 218
- 10.2 Principles of referencing 219
  - 10.2.1 Logic and importance of references 219
  - 10.2.2 Citation 220
    - 10.2.2.1 Rules 220

          10.2.2.2 Direct citations (quotations) 221
          10.2.2.3 Indirect citations (paraphrases) 223
    10.2.3 Indication 223
    10.2.4 Cross reference 224
    10.2.5 Information 224
    10.2.6 Explanation 224

10.3 Parenthetical referencing 225
    10.3.1 Major styles 225
    10.3.2 Academic styles 226
    10.3.3 Author-date method 226
    10.3.4 Author-title method/author-page method 228
    10.3.5 Unstructured bibliography or unstructured list of references 228
    10.3.6 Advantages and disadvantages 229

10.4 Footnote referencing 230
    10.4.1 Major styles and rules 230
    10.4.2 Structured bibliography or structured list of references 231
    10.4.3 Advantages and disadvantages 231

10.5 Academic abbreviations 232

10.6 Summary and exercises 234
    10.6.1 Synopsis 234
    10.6.2 Questions 234
    10.6.3 Problem 235
    10.6.4 Additional reading 235

11 Academic language and writing style 237

11.1 Context and relevance 237
    11.1.1 Context of chapter 11 237
    11.1.2 Relevance of chapter 11 238
    11.1.3 Learning objectives of chapter 11 238

11.2 Principles of academic writing 239
    11.2.1 The language of science 239

- 11.2.2 Examples of non-academic language ... 239
- 11.2.3 Academic and literary writing ... 240
- 11.2.4 Academic writing styles ... 241
- 11.2.5 Principles of accuracy and clarity ... 242
  - 11.2.5.1 Be specific ... 242
  - 11.2.5.2 Omit the needless ... 243
  - 11.2.5.3 Beware of adjectives ... 244
  - 11.2.5.4 Avoid subjectivity ... 245
  - 11.2.5.5 Apply factual tonality ... 246
  - 11.2.5.6 Focus on clear phrasing ... 247
- 11.3 Logic of argumentation, phrasing and syntax ... 248
  - 11.3.1 Logical writing ... 248
  - 11.3.2 Cohesion ... 249
    - 11.3.2.1 Links between sentences ... 249
    - 11.3.2.2 Links within sentences ... 250
    - 11.3.2.3 Linking repetition ... 252
- 11.4 Rules of spelling and punctuation ... 253
  - 11.4.1 British or American English ... 253
  - 11.4.2 British versus American English – Spelling ... 254
  - 11.4.3 British versus American English – Vocabulary ... 256
  - 11.4.4 Punctuation ... 256
    - 11.4.4.1 Comma ... 256
    - 11.4.4.2 Exclamation mark, question mark, hyphen, dash ... 258
  - 11.4.5 Special characters, symbols, figures ... 259
- 11.5 Summary and exercises ... 260
  - 11.5.1 Synopsis ... 260
  - 11.5.2 Questions ... 261
  - 11.5.3 Additional reading ... 262

12 Argumentation ... 263
- 12.1 Context and relevance ... 263
  - 12.1.1 Context of chapter 12 ... 263

    12.1.2 Relevance of chapter 12 264
    12.1.3 Learning objectives of chapter 12 264

12.2 Definitions 265
    12.2.1 Purpose 265
    12.2.2 Coverage 266
    12.2.3 Technique 267

12.3 Structure of a paragraph 268
    12.3.1 Characteristics of a paragraph 268
    12.3.2 Topic sentence 270
    12.3.3 Supporting sentences 271
    12.3.4 Concluding sentence 273
    12.3.5 Cohesion 276
    12.3.6 Indentation 277

12.4 Flow of paragraphs 278
    12.4.1 From paragraph to paragraph 278
    12.4.2 From paragraph to chapter 280
    12.4.3 Iterative character of chapter structuring 280

12.5 Reasoning 281
    12.5.1 Technical aspects 281
    12.5.2 Qualitative aspects 283
    12.5.3 Personal contribution 284

12.6 Summary and exercises 285
    12.6.1 Synopsis 285
    12.6.2 Questions 286
    12.6.3 Final problem 287
    12.6.4 Additional reading 287

List of figures 289
List of tables 295
List of abbreviations 297
Bibliography 299

Keyword index 303

1 Foundations

Abstract

Chapter 1 introduces the reader to the world of academic research and writing from a terminological and philosophical perspective. To start with, four sample cases exemplify how academic research is embedded in professional, university, institutional and collaborative scenarios. As a thread for the reader, the topic windmill financing, appearing as a recurring theme throughout this textbook, is used in each of the four sample cases; however, every sample case describes a different setting in order to illustrate different manifestations of academic research. Furthermore, relevant key terms such as academia, science and theory as well as method, set of methods and methodology are discussed, providing a terminological foundation for the content of the subsequent chapters. Philosophical considerations are presented in a concise way. The focus is on the terms truth and theories of truth as well as ontological positions and epistemic objectives. The concept of models, as simplifications of reality, is introduced. Finally, the structure of the subject matter academic research and writing is presented as a graphic.

Keywords

Academia, science, theory, method, set of methods, methodology, truth, theories of truth, ontological positions, epistemic objectives, model, subjectivism, objectivism, social constructivism, social ontology

1.1 Context and relevance

1.1.1 Context of chapter 1

This book offers an introduction to academic research and writing for readers with different levels of previous knowledge about the subject. Before any specifics are introduced in the following chapters, four key questions need to be addressed:

1. What are practical examples of academic research and writing?

2. What are major terms used in the context of academic research?

3. What is the philosophical nature of academic research and writing?

4. What forms part of this book on academic research and writing?

1.1.2 Relevance of chapter 1

The relevance of chapter 1 is to develop an understanding of the subject matter and to introduce characteristics of academic research and writing. The chapter provides a terminological framework for the subsequent chapters. Furthermore, it helps to localise the chapters within the structural design of the book.

1.1.3 Learning objectives of chapter 1

After having studied this chapter, the reader should be able to:

- understand how academic research and writing manifests itself in an academic setting as well as in a professional setting
- differentiate between key terms in the context of academic research and writing
- comprehend selected philosophical implications of academic research and writing
- understand the book's structure and its corresponding outline

1.2 Sample cases

1.2.1 Professional research

The first key question about academic research and writing is: What are practical examples of academic research and writing? In order to exemplify potential research activities, a number of sample cases will be presented in the following subchapters.

The first example deals with a case of professional research in windmill financing:

> A farmer who wants to erect a small windmill farm on his farmland has approached a local bank in a rural area. The farmer has funds available that will only cover up to 20% of the investment costs. Therefore, he applies for a loan that will make up for the remaining 80%. Besides the windmill and the income derived from electricity sales, he is not able to provide additional collateral or security to the bank. As a consequence, the electricity sales become a key factor for the financial feasibility (market risk). The farmer claims that electricity sales are guaranteed by the German renewable energy act (EEG). The bank has no experience concerning windmill project financings. Therefore, the executive committee of the bank asks the credit department to provide a memorandum that analyses the interdependencies between the EEG and project financing of windmill projects in general.

1.2.2 University research

The second sample case uses again the topic windmill financing; it exemplifies potential research activities at universities:

> A university professor has formed a research group themed "Project finance of windmill farms under the German renewable energy act (EEG)". The research group encompasses the professor who has formed it as well as several colleagues. In the course of the project, the professors decide to integrate several Ph.D., master and bachelor students into the research work. In their academic projects, the students are treating subjects connected to the main subject of the research group. In addition, the research group's activities include running a website, organising conferences and workshops where some of the research results are presented in the form of contributions and papers. Additionally, the group is publishing articles in academic journals. Simultaneously, the research results are incorporated into the academic projects that are handed in to obtain the pursued academic degree.

1.2.3 Institutional research

The third sample case uses the topic windmill financing in order to exemplify research activities within research institutes:

> The public authorities have decided to support the development and expansion of renewable energies. Therefore, the public authorities support – next to the research of technical prerequisites – the research of the legal and economic conditions. For this purpose, research institutes are receiving public funds. At the chosen institutes, researchers are analysing the conditions of the further development of renewable energies. Microeconomic and macroeconomic data and facts are collected. The processed information is provided to the interested public.

1.2.4 Collaborative research

The fourth sample case uses the topic windmill financing in order to exemplify collaborative research activities in the context of research communities:

> A federal association is dealing with the subject of renewable energies. Together with its members and sponsors, the association organises research projects referring to wind power in general as well as to related technical, legal, financial and economic subjects. Lately, questions about financing the realisation of windmill farms under the German renewable energy act (EEG) have gained importance. For this reason, the board of the association has decided to install a research platform exclusively dealing with the financing of windmill farms under the EEG. Participants are, amongst others, plant operators, rep-

resentatives of the financing banks and particularly, researchers, academics and government officials. The platform allows for the exchange of information via the Internet, at conferences and seminars as well as via publications.

1.2.5 Similarities of sample cases

At first sight, the four cases may appear different. What they all have in common are the characteristics of academic research work. Figure 1.1 illustrates the similarities.

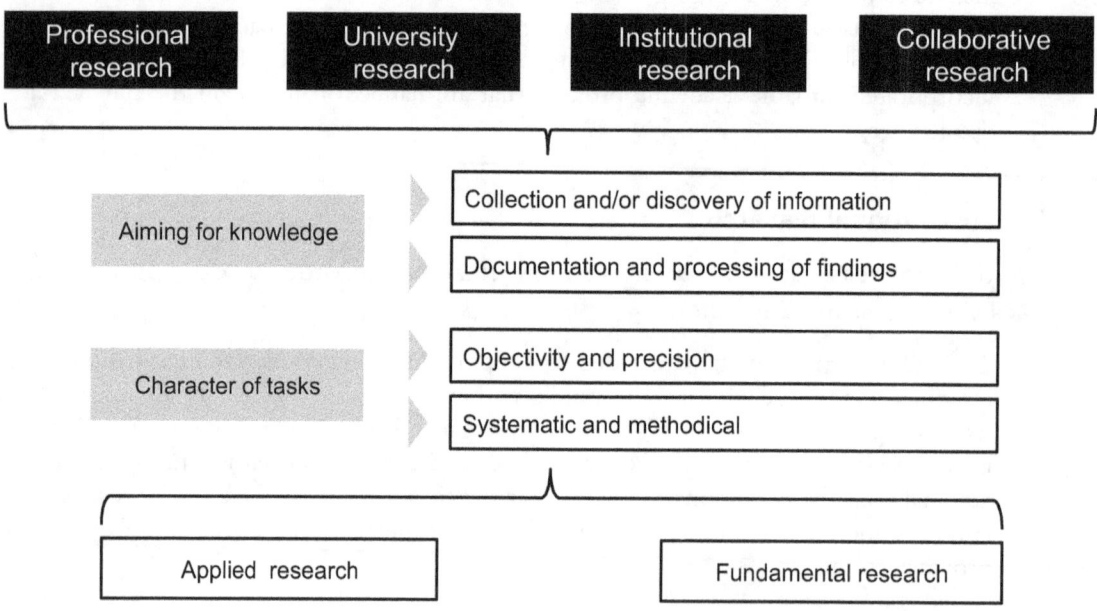

Figure 1.1: Similarities of sample cases

Be it professional, university, institutional or collaborative research, all types of research are about aiming for knowledge by collecting and/or discovering information documented and processed according to academic principles. Furthermore, it is the character of tasks that the four cases of research have in common. All tasks require the highest possible degree of objectivity and precision and have to be accomplished in a systematic and methodical way. These principles apply for practice-oriented applied research as well as for fundamental research analysing more theoretical research questions.

1.3 Terminology

1.3.1 Academia

In the following, the key question about major terms used in the context of academic research should be answered. As a starting point, Figure 1.2 gives an overview of the fields of academia.

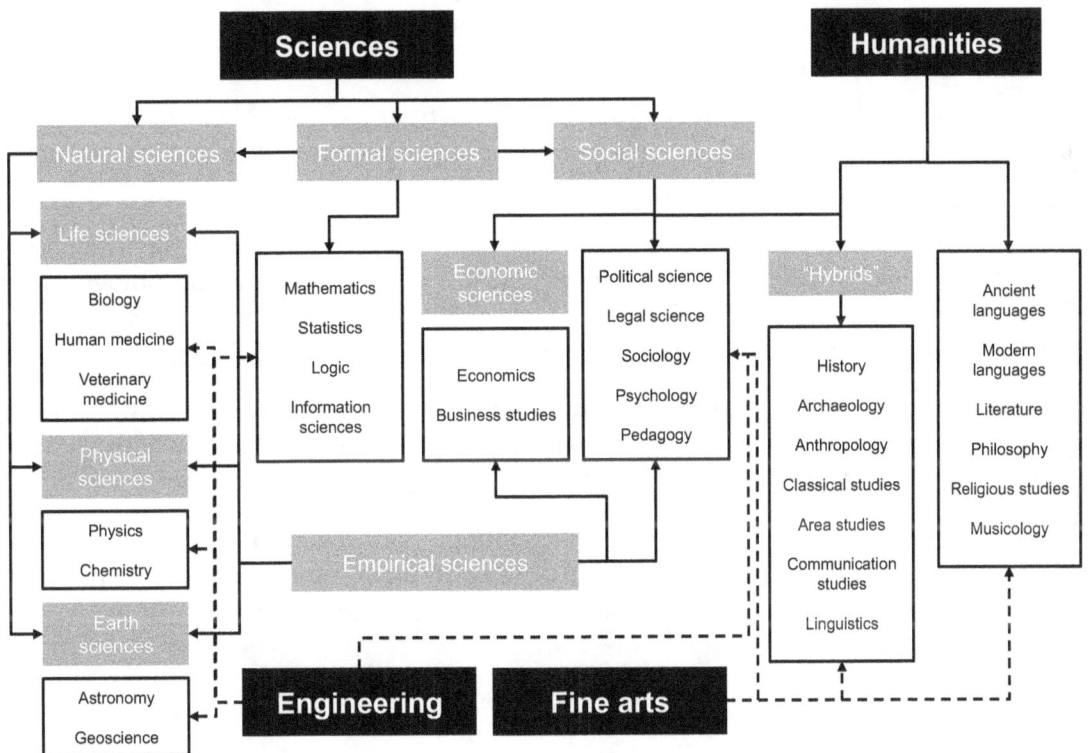

Figure 1.2: Academia – overview

Generalising, the world of academia can be divided into sciences and humanities as well as engineering and fine arts. In some cases, sciences are put on the same level as natural sciences. This is not correct. The term "sciences" encompasses natural sciences, the formal sciences and the social sciences.

Natural sciences can be divided into life sciences, physical sciences, and earth sciences. Life sciences consist of biology, human medicine and veterinary medicine. Physical sciences consist of physics and chemistry. Earth sciences consist of astronomy and geoscience.

Formal sciences are notable as they are used in other disciplines as well. Mathematics, statistics, logic and information sciences form part of the formal sciences.

Social sciences encompass disciplines that address explicitly or implicitly the interaction of human beings. Political science, legal science, psychology, sociology and pedagogy are classical social sciences. Economic sciences are a special branch of social sciences that is also heavily influenced by the formal sciences. Economic sciences encompass economics and business studies.

Natural sciences, economic sciences and social sciences are considered **empirical sciences** since they generate, collect and analyse observable quantitative and/or qualitative data.

Classical disciplines of **humanities** are ancient languages, modern languages, literature, philosophy, religious studies, and musicology. History, archaeology, anthropology, classical studies, area studies, communication studies and linguistics are considered to be "hybrids" since they carry characteristics of humanities as well as of social sciences.

Engineering addresses the application of sciences to technological problems. Engineering science has strong interconnections with natural sciences, formal sciences and to a certain degree with social sciences.

The **fine arts** encompass the disciplines painting, drawing, printmaking, calligraphy, sculpture, conceptual art, architecture, music, dancing, play-acting, prose and poetry as well as film and photography. Fine arts may have interconnections with the humanities and social sciences.

1.3.2 Science

The term "science", derived from "scientia", Latin for "knowledge", has a number of different dimensions.

1. Firstly, science can be characterised as an **activity** that systematically questions existing knowledge and generates and distributes new knowledge. The systematic and methodical **generation of knowledge** is called research. The **transfer of knowledge** is lecturing. The **reception of knowledge** is done by the reader of this book at this very moment participating in science while studying.

2. Furthermore, science can be described as the **character** of the activity or its results. Generally, the systematic and methodical approach that leads to precise and intersubjectively comprehensible and thus objective conclusions is characterised as "scientific". Please note the special use of the term "objectivity". Typically, a human being can be viewed as a subjectively acting person, who is never totally objective. However, in this context, the term objectivity refers to the intersubjective comprehensibility of results. Intersubjective comprehensibility requires that the results be documented and substantiated.
3. A further dimension of the term science is the **result** of the activity. This refers to the entirety of the findings and prevailing knowledge of an academic discipline. For example, the expression "The science of economics" implies the status quo of the discipline.
4. Moreover, as science takes place within a regulated framework, the term also conveys an **institutional dimension**. This refers to subjects such as scientists, researchers, students as well as all objects, namely institutions that participate in the research, lecturing and study process.
5. Finally, the term science may be used as a **judgement**. Depending on the circumstances, it implies either a positive or negative judgement or a neutral characterisation of human activities. In particular, the term "scientific" may be used in the sense of "non-practical" or "too theoretical". Vice versa, the term "non-scientific" may be used for criticising an approach that lacks methodology, precision and comprehensibility.

Particularly in business science, the research questions can be both of a theoretical and of a practical, application-oriented nature. As tasks increase in complexity, scientific thinking and methods have expanded into businesses.

1.3.3 Theory

The term "theory" is derived from "theoria" which is Ancient Greek for "looking at, viewing, beholding". In a figurative sense, it means "contemplating" or "understanding".

As illustrated in Figure 1.3, the term theory has a number of different dimensions.

1 Foundations

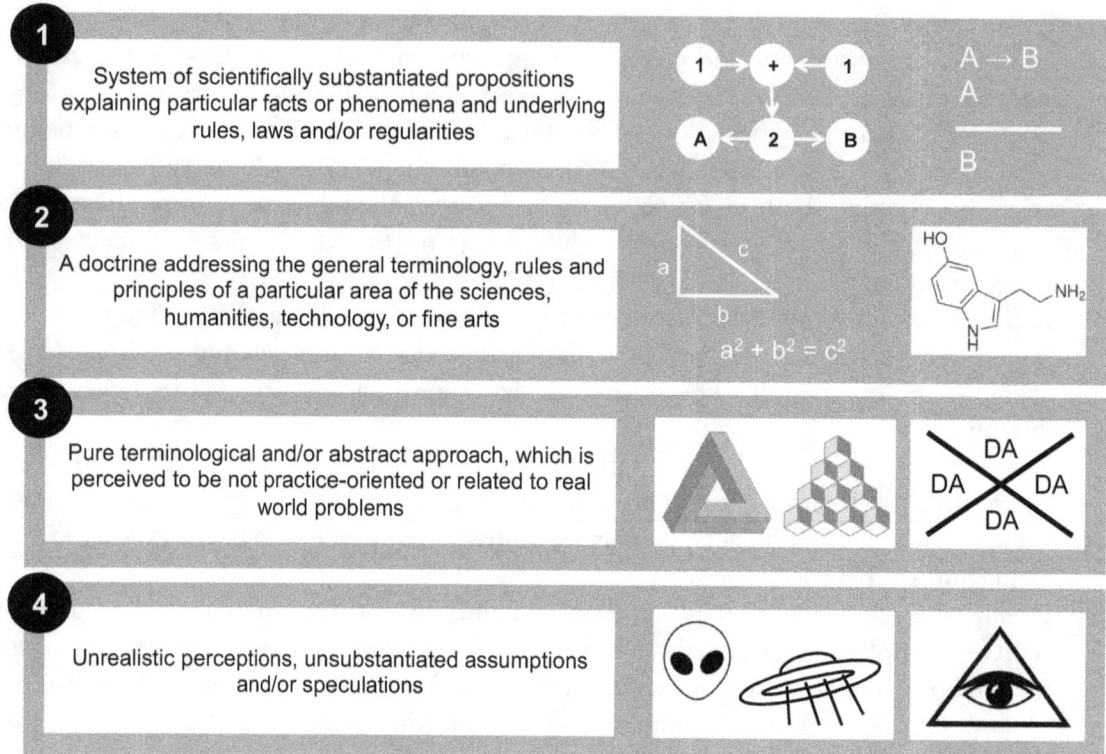

Figure 1.3: Dimensions of the term theory

First, the term theory might address a system of scientifically substantiated propositions explaining particular facts or phenomena and underlying rules, laws and/or regularities. Second, the term theory can be used for a doctrine addressing the general terminology, rules and principles of a particular area of the sciences, humanities, technology, or fine arts. Third, colloquially, the term theory might refer to a pure terminological and abstract approach, which is perceived to be neither practice-oriented nor related to real world problems. Fourth, the term theory might be used in order to characterise unrealistic perceptions, unsubstantiated assumptions and/or speculations.

1.3.4 Method, set of methods and methodology

The term "method" is derived from "méthodos" which is Ancient Greek for "a way towards something". In a figurative sense, it means "course of investigation" or "way of investigation". One of the previously addressed dimensions of science is the methodical generation of knowledge. Figure 1.4 shows how the terms "method", "set of methods" and "methodology" can be distinguished.

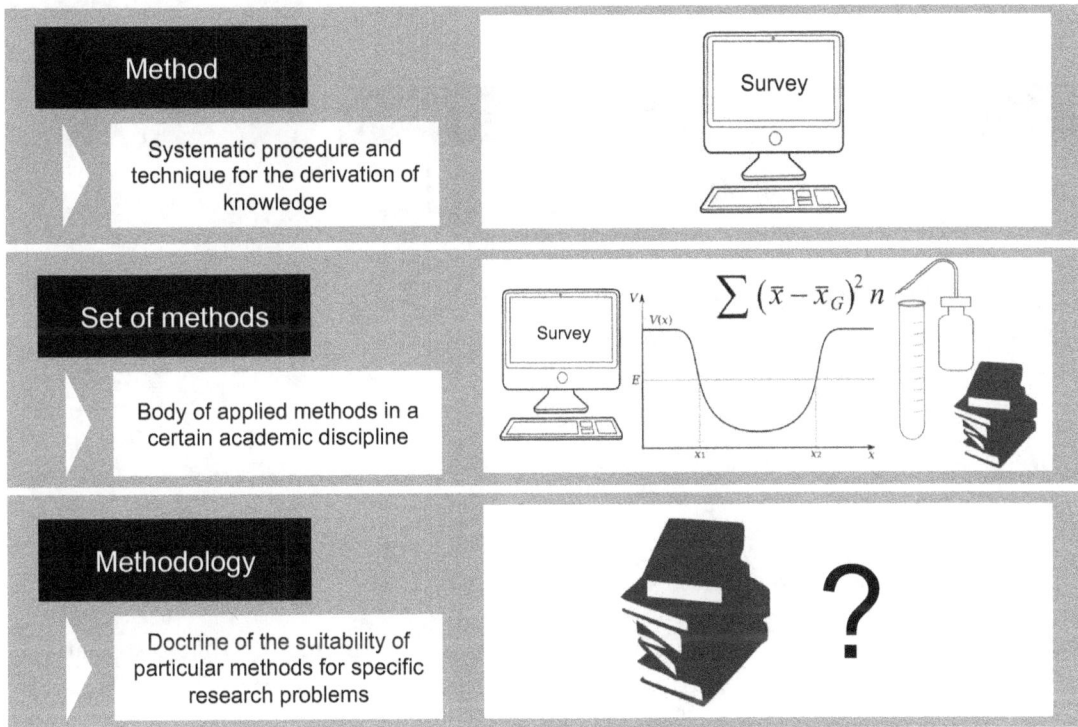

Figure 1.4: Method, set of methods, methodology

The term method refers to a systematic procedure and technique for the derivation of knowledge. In some cases, the term set of methods is used. This implies the body of applied methods in a certain academic discipline. The term methodology signifies the doctrine of the suitability of particular methods for specific research problems.

1.4 Philosophical considerations

1.4.1 Truth

As introduced above, the third key question relates to the philosophical nature of academic research and writing. To begin with, Figure 1.5 illustrates some considerations about the definition of truth.

1 Foundations

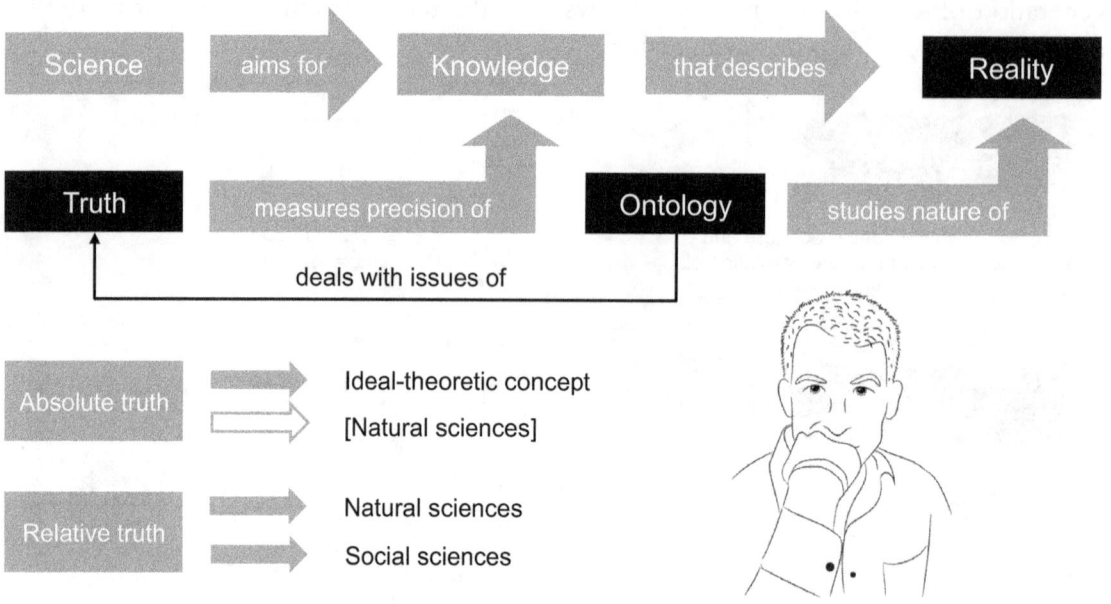

Figure 1.5: Reality, truth, ontology

As pointed out previously, science can be characterised as an activity that systematically questions existing knowledge and generates and distributes new knowledge. The term knowledge implies a description of **reality**. However, the description of a complex reality is quite an ambitious task that is doomed to fail. Knowledge is often merely an approximation of reality. Therefore, the term **truth** is used in order to measure the precision of knowledge. **Ontology** is the branch of philosophy that studies the nature of reality and deals implicitly with issues of truth.

The term truth in itself is quite vague: In an ideal world, scientists would aim for absolute truth. The concept of absolute truth should be viewed as an ideal-theoretic concept. Due to their precise character, natural sciences are sometimes viewed as disciplines dealing with matters of absolute truth. However, absolute truth should be understood as being inaccessible by human beings. Even minimal inaccuracies of measurement while conducting experimental or empirical research would fail the objective of absolute truth. In an imperfect world, scientists can only aim for relative truth. Due to their character, natural sciences are in a good position to aim for relative truth. As a result of the complex character of their research problems, social sciences face considerable obstacles while aiming for relative truth.

1.4.2 Theories of truth

Over the centuries, philosophers concerned with the nature of truth have developed different theories of truth. The complexity of these theories goes way beyond this book. Still, three theories shall be briefly mentioned in order to present different perceptions of the term truth (Figure 1.6).

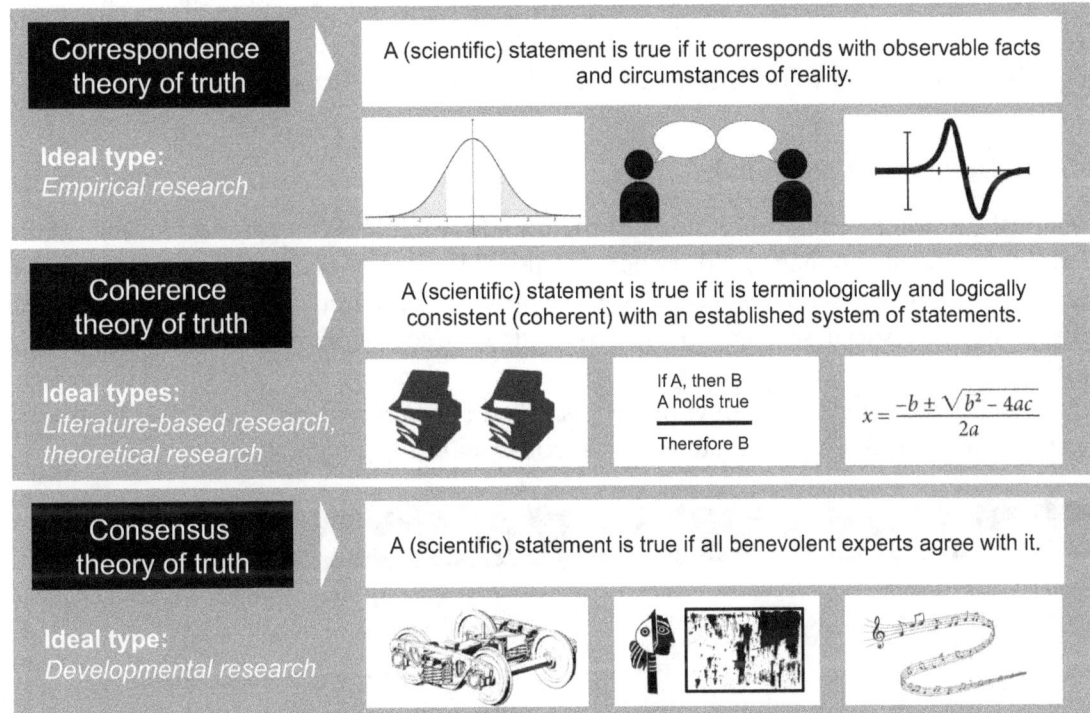

Figure 1.6: Theories of truth

The **correspondence theory of truth** postulates that a (scientific) statement is true if it corresponds with observable facts and circumstances of reality. The correspondence theory of truth predominantly matches and supports empirical research in which numerical and non-numerical data are collected in order to test hypotheses and thereby to support conclusions and propositions.

The **coherence theory of truth** postulates that a (scientific) statement is true if it is terminologically and logically consistent (coherent) with an established system of statements. The coherence theory of truth predominantly matches and supports literature-based research and theoretical research in which researchers base their thoughts on documented previous knowledge.

The **consensus theory of truth** postulates that a (scientific) statement is true if all benevolent experts agree with it. The consensus theory of truth predominantly matches and supports developmental research which can be found inter alia in engineering sciences as well as in fine arts and other disciplines. Here, the research task lays in the development of a prototype or object that satisfies certain predetermined objectives. Typically, more than one possibility exists that satisfies the objectives. Hence, the opinion of experts might be used in order to determine the "truth" of the scientific statement.

1.4.3 Ontological positions

Previously, ontology has been defined as the branch of philosophy that studies the nature of reality and deals implicitly with issues of truth. More precisely, social ontology studies the nature of reality with respect to social entities. Compared to natural sciences and formal sciences, social sciences are confronted with social phenomena posing specific problems for the research process. There are two competing major philosophical positions that address social ontology: objectivism and subjectivism; the latter one is alternatively called social constructionism or social constructivism (Figure 1.7).

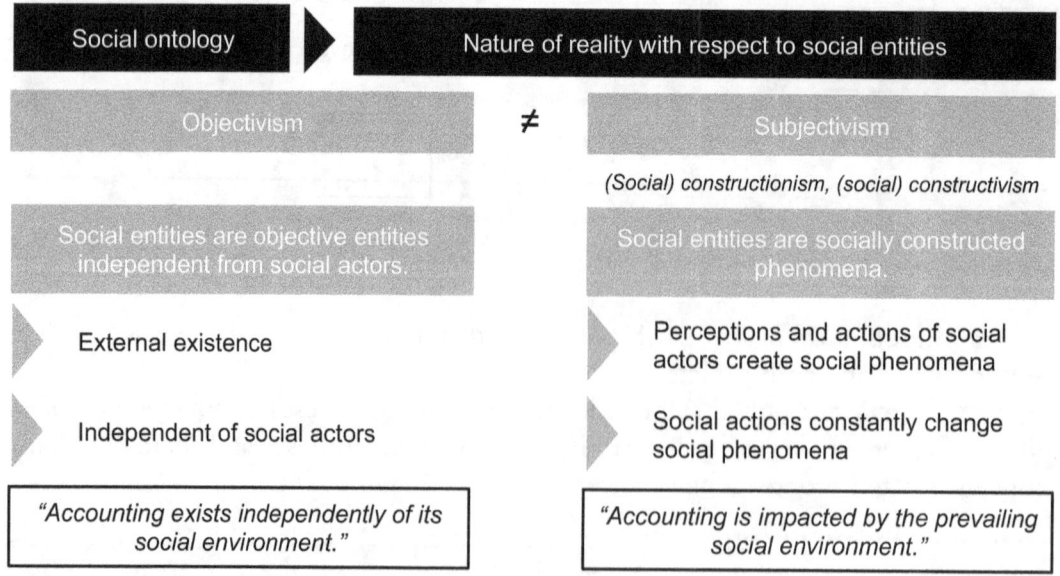

Figure 1.7: Ontological positions

Objectivism postulates that social entities are objective entities independent from social actors. Accordingly, social entities exist as external phenomena. Furthermore, social entities are independent of social actors.

In contradiction, subjectivism postulates that social entities are socially constructed phenomena. Accordingly, perceptions and actions of social actors create social phenomena. Moreover, social actions constantly change social phenomena.

The relevance of ontological positions for research can be exemplified by the following case of "accounting research":

> A researcher who favours objectivism could assert that accounting exists independently of its social environment. As a result, the researcher would ignore social aspects while merely focussing on technocratic aspects of accounting. An objectivist position for example might be helpful if a researcher wants to analyse different techniques of double entry bookkeeping on an abstract basis. A second researcher who favours subjectivism could assert that the prevailing social environment impacts accounting. In addition to technocratic aspects, the researcher would address social aspects of accounting. A subjectivist position for example might be helpful if a researcher wants to analyse accidental bookkeeping errors or deliberate accounting fraud. Obviously, the behaviour of social actors plays an important role for the analysis of these issues.

Generally, both ontological positions are justified. Nevertheless, they imply the application of different methods to the problem. Some researchers favour a proximity to natural sciences and formal sciences, often viewed as "hard sciences". These researchers might orientate their work towards objectivism. However, an ontological position of objectivism does not automatically provide credit to research output if it is not suitable for a research problem at hand. Therefore, one should keep in mind that an ontological position, be it objectivism or subjectivism, has to be carefully chosen.

1.4.4 Epistemic objectives

Sciences aim for knowledge about reality. The goals for the derivation of knowledge are called epistemic objectives. Four principal epistemic objectives need to be introduced and discussed (Figure 1.8).

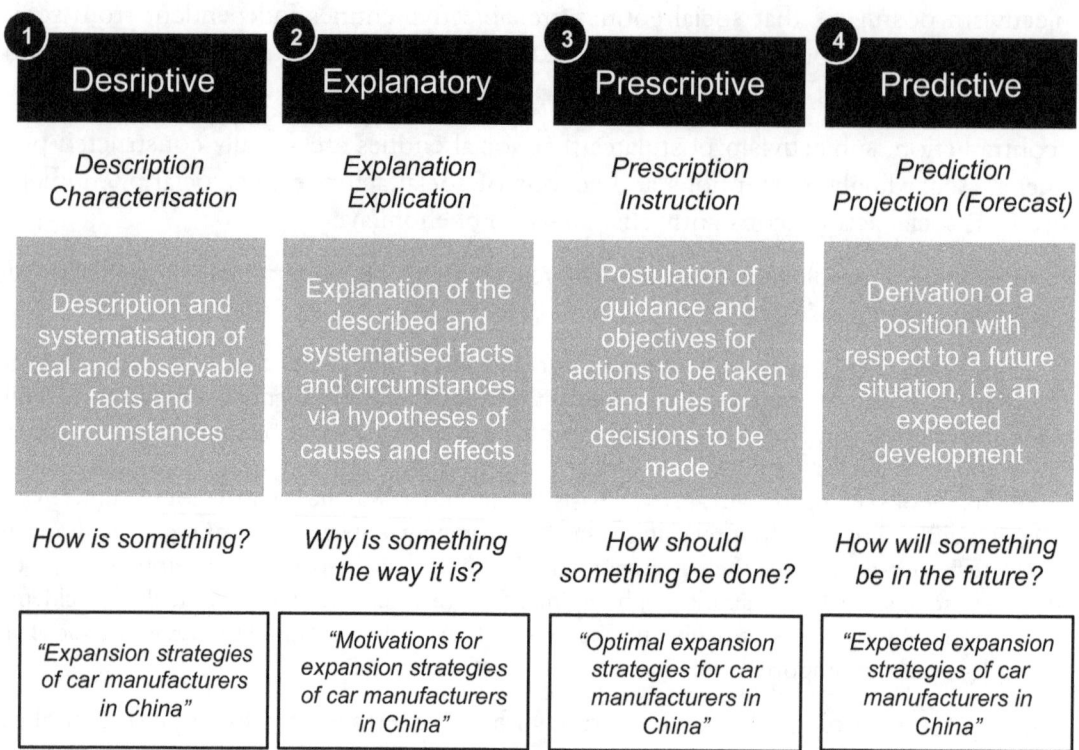

Figure 1.8: Epistemic objectives

A descriptive objective serves the description or characterisation. The descriptive objective addresses the description and systematisation of real and observable facts and circumstances. The researcher asks the question: "How is something?"

An explanatory objective serves the explanation or explication. The explanatory objective addresses the explanation of the described and systematised facts and circumstances via hypotheses of causes and effects. The researcher asks the question: "Why is something the way it is?"

A prescriptive objective serves the prescription or instruction. The prescriptive objective addresses the postulation of guidance and objectives for actions to be taken and rules for decisions to be made. The researcher asks the question "How should something be done?"

A predictive objective serves the prediction or projection. The predictive objective addresses the derivation of a position with respect to a future situation, i.e. an expected development. The researcher asks the question: "How will something be in the future?"

The four epistemic objectives can be exemplified by the following research topics:

- If the topic of a research project is "Expansion strategies of car manufacturers in China", it would imply a descriptive objective. The researchers would have to elaborate on a given situation in a special market segment.
- If the topic of a research project is "Motivations for expansion strategies of car manufacturers in China", it would imply an explanatory objective. The researchers would have to elaborate on the reasons for the application of different strategies in a given market segment.
- Another topic of a research project could be "Optimal expansion strategies for car manufacturers in China". This topic would imply a prescriptive objective. The researchers would have to elaborate on instructions for different strategies in a given market segment.
- Finally, if the topic of a research project is "Expected expansion strategies of car manufacturers in China", it would imply a predictive objective. The researchers would have to project the expected application of different strategic options in a given market segment.

1.4.5 Model

In subchapter 1.3.2, science was characterised as an activity that systematically aims for knowledge that describes reality. In the majority of cases, it is not possible to fully describe the complexity of a given segment of reality. Therefore, a simplification of reality is needed. Models are simplified illustrations of real situations. Their purpose is to solve problems that cannot be solved based on reality. The main characteristic of models is the simplification of a given or expected situation. Accordingly, complexity should be decreased by selecting the relevant phenomena and connections.

In principle, two different procedures of model deduction can be distinguished (Figure 1.9):

- Reductive models
- Constructive models

1 Foundations

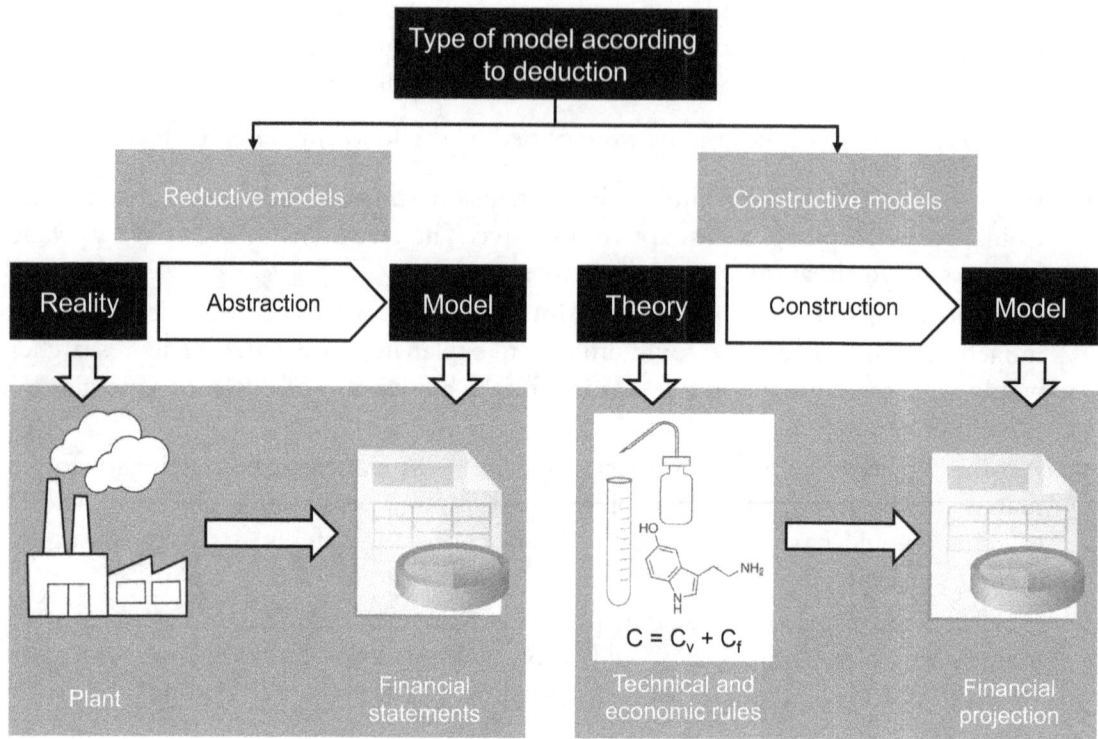

Figure 1.9: Reductive models and constructive models

Reductive models reduce reality by isolating and selecting individual observed phenomena and connections. In other words, one reaches from reality to the model via abstraction. Constructive models construct – based on a theory and selected general phenomena and connection of reality – a simplified model of a fictitious reality. In other words, one reaches from a theory to a model via construction.

This logic can be explained with a simple example: A company runs a plant abroad. The reality of this plant can be illustrated in an abstract and isolated way within the framework of accounting. Obviously, it can solely be an abstract illustration, as the accounting for the plant is not the plant itself. In other words, accounting is a model that illustrates the economic activities of the plant in a simplified way. Consequently, the accounting for the plant is based on a reductive model. In a second step, the company intends to build an additional plant in another country. In order to be able to decide whether to undertake the investment, the management needs a financial projection that will be realised with the help of spreadsheet software. However, this financial projection is not based on a real plant. Instead its construction is based on generally accepted technical and economic rules. Together with empirical values and anticipated data, these technical and economic rules form the basis for the financial projection. Consequently, the financial projection is a constructive model.

1.5 Book structure

1.5.1 Topic structure

The fourth key question stated above is: What forms part of this book on academic research and writing?

Academic research and writing encompasses a number of different aspects that can be found in a research project. Visualising these different aspects, Figure 1.10 gives an overview of the topic structure of academic research and writing.

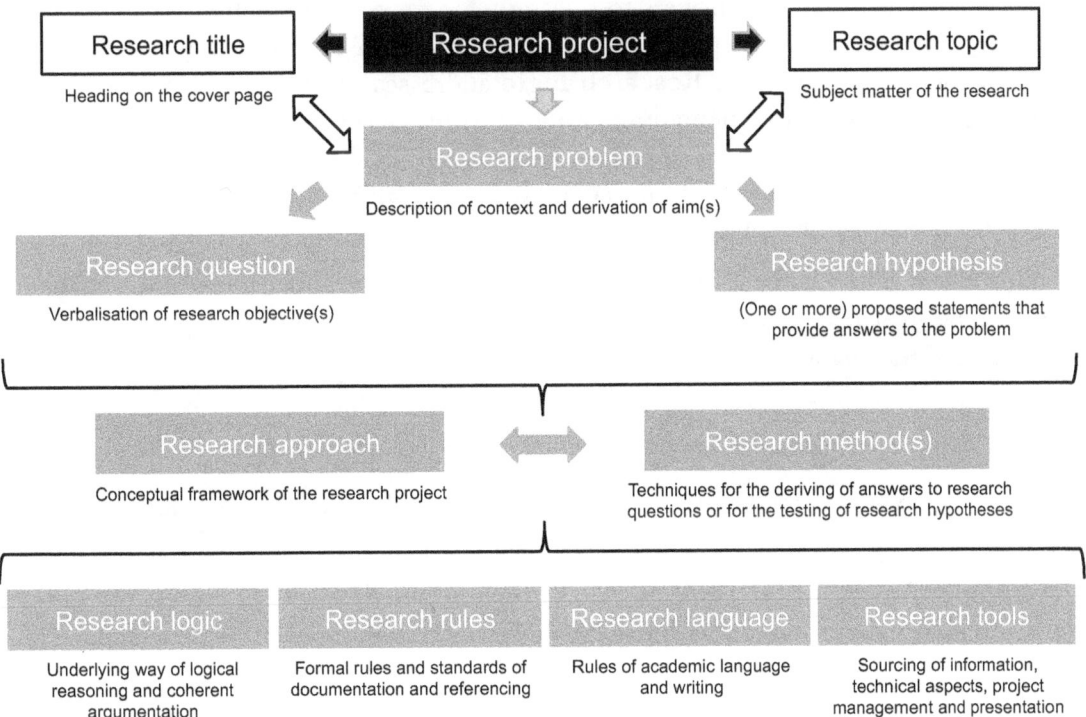

Figure 1.10: Topic structure of academic research and writing

Typically, the findings of a **research project** will be documented in a research report or a research paper. The **research title** is the heading that appears on the cover page of a research report or a research paper. In some cases, the research title is identical with the research topic. In other cases, it might be different. The **research topic** is the subject matter of the research. In all cases, an underlying **research problem** is at hand. It encompasses a description of the context and the derivation of one or more aims to be investigated in the research project. Principally, one or more **research questions** have to be formulated that explicate the aim of the research project. Typically, the verbalisation of the objectives takes place by formulating an indirect question. Moreover, some research projects require the formulation of a research hypothesis. A **research hypothesis** is a proposed statement that provides an assumed answer to the research problem. Depending on the complexity of the research problem, there can be one or more proposed statements. It has to be noted that not all research projects require the formulation of a research hypothesis. Whether a research hypothesis has to be formulated or not depends on the chosen research approach and the applied research methods. A **research approach** is the conceptual framework of a research project. **Research methods** are specific techniques for deriving answers to questions or for testing whether an assumed research hypothesis can be accepted or should be rejected. Additional issues will interact with the described framework: **Research logic** addresses the underlying way of logical reasoning and coherent argumentation; **research rules** cover formal rules and standards of documentation and referencing; **research language** deals with the rules of academic language and writing; **research tools** cover the sourcing of information, technical aspects, project management and presentation.

The illustration of the topic structure serves as a recurring point of orientation throughout this book. It will appear at the beginning of each of the following chapters, indicating the context of the chapter.

1.5.2 Chapter structure

This book is divided into twelve chapters introducing the reader to academic research and writing.

In **chapter 2**, five major academic principles are presented. These principles are broken down into sub-principles that provide general guidance while performing research.

In **chapter 3**, research logic is addressed. In this context, the underlying mechanisms of logical reasoning and coherent argumentation in research projects are introduced.

Chapter 4 is about the research process. Here, different aspects of academic research are affected: the research problem, the research question, the research hypothesis, the research approach, and the research methods. Accordingly, the chapter aims at combining related aspects of academic research in a coherent way.

In **chapter 5**, the task of identifying a (research) topic, is addressed. The chapter aims at clarifying the characteristics of a research topic. Identification of a topic becomes important if one has been asked to submit a research proposal.

Chapter 6 deals with sourcing of information. The chapter focuses on literature search, specifically, the exemplification of different types of literature and the academic appraisal of references.

In **chapter 7**, the elements of a research paper are introduced. The chapter aims at providing a comprehensive overview of formal rules and standards of documentation.

In **chapter 8**, the interpretation of a topic, or more specifically, the selection of an aim is explicated. The chapter demonstrates the importance of isolating and deciding for potential research objectives.

In **chapter 9**, common structuring techniques are explained. The chapter elaborates on logically aligning different elements that form part of a research paper. Furthermore, aim-related and advanced structuring options are introduced.

In **chapter 10**, formal rules and standards of referencing are addressed. After the discussion of the objectives of referencing, the techniques of parenthetical referencing and footnote referencing are explained.

Chapter 11 deals with the language of research, or more specifically, rules of academic language and writing. The chapter focuses on the impact of academic principles on the use of language as well as the means of giving coherence to an academic text.

In **chapter 12**, the aspects and techniques of argumentation are discussed. The chapter aims at creating a nexus between logical reasoning, academic language and writing as well as referencing.

There are more aspects and issues in academic research and writing that might be important in some cases but will not be covered by this book:

- Project management including time management and problem management is important in order to organise a research project.

- Academic presentation can take place via presentations and/or posters and might be important for an oral examination.
- Empirical research or empirical social research methods are prerequisites for some research projects where data have to be collected and analysed.
- Technical aspects relate to application software used for the preparation of research papers.

Due to the comprehensive nature and inherent complexity of project management, academic presentation and empirical research, a depiction of these topics would go beyond the potentialities of a concise introduction of academic research and writing. Furthermore, a discussion of technical aspects would have to be related to the applied word processing programmes as well as illustration and presentation programmes and their individual specificities. Here, a comprehensive depiction of all possible technical scenarios seems to be impossible and out of place.

1.6 Summary and exercises

1.6.1 Synopsis

In this chapter, foundations of academic research and writing were laid:

- Business, university, institutional and collaborative research are manifestations of academic research.
- Common aims of these manifestations are the collection and/or discovery of information as well as the documentation and processing of findings.
- Common characteristics of these manifestations are to strive for objectivity and precision as well as a systematic and methodical approach to problem solving.

Understanding and proper use of terminology are important in academic research and writing:

- Academia can be divided into sciences, humanities, engineering and fine arts.
- Sciences can appear in the form of natural, formal, social and empirical sciences.
- The terms "science" and "theory" have different dimensions and connotations.
- The terms "method", "set of methods" and "methodology" have to be distinguished from each other.

Philosophical considerations help to understand the nature of science and research:

- The term "truth" is an ambivalent attribute for the precision of knowledge that aims to describe reality.
- Different theories of truth provide practical approaches for analysing the truth of scientific statements.
- Objectivism and subjectivism (social constructivism) are social ontological positions towards social phenomena.
- Epistemic objectives can be descriptive, explanatory, prescriptive and predictive.
- Models as simplifications of a complex reality can be deduced by way of reduction or construction.

Finally, the topic academic research and writing was structured into logical units that serve as a basis for the subsequent chapters of this textbook.

1.6.2 Questions

Knowledge

1. What is professional research?
2. What is academic research?
3. What institutional research?
4. What is collaborative research?
5. Which disciplines form part of natural sciences?
6. Which disciplines form part of formal sciences?
7. Which disciplines form part of social sciences?
8. Which disciplines form part of humanities?
9. Why are some humanities considered to be "hybrids"?
10. Which sciences are empirical sciences?
11. What are engineering sciences?
12. Which disciplines form part of fine arts?
13. What are the five dimensions of the term science?
14. How are research, lecturing and teaching related to each other?
15. What are different meanings of the term theory?
16. What is a method?
17. What is a set of methods?
18. What is methodology?
19. How are sciences related to reality?
20. What is the meaning of truth in the context of sciences?
21. What is ontology?

1 Foundations

22. What is the difference between absolute truth and relative truth?
23. What is the central proposition of the correspondence theory of truth?
24. What is the central proposition of the coherence theory of truth?
25. What is the central proposition of the consensus theory of truth?
26. What is social ontology?
27. What is the essence of objectivism?
28. What is the essence of subjectivism?
29. What are epistemic objectives?
30. What is the intention of a descriptive objective?
31. What is the intention of an explanatory objective?
32. What is the intention of a prescriptive objective?
33. What is the intention of a predictive objective?
34. What is a model?
35. What is a reductive model?
36. What is a constructive model?

1.6.3 Problems

1.6.3.1 Science in politics

Application

Learning target

Being able to characterise the term science

Mini case

A minister submits a proposal for a reform of the pension system to the national parliament. In the process, data regarding the projected population development are presented. During the parliamentary debate, a member of the parliament criticises the proposal together with the data basis and condemns the documents as "unscientific".

Question

What are prerequisites for characterising the proposal and/or the data basis as "unscientific"?

1.6.3.2 Science at a party

Comprehension **Application**

Learning targets

Being able to characterise the term science and to spot its connotations

Mini case

You meet someone at a private party and give an enthusiastic account about your studies of academic research and writing via this textbook and corresponding e-learning tutorials. Your conversational partner replies with the question: "But this is not a scientific course, is it?"

Questions

What are potential connotations of the question?

How would you answer this in a truthful and friendly manner?

1.6.3.3 Financial research

Analysis

Learning target

Being able to characterise the term research

Background

Typically, larger banks have research units that frequently generate research reports.

Instruction

Please investigate the term research (in the context of banking) by using the Internet.

Questions

What are tasks of a research unit in a bank?

Why are these tasks labelled with the term research?

1.6.3.4 Epistemic objectives

Synthesis

Learning target

Being able to design problems taking into account different epistemic objectives

Instruction

Please create four examples of topics that each applies a different epistemic objective.

1.6.3.5 Reductive and constructive models

Synthesis

Learning target

Being able to design problems implying a specific model

Instruction

Please create an example of a reductive model and an example of a constructive model.

1.6.4 Additional reading

Mallon, R. (2013), Naturalistic Approaches to Social Construction. In E. N. Zalta (Ed.), *The Stanford Encyclopedia of Philosophy*, (Winter 2014 ed.), Retrieved from http://plato.stanford.edu/archives/win2014/entries/social-construction-naturalistic/

2 Academic principles

Abstract

In chapter 2, five major academic principles are introduced. They represent sets of unwritten rules prescribing a certain formal and material behaviour in academic research and writing. Although there is often no legally binding rule set in academic research and writing, certain conventions have been developed and generally accepted by academia. The five major principles presented here are a way to collect dispersed rules and standards and to organise them in a systematic way. The five principles are defined as accuracy, completeness, clarity, comparability and materiality. The principle of accuracy implies the observation of applicable rules and norms, the intersubjective comprehensibility of the research output, the timeliness and currency of processed information as well as the true and fair representation of the research project. The principle of completeness demands qualitative completeness and quantitative completeness. The principle of clarity requires the clearness and the proper composition of academic texts. The principle of comparability implies obeying the status quo of the discipline and explaining deviations. The principle of materiality prescribes an adequate reduction of inherent complexity and demands adequate decision usefulness for the recipients of a research project.

Keywords

Academic principles, accuracy, completeness, clarity, clearness, comparability, falsifiability, intersubjective comprehensibility, materiality, perceptibility, proper composition, reliability, traceability, validity

2.1 Context and relevance

2.1.1 Context of chapter 2

In the previous chapter, a basic understanding of academic research in theory and practice has been developed. The next step would be to come up with a more structured and systematic approach to characterise academic research. Therefore, the context of chapter 2 is to deepen the understanding of the characteristics of academic research and writing.

Figure 2.1 shows how chapter 2 is embedded within the setting of a research project.

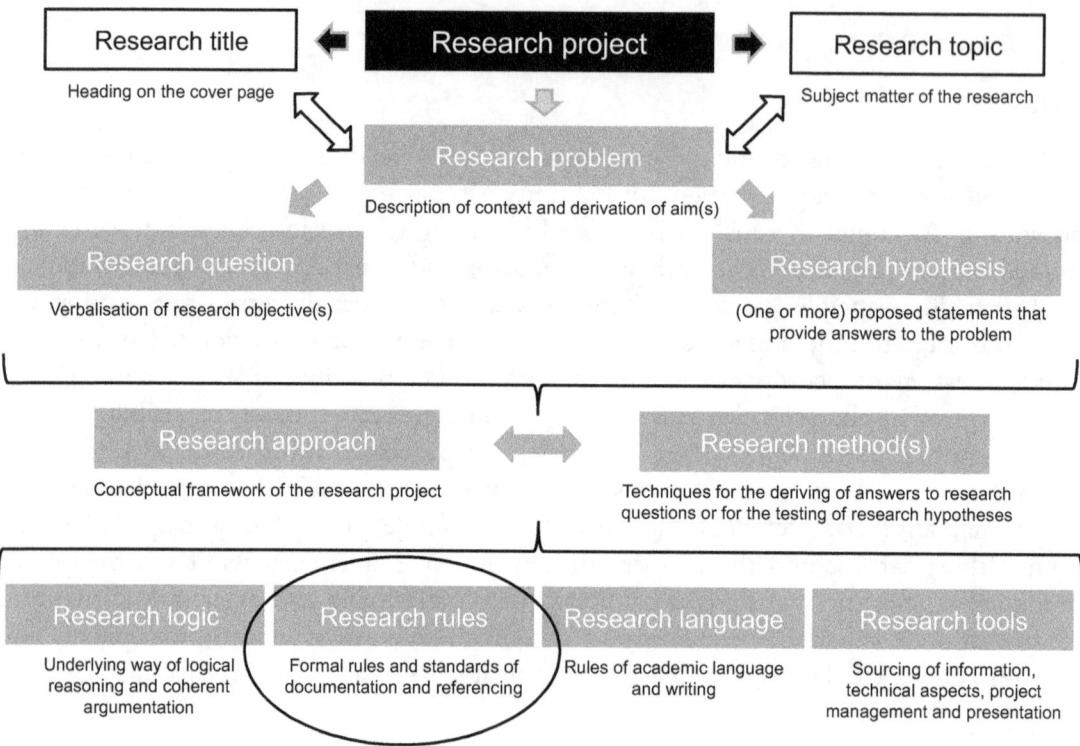

Figure 2.1: Context of chapter 2

In this chapter, formal rules and standards of academic research are addressed.

2.1.2 Relevance of chapter 2

Academic principles provide general guidance for individual research and writing processes. Furthermore, academic principles clarify norms and rules employed in the process of grading academic research projects.

The five fundamental academic or scientific principles to be addressed in this chapter are:

- Accuracy
- Completeness
- Clarity
- Comparability
- Materiality

As the five principles constitute an abstraction on a very high level, they will be broken down into subcategories in the following subchapters.

It should be mentioned that this classification is also used for reporting and forecasting purposes and is thereby generally accepted and legally tested, for example in the field of accounting. However, these five principles are not restricted to a specific academic discipline.

2.1.3 Learning objectives of chapter 2

After having studied this chapter, the reader should be able to:

- understand the five fundamental academic principles and their subcategories
- identify academic misbehaviour

2.2 Accuracy

2.2.1 Observation of applicable rules and norms

The principle of accuracy implies that applicable rules and norms are obeyed.

Certain rules and norms exist inside as well as outside the academic world or scientific community:

- **Spelling and grammar**

    Correct spelling and grammar are important in order to enhance receptiveness and to avoid ambiguity of presented research work.

- **Algorithms and calculation rules**

    It should be self-evident that calculations are free of any mistakes. The value of academic work and its credibility are based inter alia on correct computations.

Furthermore, there are rules and norms that exist predominantly in the academic world:

- **Referencing and citation**

    The verifiability of propositions and conclusions is of utmost importance in the world of sciences. Correct referencing and citation allow for the verifiability of research work in a consistent and traceable way.

2 Academic principles

- 🎓 **Tip**

    It is advisable to clarify the applicable rules of referencing and citation before starting the writing process.

- **Formatting and presentation**

    Academic documents and academic presentations imply an appropriate formatting of the work to be prepared, submitted and presented. Although different forms of documenting and presenting might be adopted, seriousness and academic credibility are expected.

- 🎓 **Tip**

    It is advisable to clarify the applicable rules of formatting such as font type, font size, spacing and margining before starting the writing process.

2.2.2 Intersubjective comprehensibility

In the context of scientific work, the terms "objective" and "objectivity" are often used in order to characterise the research process and the research output. However, this wording is incorrect. Figure 2.2 reveals the underlying problem.

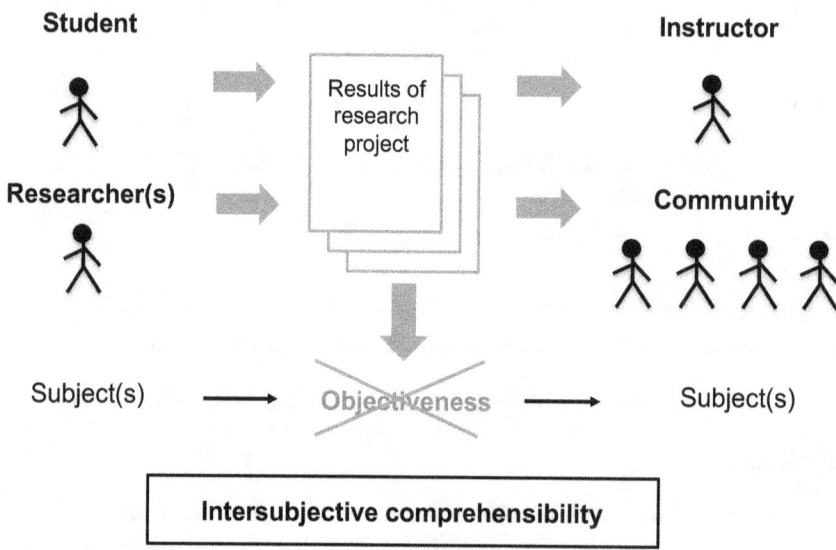

Figure 2.2: Intersubjective comprehensibility

The often-stated idea that a research project has been conducted with objectiveness is a misconception. Although desired, objectiveness can never be achieved by human beings. Subjects can only report from a subjective perspective. Therefore, it is preferable to use the concept of intersubjective comprehensibility in order to characterise a given research output.

Intersubjective comprehensibility means: What has been researched by one or more subjects can be comprehended, reproduced, retraced and/or understood by one or more subjects that are the recipients of the research results.

🎓 Tip

It is advisable to avoid the use of the words objective and objectivity.

In this sense, one should be suspicious if the words objective and objectivity are used in an academic context.

The principle of accuracy aims to provide intersubjective comprehensibility. There are five aspects that can be used in order to determine whether the research output is intersubjectively comprehensible:

- **Perceptibility**

  Perceptibility means that the research question and/or the underlying hypothesis of a research project have to be formulated in an apprehensible way. If recipients do not understand what the research is about, it is not intersubjectively comprehensible.

- **Traceability**

  Traceability means that the research output has to be presented in a documented way that allows third parties the reproduction of conclusions. If an educated third party cannot reproduce the researcher's conclusions, they are not intersubjectively comprehensible.

- **Reliability**

  The aspect of reliability is closely linked to traceability. However, it addresses a specific aspect of research. Reliability means that the research output that has been generated by experimental or empirical research methods can be reproduced. There are two dimensions: First, researchers should be able to reproduce their own research output. Second, other researchers should be able to reproduce the research output as well.

> Example
> A student uses statistical software in order to simulate business scenarios for a master's thesis project. Although the student uses the same data and the same settings, the generated probability distributions of the simulations are varying with each simulation run. The student is not able to reproduce the initial output. Here, a more or less substantial problem with the code of the statistical software can be suspected.

- **Validity**

The aspect of validity is closely linked to reliability. However, it addresses another problem. Validity means that the research output has to be generated with an adequate degree of precision regarding the problem to be considered.

> Example
> A student designs a market survey in order to analyse a given research problem. A questionnaire has been sent to 2,000 companies. The response rate is 0.1%, meaning that two companies have answered the questionnaire. Obviously, the results of the empirical analysis should not be used in order to support a precise conclusion.

- **Falsifiability**

Falsifiability means that the research output has to be formulated in a way so that it is disputable, i.e. it is falsifiable.

> Example 1
> A professor for marketing prepares a research paper that ends with the conclusion: "Perfect marketing strategies exist." This conclusion is not falsifiable due to the imprecise adjective "perfect".

> Example 2
> A professor for human resource management claims in a statement: "Leadership training will have an impact on the management of companies." Again, this statement is not falsifiable because it lacks precision.

2.2.3 Timeliness and currentness

The principle of accuracy implies paying attention to timeliness and currentness.

- **Timeliness of references**

    Timeliness of references means that references have to be selected in a way so that they reflect the current status of publications in the field to be investigated.

    It should be noted, however, that major theories as well as ground-breaking thoughts and achievements should be cited by referring to the historic sources.

- **Currentness of data**

    Currentness of data refers to the requirement that data in the form of quantitative and qualitative information used in a research project have to be up to date.

    It should be noted, however, that historic data might be needed while working with time series or conducting longitudinal studies in order to derive trends.

2.2.4 True and fair representation

The principle of accuracy implies a true and fair representation of one's research work. True and fair representation means that one has to act with integrity, impartiality and honesty.

There are four aspects that can serve as indicators of a true and fair representation:

- **Identification of a research problem**

    One or more research questions have to be clearly identified and documented in a comprehensible way. The research problem has to be deduced from the title or inherent topic of the research project.

- **No redrafting of title**

    A change of the title of a research project is strictly forbidden. Even if one is not able to deduce a research problem from the title of a given project, changes to the title must not be made. This holds true for an examination situation as well as for officially sponsored research projects.

- **No reinterpretation of the topic**

    Every title of a research project implies an underlying topic. A reinterpretation of the underlying or implicit topic of a research project is not allowed.

- **No manipulation**

    While stating data, references and other information, modifications that change the nature of the evidence have to be avoided.

Unfortunately, there are cases of academic misconduct. If intentionally manipulating their research work, students might face internal penalties imposed by the examination board, and professional researchers might face criminal charges and civil actions as well as the end of their academic careers.

2.3 Completeness

2.3.1 Qualitative completeness

The principle of completeness demands qualitative completeness of the research work. Qualitative completeness requires:

1. a **comprehensive analysis of the research topic**. All aspects relevant in order to answer the research question have to be addressed.

2. the **consideration of all relevant information sources**. Upon availability, the researcher has to use all existing information, e.g. literature or data, which stems from previous research. Alternatively or additionally, the researcher has to collect new information by way of surveys or experiments.

It has to be noted that the principle of qualitative completeness is closely linked to the principle of accuracy. Naturally, if a piece of research is not complete, it is not accurate. Therefore, the principle of qualitative completeness is meant to be a clarification of the principle of accuracy.

2.3.2 Quantitative completeness

Quantitative completeness depends upon the nature and requirements of the research project. In academic research projects, there is a range of elements to be considered in terms of quantitative completeness. These elements might be named differently depending on the research context (e.g. "research purpose" instead of "research problem"). However, every research project should incorporate elements that deal with the followings aspects:

- **Research problem**

    The research question has to be clarified. In some cases, an explicit research hypothesis has to be developed and documented as well.

- **Course of investigation**

    The research approach has to be laid out, and the applied methodology has to be explained.

- **Conclusion**

    A conclusion summarising the findings has to be provided. Furthermore, a critical acclaim and, in some cases, an outlook that goes beyond the investigated research question might be expected.

- **Relevant lists**

    The documentation of a research project should include all relevant lists that help the reader's perception and enhance the traceability of conclusions. This would encompass inter alia a list of figures, a list of tables, a list of abbreviations, and a list of references.

Last but not least, compliance with an adequate number of pages according to prevailing circumstances or guidelines is expected. In the case of academic research projects, the instructor or thesis advisor should provide the relevant information to the student researchers.

2.4 Clarity

2.4.1 Clearness

The principle of clarity implies a sufficient degree of clearness of the research work in order to avoid ambiguities with respect to the research project and its conclusions. There are a number of aspects that have a direct impact on the clearness of a research project:

- **Description of methodology**

    The methodical approach of a research project should be laid out in clear and precise wording.

- **Definition of relevant terminology**

    In order to avoid misconceptions, it is important to clarify the intended meaning of terms used in a research project.

- **Accurate and academic language**

    A clear linguistic and terminological application enhances the comprehensibility of the research output.

- **Consistent argumentation**

    Consistent argumentation is important because contradictions and inconsistencies reduce the clearness of the research output.

2.4.2 Proper composition

Proper composition is the clear arrangement of a written documentation of a research project. There are several aspects reflecting proper composition of a research paper:

- **Logic of structure**

    A logical structure and a well-organised outline of the research paper enhance the intersubjective comprehensibility.

- **Focus on topic**

    The uncompromising focus on the topic of the research paper without any off-topic remarks is an absolute condition for every research project.

- **Deduction of structure**

    The adequate and formally correct deduction of chapters and subchapters of the research paper is a prerequisite for proper reasoning.

- **Formal correctness**

    The formally correct structuring and numbering of the research paper should be self-evident and serves as guidance for the recipients.

- **Thread**

    The perceptibility of a recurrent theme or leitmotif increases the readability and the intersubjective comprehensibility of the research documentation.

2.5 Comparability

2.5.1 Status quo of discipline

The principle of comparability implies obeying the status quo of the relevant academic discipline (Figure 2.3). Only in rare cases will ground-breaking theoretical findings be generated in the context of research projects. The theoretical foundation of academic research papers should be based as much as possible upon the status quo of the relevant discipline. If applying the status quo of one's discipline, one will comply with the principle of comparability.

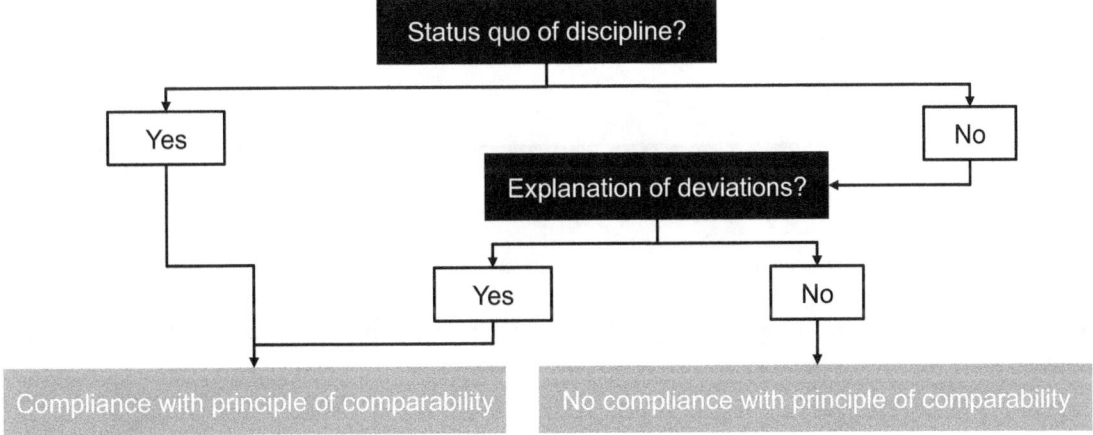

Figure 2.3: Status quo of discipline

Any departures from prevailing views are indeed possible and – if reasonable – favoured. However, it is compulsory to give reasons for deviations and to explain them in detail:

- If deviations are explained, one will again comply with the principle of comparability.
- If deviations are not explained, one will not comply with the principle of comparability.

2.5.2 Expectancy of deviations

In the previous subchapter, it was stated that deviations from the status quo of a discipline are possible, but have to be explained. Figure 2.4 shows the idealised positioning of academic research projects regarding the expectancy of deviations and the inherent level of sophistication.

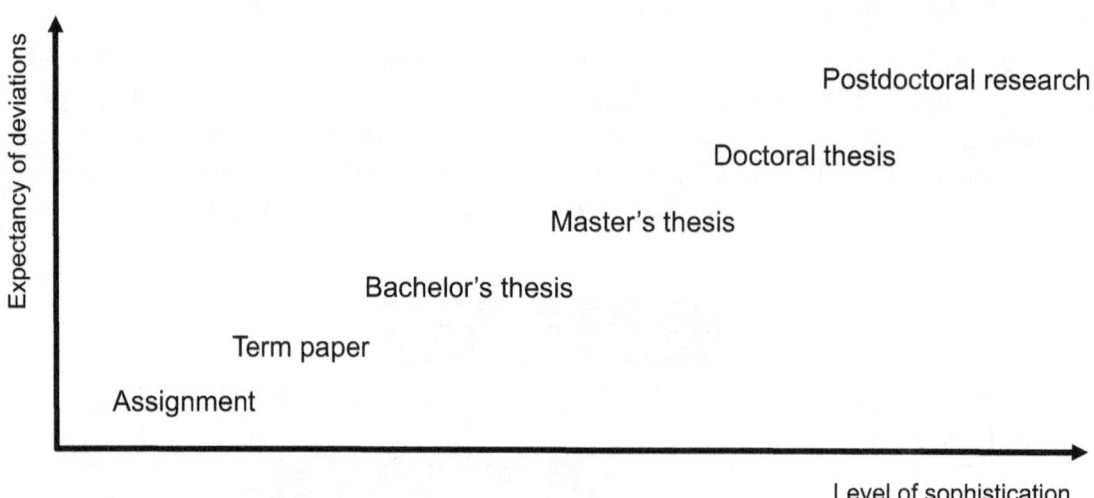

Figure 2.4: Expectancy of deviations

Generally speaking, the room for deviations increases as the complexity of the work increases.

2.6 Materiality

2.6.1 Adequate reduction of inherent complexity

The principle of materiality implies an adequate reduction of the inherent complexity of a research question (Figure 2.5). Information and facts are processed while pursuing a given aim. Selected theories and methods are used in order to derive conclusions.

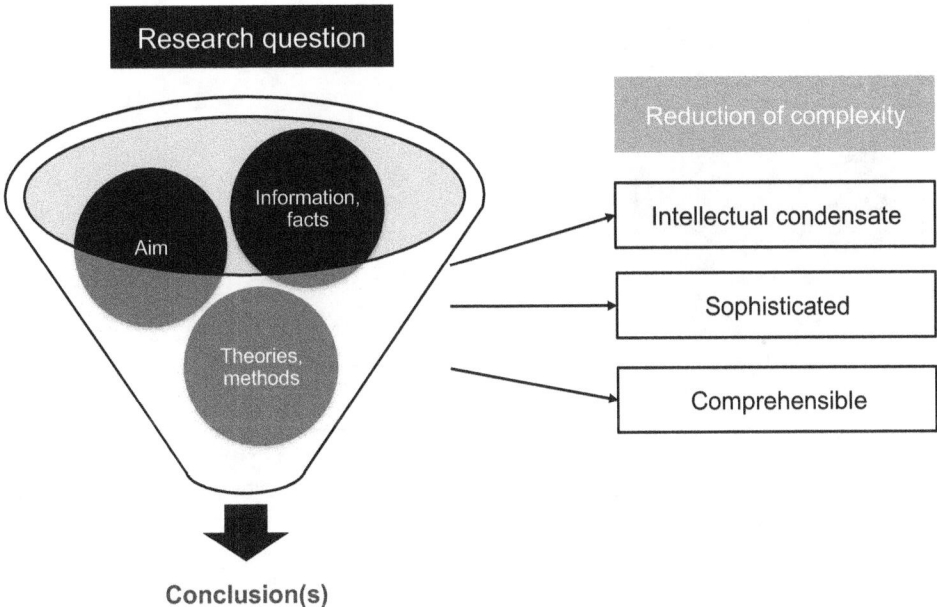

Figure 2.5: Reduction of inherent complexity

The adequate reduction of inherent complexity means that the research output has to be the intellectual condensate of a proper research process. The research output has to be free of trivial as well as overly complicated statements. It should demonstrate a certain level of sophistication while simultaneously being comprehensible for the recipients.

2.6.2 Adequate decision usefulness

In addition to the adequate reduction of inherent complexity, the principle of materiality implies adequate decision usefulness (Figure 2.6). Adequate decision usefulness means that conclusions have to provide meaningful answers to the problems at hand.

2 Academic principles

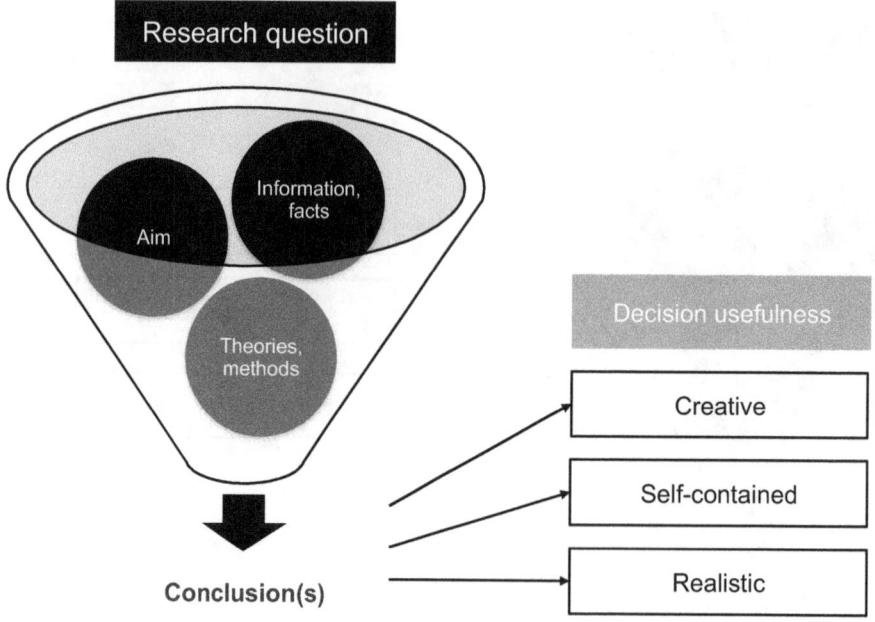

Figure 2.6: Decision usefulness

Researchers should demonstrate sufficient academic creativity while addressing the research question. Hence, the extent of self-contained conclusions is an important criterion for the evaluation of the research output. Particularly in business and social sciences, the consideration of the empirical environment or operational reality might become important.

2.7 Summary and exercises

2.7.1 Synopsis

In this chapter, five major academic principles that characterise academic or scientific work have been addressed:
- The principle of accuracy implies the observation of rules and norms, intersubjective comprehensibility, timeliness and currentness of data as well as a true and fair representation.

- The principle of completeness implies qualitative and quantitative completeness of a research project.
- The principle of clarity implies clearness of the research work and proper composition of the research documentation.
- The principle of comparability implies paying attention to the status quo of the discipline and providing an explanation of any deviations.
- The principle of materiality implies the adequate reduction of inherent complexity and allowing for an adequate decision usefulness of the conclusions.

2.7.2 Questions

Knowledge

1. Why is it relevant to have a sound knowledge of academic principles?
2. What are the five fundamental academic principles?
3. What are general rules and norms to be obeyed while performing research?
4. What are specific rules and norms to be obeyed while performing research?
5. What is meant by the principle of intersubjective comprehensibility?
6. What is meant by the principle of perceptibility of academic research?
7. What is meant by the principle of traceability of academic research?
8. What is meant by the principle of reliability of academic research?
9. What is meant by the principle of validity of academic research?
10. What is meant by the principle of falsifiability of academic research?
11. In which cases is the timeliness of references not relevant?
12. In which cases is the currentness of data not relevant?
13. What is meant by true and fair representation in academic research?
14. What are indicators of a true and fair representation in academic research?
15. What is qualitative completeness of a research project?
16. What is quantitative completeness of a research project?
17. How can clearness be achieved in academic research?
18. What are indicators of proper composition of a research project and its written documentation?
19. Why is the status quo of a discipline relevant for a research project?
20. Why is it necessary to explain deviations from the status quo of a discipline?
21. Why is an adequate reduction of the inherent complexity of a research project important in academic research?
22. What is meant by adequate decision usefulness of academic research?

2.7.3 Problems

Application

Learning targets

Being able to recognise and to explain academic misbehaviour.

Instructions

Analyse the following mini cases with respect to academic misbehaviour and identify violations of academic principles.

Please note that one or more principles could be violated.

Mini cases

1. A student prepares a master's thesis that is comprised of a complex set of calculations prepared with MS EXCEL. The printed version of the thesis is handed in without a soft copy of the calculations (i.e. an Excel file).
2. A student prepares a master's thesis that comprises a complex set of calculations prepared with MS EXCEL. The printed version of the thesis is handed in with a soft copy of the calculations. The soft copy does not match the printed version of the calculations attached as appendices to the master's thesis.
3. A student prepares a bachelor's thesis that comprises a complex set of calculations that include some major arithmetic errors.
4. A student prepares a bachelor's thesis that comprises a complex set of calculations that include some minor arithmetic errors.
5. A German minister submits a doctoral thesis that is based on literature research. An academic identifies that the minister has copied excessively from other authors without proper citation.
6. A German minister submits a doctoral thesis that is partially based on an empirical survey via a questionnaire. While the empirical survey is organised, processed and compiled by her staff, she has written the text of the thesis.
7. A student has to submit a term paper entitled "Green fashion: Sustainability and ethics in the textile industry". Her paper includes a chapter on the historic development of environmental friendly business activities and the role of Greenpeace in changing the general sentiment towards ecological issues.
8. A student submits a term paper that misses a list of abbreviations.
9. A student submits a term paper that is not structured in chapters.

10. A student submits a term paper that is structured in chapters that are not numbered.
11. While a student submits a master's thesis that delivers innovative findings in the chapter "conclusions", the evaluators cannot trace these conclusions while reading other chapters of the master's thesis.
12. In 2012, a student submits a thesis on "Migration trends of highly educated human resources" which is based on data that have been published by the World Bank in 1995.
13. A student submits a term paper that is printed on purple paper.
14. A student submits a term paper with chapters that are not numbered but are denoted with symbols of little animals.
15. A student submits a critical acclaim that states excuses for the small amount of literature that has been used for referencing arguments.
16. In the context of a survey on "Personal biases in forecasting processes", a student conducts a number of experiments with test persons. The final results of the experiments are summarised in the thesis. All protocols of the experiments have been destroyed.
17. A student has to submit a term paper for the course "Academic Research and Writing". Since he is not able to come up with a proper list of references, he fakes a number of articles.
18. A researcher publishes a paper on spending power of students studying in Hamburg. Other researchers try but are not able to replicate the conclusions.
19. A student has to submit a term paper on haptic marketing strategies for hair care products. Since she has a weakness for fragrances, she changes the topic to "Olfactory marketing strategies for hair care products".
20. A student has to submit a term paper on haptic marketing strategies for hair care products. She keeps the title but includes a chapter on olfactory marketing aspects.
21. A student submits a term paper entitled "Adaption of International Financial Accounting Standards (IFRS) in India". The paper comprises two main chapters: one chapter about India and one chapter about IFRS.
22. A student submits a handwritten term paper.
23. A student submits a term paper that makes heavy use of personal pronouns, especially "I", "me" and "we".
24. A German student submits a thesis about "Accounting for banking activities". The thesis solely analyses the rules of the German commercial code (Handelsgesetzbuch) although the majority of banks have to prepare finan-

cial statements according to International Financial Accounting Standards (IFRS).
25. A student has to submit a thesis entitled "The role of the European Central Bank in the sovereign debt crisis". He changes the title to "The sovereign debt crisis and the role of the European Central Bank".

2.7.4 Additional reading

Anonymous (2013, February 9). Merkel Loses Minister: Schavan Steps Down amid Plagiarism Scandal. *Spiegel Online International*. Retrieved from http://www.spiegel.de

Bhattacharjee, Y. (2013, April 26). The Mind of a Con Man. *New York Times*. Retrieved from http://www.nytimes.com

3 Research logic

Abstract

Chapter 3 introduces the reader to the underlying philosophical or, more precisely, logical aspects of research. The basic understanding of research logic is a necessary foundation for every research project. Induction and deduction are two major types of reasoning frequently applied in research. Both types provide a framework for generating intersubjectively comprehensible conclusions and projections. The understanding of the basic structure of syllogisms, the ancient Greek sets of logical conclusions as laid out by Aristotle, helps to differentiate between universal and existential propositions as well as affirmative and negative statements. The deductive-nomological model and the inductive statistical model provide techniques to formally describe logical reasoning. These thoughts and ideas help to comprehend the concepts of falsification and falsifiability. Finally, indicator and causal hypotheses are introduced in order to discuss individual limitations of induction and deduction and the benefit of a combination of both types of reasoning.

Keywords

Deduction, induction, DN model, IS model, logical reasoning, nomological hypothesis, statistical hypothesis, syllogism, falsification, falsifiability, existential propositions, universal propositions, indicator hypothesis, causal hypothesis

3.1 Context and relevance

3.1.1 Context of chapter 3

In previous chapters, a basic understanding of academic research in theory and practice as well as corresponding academic principles has been developed. The next step is to look at the underlying logic of research processes. Before turning to other aspects of academic research and writing, one should understand how conclusions and answers to research questions are derived.

Figure 3.1 shows how chapter 3 is embedded within the setting of a research project.

3 Research logic

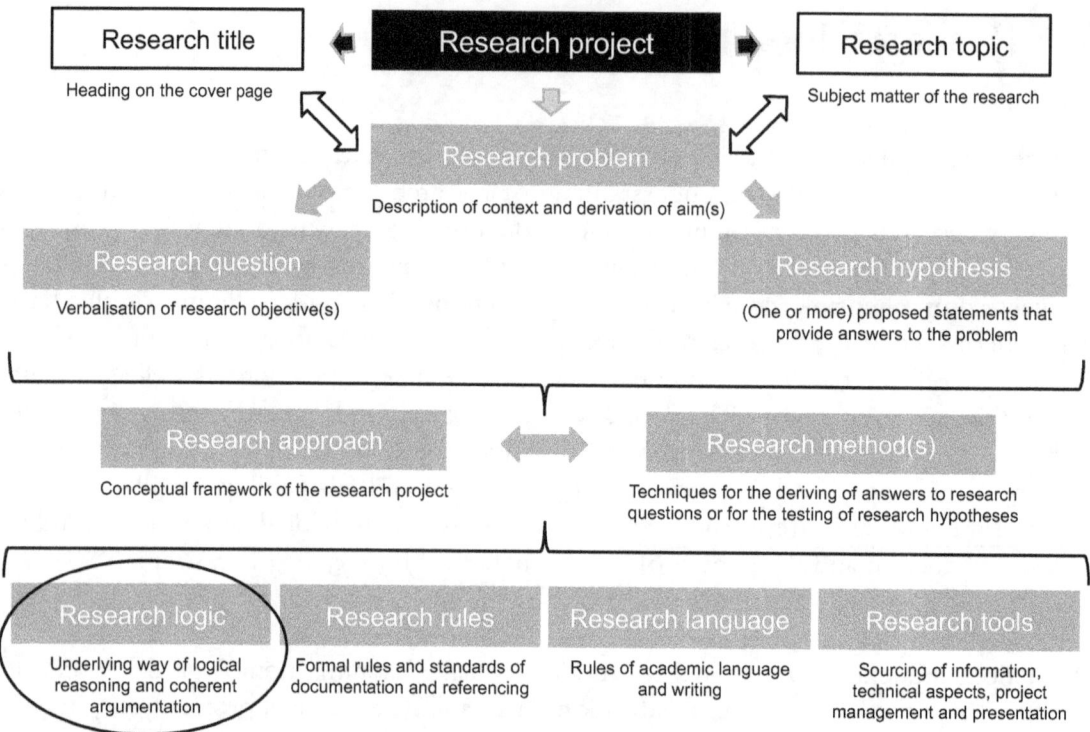

Figure 3.1: Context of chapter 3

In this chapter, the underlying way of logical reasoning and coherent argumentation is addressed.

3.1.2 Relevance of chapter 3

The research process has to be structured in a logical way. Understanding the principles of research logic helps to avoid illogical reasoning that might lead to false conclusions and, ultimately, to the failure of the research project. Therefore, understanding the principles of research logic is essential for a successful research project.

3.1.3 Learning objectives of chapter 3

After having studied this chapter, the reader should be able to:

- understand different ways of reasoning

- differentiate between inductive and deductive reasoning
- explain the structures of modus ponens and modus tollens
- understand the terms falsification and falsifiability
- differentiate between indicator and causal hypotheses

3.2 Reasoning

3.2.1 Types of reasoning

Generally, one can distinguish between two major types of reasoning: induction and deduction (Figure 3.2).

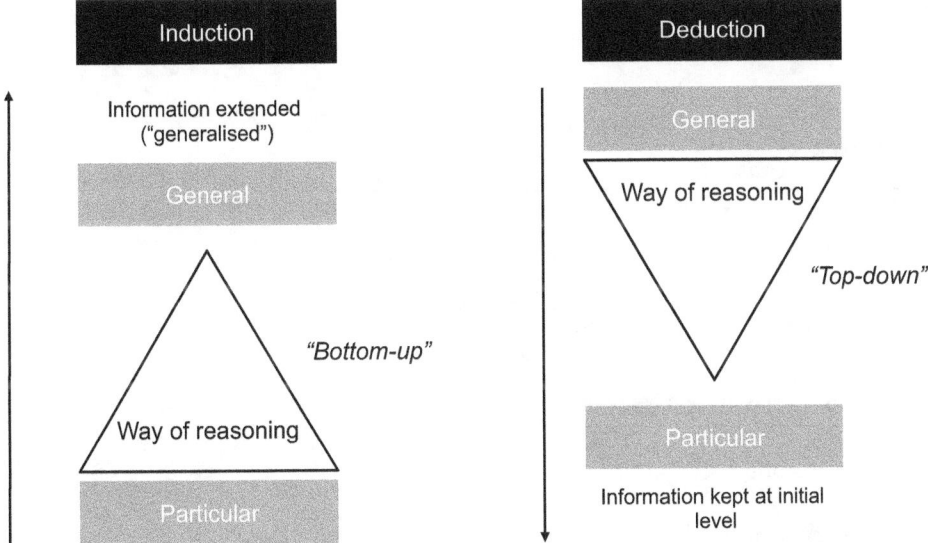

Figure 3.2: Types of reasoning

By way of inductive reasoning, a particular proposition is extended to a generalising proposition. Induction means that the way of reasoning takes place bottom-up. The limited initial information is extended, i.e. generalised.

While applying deductive reasoning, a general proposition is applied to a specific incident in order to derive a particular proposition. Deduction means that the way of reasoning takes place top-down. The initial information is kept at the same level. In other words, it remains unchanged.

3.2.2 Inductive reasoning

Inductive reasoning can be used in order to generate forecasts or explanations (Figure 3.3).

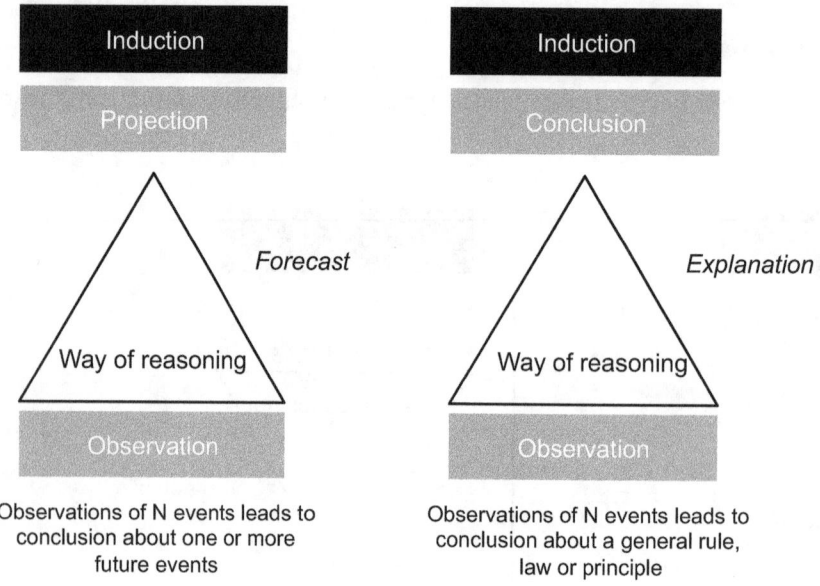

Figure 3.3: Inductive reasoning

In a forecast, an observation of N events leads to a conclusion about one or more future events. The starting point is the observation, which is used in order to come up with a more generalised projection of future events.

For an explanation, an observation of N events leads to a conclusion about a general rule, law, or principle. Again, the starting point is the observation, which is used in order to come up with a more generalised conclusion.

3.2.3 Deductive reasoning

Deductive reasoning can be used in order to generate forecasts or explanations (Figure 3.4).

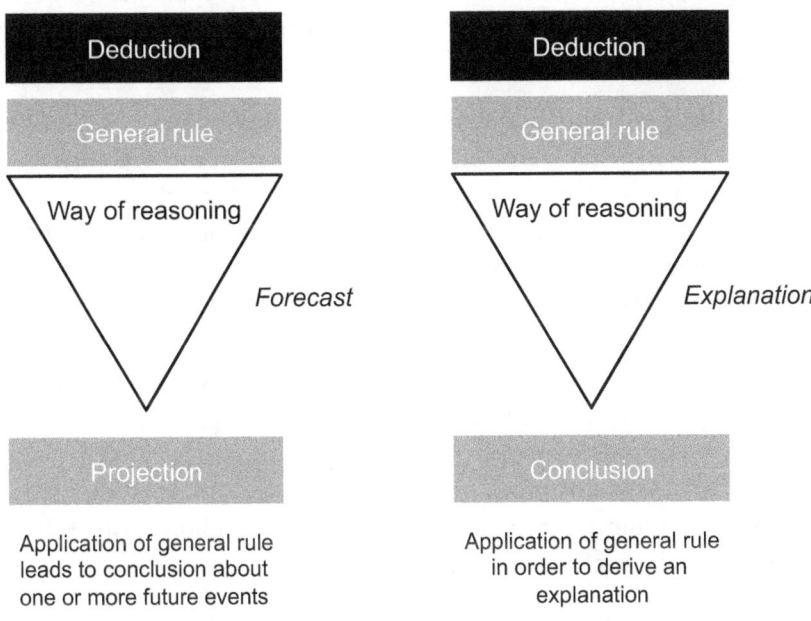

Figure 3.4: Deductive reasoning

In a forecast, the application of a general rule leads to a statement about one or more future events. The starting point is the general rule, which is used in order to come up with a projection of future events.

For an explanation, a general rule will be applied in order to derive an explanation. Again, the starting point is the general rule, which is used in order to come up with a conclusion.

3.3 Syllogism

3.3.1 Logical reasoning

There have been numerous philosophers and scientists who devoted their academic life to logical reasoning. Three outstanding philosophers shall be named in order to give credit for their ideas:

1. **Aristotle**, the Greek philosopher and polymath, devoted a major part of his life's work to logical reasoning and a special form of logical conclusions, the syllogism.
2. **Sir Karl Popper**, the Austrian-British philosopher, used, amongst others, the techniques of logical reasoning in order to develop his school of thought named critical rationalism and falsificationism. Critical rationalism could be described in simple words as a critical attitude towards scientific knowledge. All scientific knowledge should be questioned, challenged and scrutinized in order to come up with scientific progress. Falsificationism forms the basis of critical rationalism. Its basic idea is that certain academic propositions can never be verified, but only falsified.
3. **Carl Gustav Hempel**, a German philosopher, mathematician and physicist, developed, together with **Paul Oppenheim**, formal notations of the deductive-nomological model and the inductive-statistical explanation providing more formalised ways for describing logical conclusions.

A syllogism is a logical conclusion or a form of logical reasoning. The word stems from the ancient Greek word "syllogismo". Syllogisms are a set of logical conclusions as laid down by Aristotle. Figure 3.5 shows an example of a syllogism.

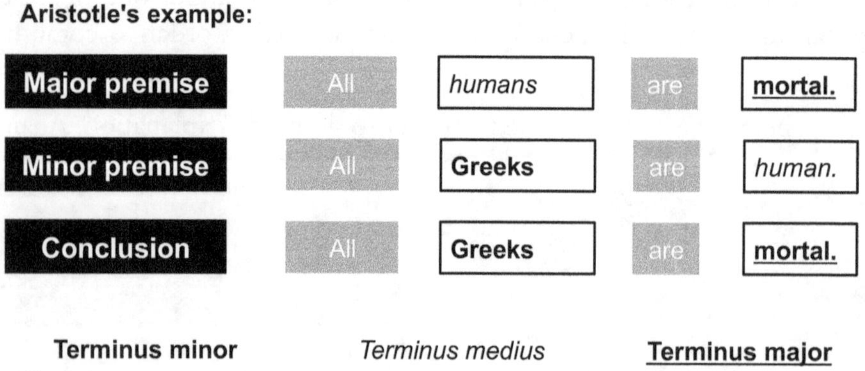

Aristotle's example:

Major premise	All	humans	are	mortal.
Minor premise	All	Greeks	are	human.
Conclusion	All	Greeks	are	mortal.
Terminus minor		*Terminus medius*		**Terminus major**

Figure 3.5: Syllogism

Each sentence of a syllogism has a subject and a predicate, which traditionally carry Latin names:

- The word "Greeks" is called terminus minor.
- The words "humans" and "human" are called terminus medius.
- The word "mortal" is called terminus major.

A closer look at Aristotle's example reveals more structural elements (Figure 3.6).

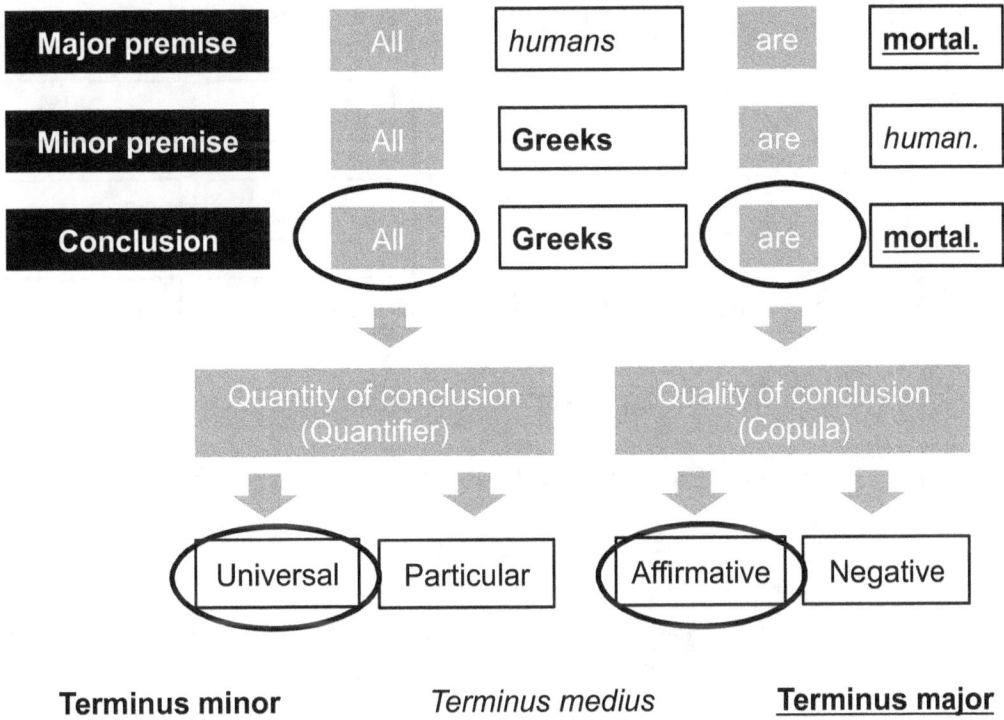

Figure 3.6: Quantity and quality of conclusions

There are two more words in the structure of the sentences that have not been described yet:

- The numeral "all" describes the quantity of a conclusion or the quantifier. The quantifier can be universal or particular. In this case it is universal.
- The auxiliary verb "are" describes the quality of a conclusion or the copula. The copula can be affirmative or negative. In this case it is affirmative.

The quantifier and the copula can be used in order to describe the possible combinations of logical conclusions and thereby the types of statements (Figure 3.7).

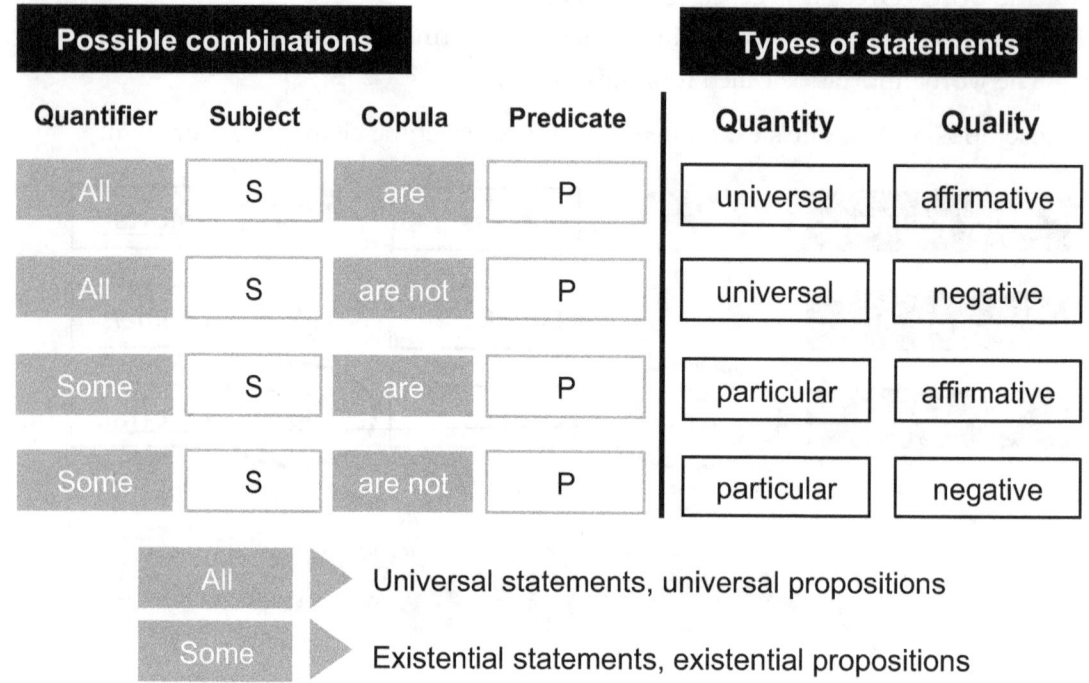

Figure 3.7: Types of propositions

The structure of each sentence can be described by using quantifier, subject, copula and predicate. The type of statement can be described by quantity and quality:

- The first possible combination is "All S are P." Due to the quantifier "all" and the copula "are", it is a universal and affirmative statement.
- The second possible combination is "All S are not P." Due to the quantifier "no" and the copula "are", it is a universal and negative statement.
- The third possible combination is "Some S are P." Due to the quantifier "some" and the copula "are", it is a particular and affirmative statement.
- The fourth possible combination is "Some S are not P." Due to the quantifier "some" and the copula "are not", it is a particular and negative statement.

The sentences which start with "all" are called universal statements or universal propositions. The sentences that start with "some" are called existential statements or existential propositions. As will be described in one of the following subchapters, it is important to distinguish between universal and existential propositions.

As previously pointed out, the deductive-nomological model was developed by Carl Gustav Hempel and Paul Oppenheim. The model has its roots in the logical reasoning of Aristotle. It is also known as the DN model, HO-Scheme, Hempel-Oppenheim model, Popper-Hempel model or Hempel's model (Figure 3.8).

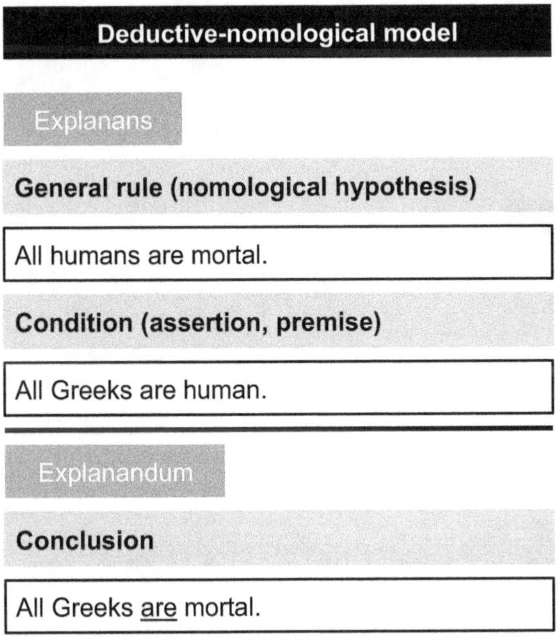

Deductive-nomological model

Explanans

General rule (nomological hypothesis)

All humans are mortal.

Condition (assertion, premise)

All Greeks are human.

Explanandum

Conclusion

All Greeks are mortal.

Figure 3.8: Deductive-nomological model – explanation

The model has two parts: The explanans, Latin for "the explaining", and the explanandum, Latin for "that what is to be explained".

Again, the explanans consists of two elements:

- The first part comprises a general rule, which is also called a nomological hypothesis. The word "nomological" stems from the Greek word "nomos", which means "law" or "rule". The word "hypothesis" stems from the Greek word "hypotithenai", which means "to suppose". An example of a general rule is Aristotle's statement "All humans are mortal."

- The second part comprises a condition, which is sometimes called "assertion" or "premise". An example of a condition is Aristotle's statement "All Greeks are human."

The explanandum contains the conclusion. The apparent conclusion that can be derived from the first two sentences is "All Greeks are mortal."

Evidently, the deductive-nomological model applies a specific way of writing down a logical explanation. However, in addition to the formal representation it is important to note that conclusions can only be derived from a nomological hypothesis in the form of a general rule or law.

The deductive-nomological model can also be used for forecasts and projections (Figure 3.9).

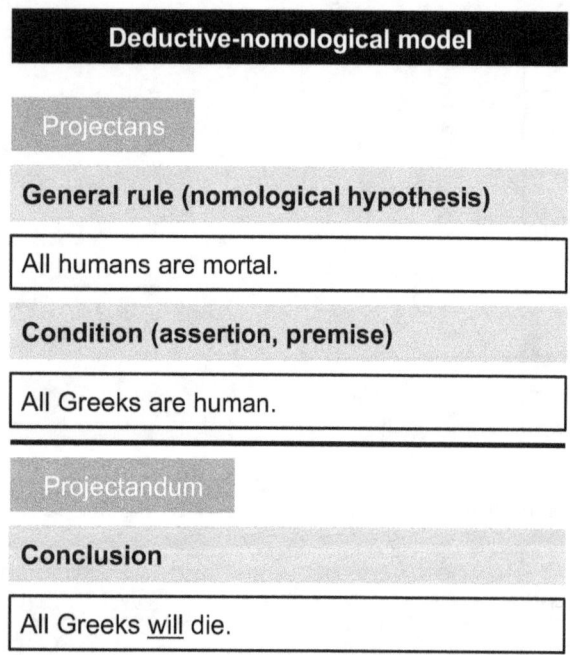

Figure 3.9: Deductive-nomological model – forecast

Again, the model has two parts: The projectans, Latin for "the projecting", and the projectandum, Latin for "that what is to be forecasted".

Again, the projectans consists of two elements:

- As a general rule one can use the previous example of Aristotle: "All humans are mortal."
- Again, the second part comprises a condition, sometimes called assertion or premise, which in our example is "All Greeks are human."

The projectandum contains the conclusion. The conclusion that can be derived from the first two sentences is "All Greeks will die."

At first glance, this does not appear to deviate from the formal notation of the deductive-nomological model for an explanation. However, one has to keep in mind that the conclusion addresses aspects that will only take place in the future.

In the deductive-nomological model conclusions can only be derived from a nomological hypothesis. This leads to a problem because often such a nomological hypothesis is not available. Especially in business and social sciences, it is common to work with statistical data. Here, the inductive-statistical model might provide another way of logical reasoning (Figure 3.10).

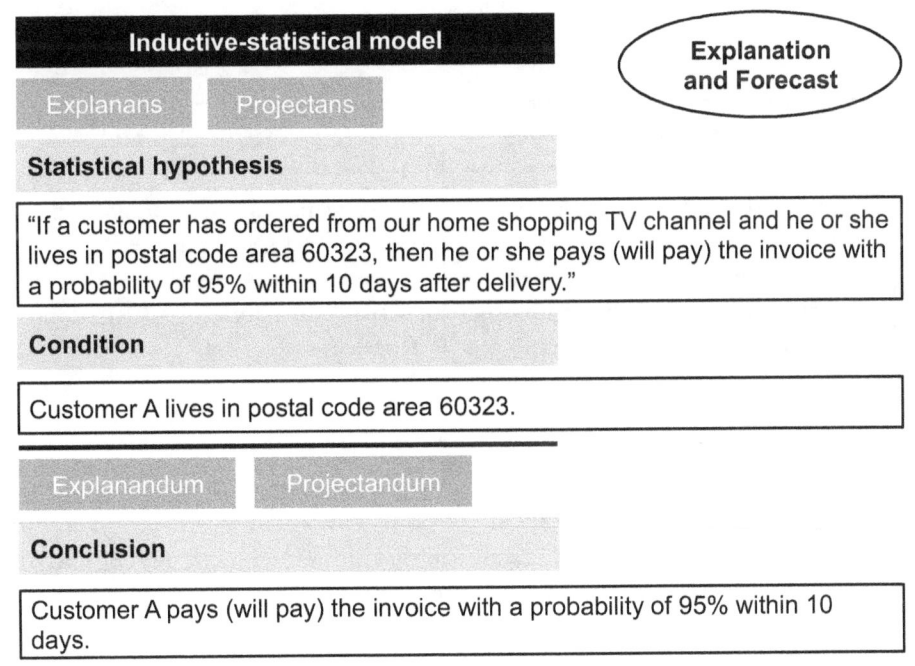

Figure 3.10: Inductive-statistical model

Again, the scientific notation of Hempel and Oppenheim helps to describe a logical explanation or forecast.

The model has two parts: The explanans or projectans and the explanandum or projectandum.

Again, the explanans or projectans consists of two elements:

- The first part comprises a statistical hypothesis, which needs to have a certain statistical reliability. For example: "If a customer has ordered from our home shopping TV channel and he or she lives in postal code area 60323, then he or she pays (will pay) the invoice with a probability of 95% within 10 days after delivery."
- The second part comprises a condition. In the example, the condition could be as follows: "Customer A lives in postal code area 60323."

The explanandum or projectandum contains the conclusion. In the example, the conclusion could be as follows: "Customer A pays (will pay) the invoice with a probability of 95% within 10 days."

Both the deductive-nomological model and the inductive-statistical model have advantages and disadvantages as pointed out in Table 3.1.

	Deductive-nomological model	Inductive-statistical model
Advantage	Deterministic nature of explanation (forecast)	Probabilistic rules are common in business and social sciences
Disadvantage	Deterministic rules are not common in business and social sciences	Probabilistic nature of explanation (forecast)

Table 3.1: Advantages and disadvantages of models

The inductive-statistical model or IS model leads to explanations or forecasts within business and social sciences that are often logically incomplete and require time stability. A closer look at a statistical hypothesis that tries to provide a rule with respect to the payment behaviour of customer A reveals the problem (Figure 3.11).

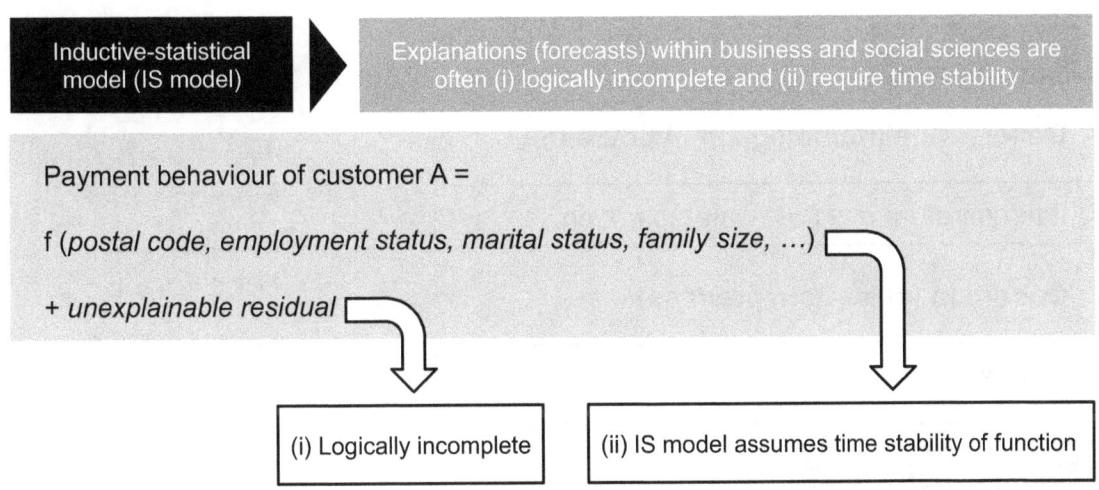

Figure 3.11: Problems of inductive-statistical reasoning

The payment behaviour of customer A is equal to the function of postal code, employment status, marital status, family size, and maybe some other variables as well as an unexplainable residual.

The inductive-statistical model implies that what has been true in the past (in terms of historic observations) will also be true in the future (in terms of future observations).

Therefore, this type of reasoning has two shortcomings:

1. Due to its probabilistic nature, the statistical rule is logically incomplete. The unexplainable residual allows only for a rule or hypothesis with a certain probability.
2. The function itself is based on historic observations of the past. The inductive-statistical model assumes time stability of the observed function.

3.3.2 Modus ponens

Modus ponens is Latin and means "the way that affirms by affirming". It is a logical figure that was known in the ancient world. Modus ponens is explained by using the formalised way of the Hempel-Oppenheim model for describing nomological-deductive conclusions (Figure 3.12).

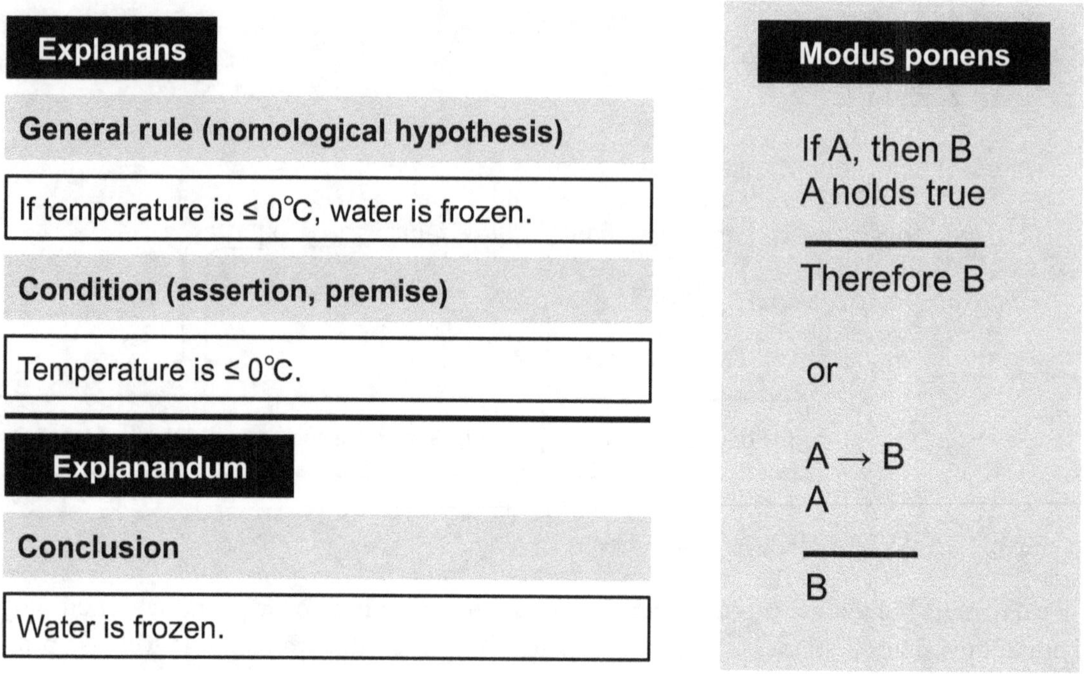

3 Research logic

Explanans	Modus ponens
General rule (nomological hypothesis)	If A, then B
If temperature is ≤ 0°C, water is frozen.	A holds true
Condition (assertion, premise)	Therefore B
Temperature is ≤ 0°C.	or
Explanandum	$A \rightarrow B$
Conclusion	A
Water is frozen.	B

Figure 3.12: Modus ponens

The explanans contains the general rule or nomological hypothesis "If the temperature is ≤ 0°C, water is frozen" and the condition "The temperature is ≤ 0°C". The explanandum contains the conclusion "Water is frozen".

There is also a more formalised way of describing modus ponens that can be written in mathematical terms.

3.3.3 Modus tollens

Modus tollens is Latin and means "the way that denies by denying". The formal notation of the Hempel-Oppenheim model helps to describe nomological deductive conclusions (Figure 3.13).

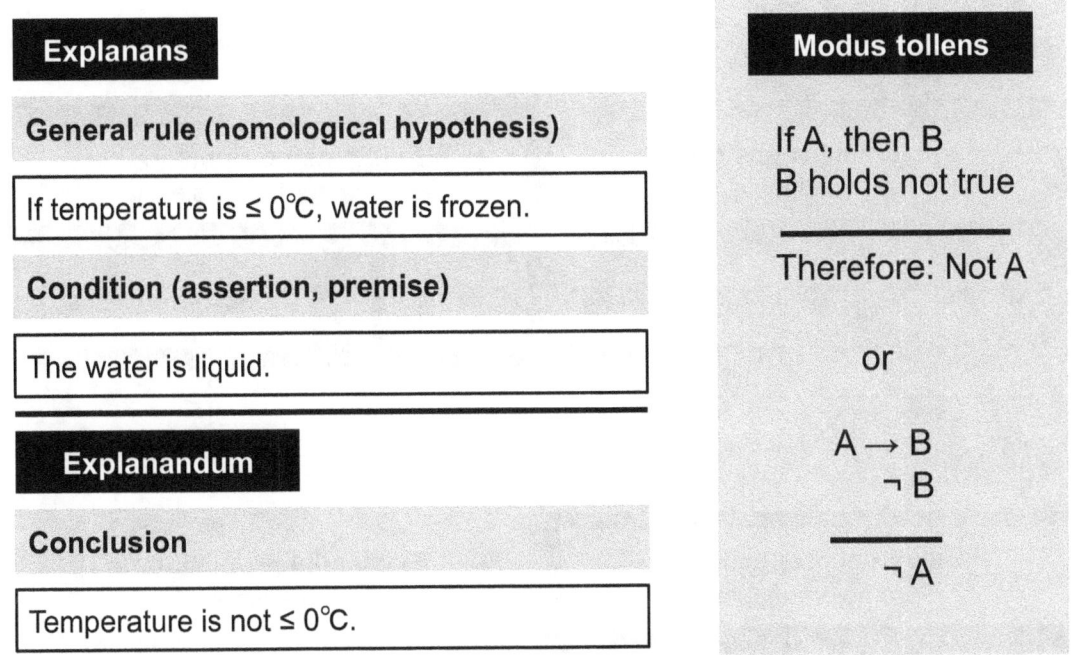

Figure 3.13: Modus tollens

The explanans contains the general rule or nomological hypothesis "If the temperature is ≤ 0°C, water is frozen" and the condition "The water is liquid". The explanandum contains the conclusion "Temperature is not ≤ 0°C".

In the following chapter, Modus tollens is used in order to explain the process of falsification.

3.4 Falsification

3.4.1 Falsifiability and verifiability of propositions

Generally, one distinguishes between falsification and verification (Figure 3.14).

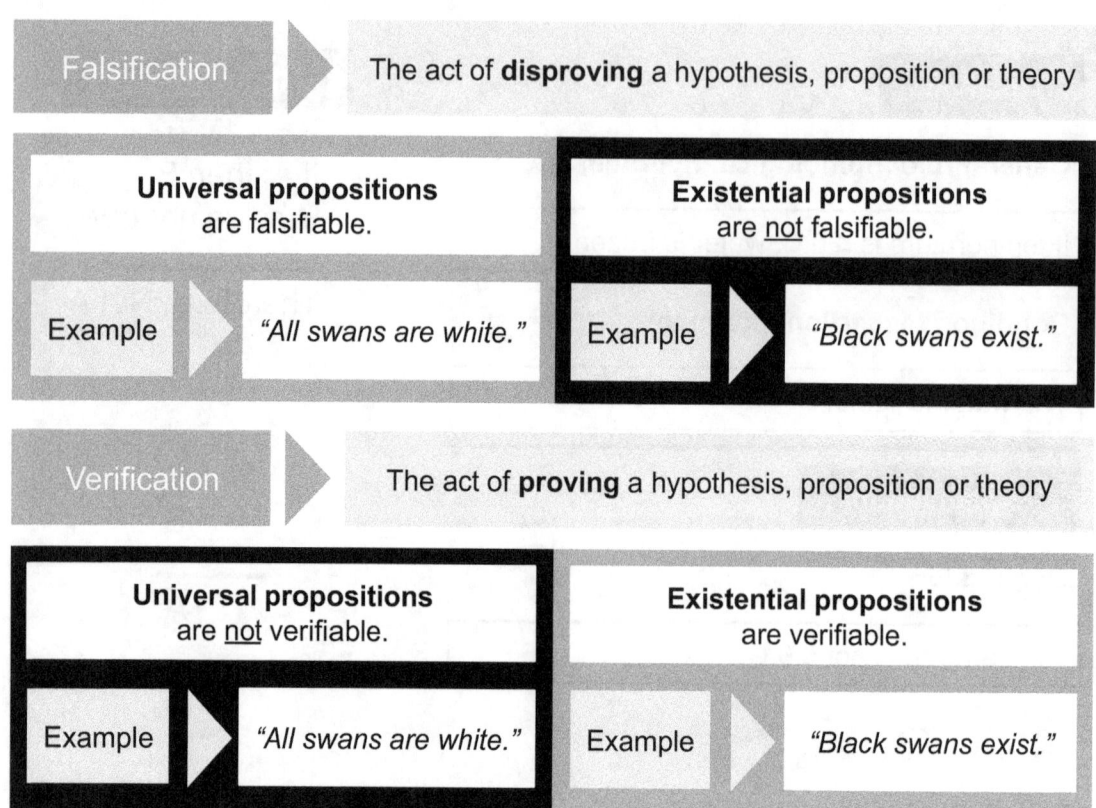

Figure 3.14: Falsification, verification

Falsification can be defined as the act of disproving a hypothesis, proposition or theory. In subchapter 3.3.1, it was pointed out that a distinction has to be made between universal propositions and existential propositions. In the context of falsification, this differentiation becomes important.

- Universal propositions are falsifiable.

    An example of a universal proposition is "All swans are white". This sentence is falsifiable – either because of the fact that someone discovers a black swan, or because of the possibility that someone might identify a swan with a colour that is not white.

- Existential propositions are not falsifiable.

    An example of an existential proposition is "Black swans exist". This sentence is not falsifiable – either because of the proof that black swans exist or because of the possibility that someone might proof the existence of black swans. The problem of non-falsifiability might become evident if one changes the sentence to "Blue swans exist". Nobody knows whether blue swans exist or not. There is always a possibility that someone discovers a blue swan.

Verification can be defined as the act of proving a hypothesis, proposition or theory.

- Universal propositions are not verifiable.

    Again, the example of a universal proposition is "All swans are white". This sentence is not verifiable – either because it is already known that swans with other colours exist or because of the possibility that someone might discover swans with a colour that is not white.

- Existential propositions are verifiable.

    Again, the example of an existential proposition is "Black swans exist". This sentence is verifiable – either because of the proof that black swans exist or because of the possibility that someone might prove the existence of black swans.

In an academic or scientific context, the attribute or characteristic of **falsifiability** becomes important. Falsifiability is the fact that a hypothesis, proposition, statement, sentence or theory has to be formulated in a way that it is disputable, meaning that it is falsifiable. The following examples of non-falsifiable statements illustrate the problem:

The sentence "The sun will shine tomorrow, or not" is non-falsifiable because it is tautological. The statement is always true.

The sentence "Actions will have consequences" is non-falsifiable because it is meaningless. The statement lacks precision.

The sentence "The German renewable energy act has (or could have) a strong impact on the financial feasibility" is non-falsifiable because it is meaningless. The statement lacks precision due to the imprecise adjective "strong".

3.4.2 Falsification with modus tollens

In the following, modus tollens is used in order to explain the logical structure of falsification (Figure 3.15).

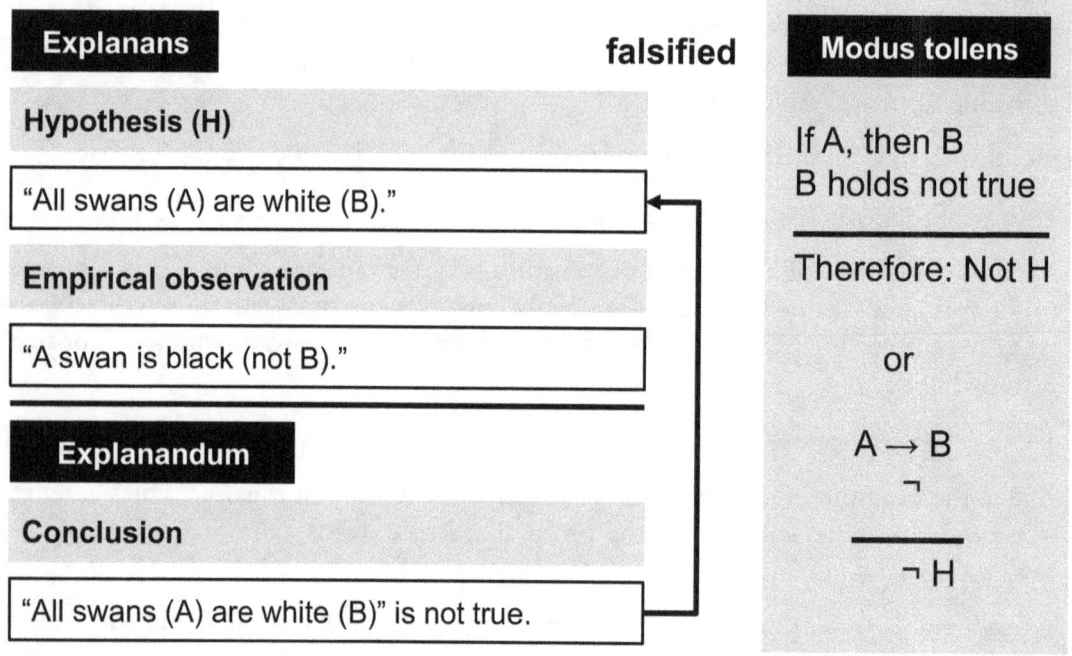

Figure 3.15: Falsification of a hypothesis with modus tollens

Provided that a hypothesis is "All swans are white", an empirical observation might lead to the statement "A swan is black." This leads to the conclusion that the initial hypothesis "All swans are white" is not true. Thus, the initial hypothesis has been falsified.

3.4.3 Indicator and causal hypotheses

In business and social sciences, it is common to generate indicator hypotheses by way of induction. More precisely, observations are extended in order to generate an indicator hypothesis. Figure 3.16 explains the underlying reasoning, using the "White and black swan example".

3.4 Falsification

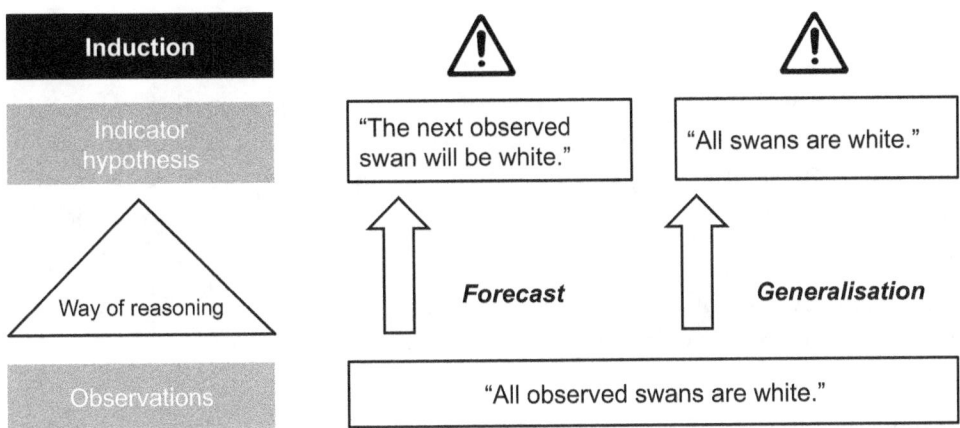

Figure 3.16: Generation of indicator hypotheses

From "All observed swans are white" one can derive the projecting indicator hypothesis "The next observed swan will be white" or the generalising indicator hypothesis "All swans are white". As previously explained, this type of reasoning is problematic as evident in the "White and black swan example".

The shortcomings of this reasoning can be illustrated with the help of the management problem "Credit risk and the equity ratio" (Figure 3.17).

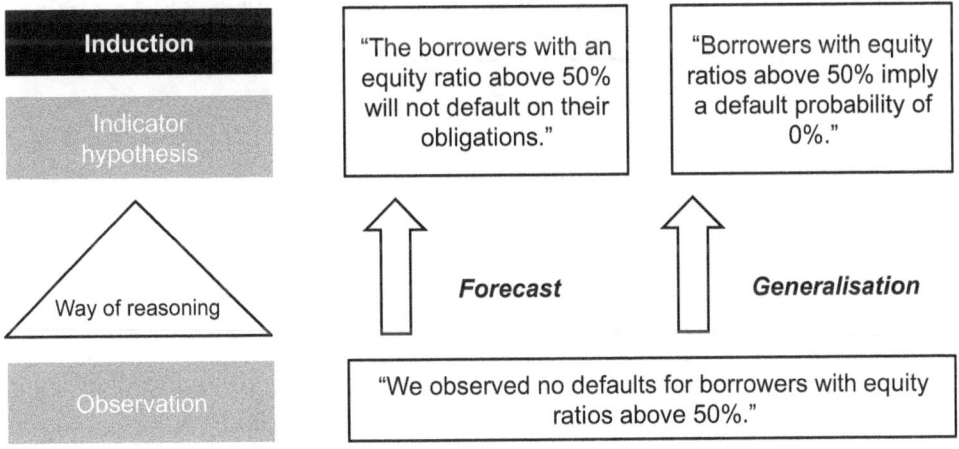

Figure 3.17: Indicator hypotheses – examples

From the statement "We observed no defaults for borrowers with equity ratios above 50%" we could derive a projecting indicator hypothesis such as "The borrowers with an equity ratio above 50% will not default on their obligations" or a generalising indicator hypothesis such as "Borrowers with equity ratios above 50% imply a default probability of 0%". Again, this type of reasoning is problematic because there might be borrowers, which default although they have an equity ratio above 50%. In other words, they are "black swans".

If inductive reasoning by way of an indicator hypothesis is problematic, the question is whether one can apply deductive reasoning as an alternative (Figure 3.18).

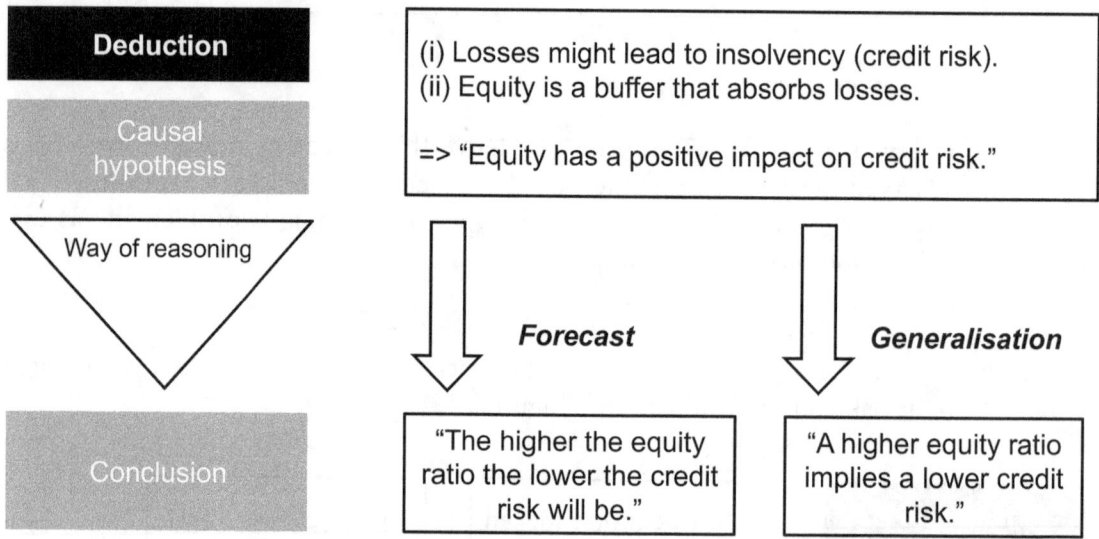

Figure 3.18: Causal hypothesis – example

While applying deductive logic, one could state the following line of thought:

- Losses might lead to insolvency (credit risk).
- Equity is a buffer that absorbs losses.

Therefore, one could develop the causal hypothesis "Equity has a positive impact on credit risk". From the causal hypothesis one can generate either the forecast "The higher the equity ratio the lower the credit risk will be" or the generalisation "A higher equity ratio implies a lower credit risk". Again, this type of reasoning might be problematic because the causal hypothesis is only an assumed relationship but not a general law of nature.

A comparison of induction and deduction reveals the inherent characteristics of the two types of hypothesis (Table 3.2).

Reasoning	Induction	Deduction
Method	Empirical-statistical methods	Logical-deductive methods
Example	"We observed no defaults, i.e. no credit risk, for borrowers with equity ratios above 50%."	"Equity has a positive impact on credit risk because it serves as buffer against losses."
Hypothesis	Indicator hypothesis	Causal hypothesis
Explanation	Statistical explanation of credit risk drivers ("indicators")	Logical explanation of credit risk drivers ("causalities")
Problem	No logical explanation	No statistical proof

Table 3.2: Comparison of induction and deduction

Inductive reasoning uses empirical-statistical methods. The statement "We observed no defaults (credit risk) for borrowers with equity ratios above 50%" is an indicator hypothesis that is based on a statistical explanation of credit risk drivers. The downside is that it does not necessarily provide a logical explanation.

Deductive reasoning applies logical-deductive methods. The statement "Equity has a positive impact on credit risk because it serves as buffer against losses" is a causal hypothesis based on a logical explanation of credit risk drivers. The downside is that it is not necessarily based on a statistical proof.

Both induction and deduction have their shortcomings. In order to reduce the inherent problems, both methods are typically combined in the world of sciences (Figure 3.19).

3 Research logic

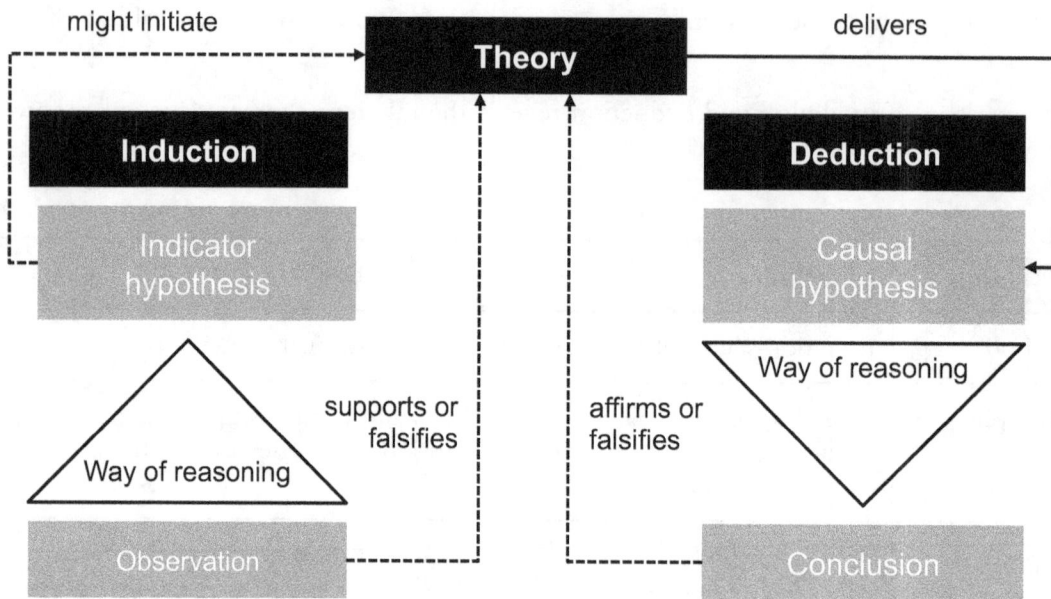

Figure 3.19: Induction, deduction and theory

An observation might be the starting point for deriving an indicator hypothesis. An indicator hypothesis might initiate a theory. Typically, a theory delivers a causal hypothesis that can be used in order to derive a conclusion. Observations might be used in order to support or falsify the theory. Conclusions might affirm or falsify the theory.

3.5 Summary and exercises

3.5.1 Synopsis

In this chapter, principles of reasoning were addressed:

- By way of inductive reasoning, a particular proposition will be extended to a generalising proposition.
- Via the method of deductive reasoning, a general proposition will be applied to a specific incident in order to derive a particular proposition.
- Both ways of reasoning can be used in order to create forecasts or to derive explanations.

The syllogism is a special form of deriving logical conclusions:

- Logical reasoning can be explained by using Aristotle's example of the structure of syllogisms.
- The quantity and quality of statements and conclusions become important.
- The deductive-nomological model and the inductive-statistical model provide more formalised ways of reasoning.
- The logical figures of modus ponens and modus tollens are similar ways to describe reasoning.

Falsification and verification of propositions are fundamental to academic research:

- There are two important rules to keep in mind:
  1. Universal propositions are falsifiable, but not verifiable.
  2. Existential propositions are not falsifiable, but verifiable.
- Falsification is the act of disproving a hypothesis, proposition, statement, sentence, or theory.
- Falsifiability is the fact that a hypothesis, proposition, statement, sentence, or theory has to be formulated in a way that it is disputable, meaning that it is falsifiable.
- Falsification with modus tollens is a formalised way of describing the falsification of a hypothesis.

Empirical-statistical methods use indicator hypotheses and logical-deductive methods use causal hypotheses:

- Observations can be used order to generate an indicator hypothesis.
- Logical reasoning might lead to a causal hypothesis.
- Both the indicator hypothesis and the causal hypothesis imply advantages and disadvantages. In order to overcome shortcomings, both methods can be employed while deriving new theories or falsifying existing theories.

3.5.2 Questions

Knowledge

1. What is induction?
2. What is deduction?
3. What is a syllogism? What are syllogisms?

3 Research logic

4. What is the structure of a syllogism?
5. What are terminus minor, terminus medius, and terminus major?
6. What are quantifier and copula?
7. What are the two types of statements used in syllogisms?
8. What is the formal notation of the deductive-nomological model in case of an explanation?
9. What is the formal notation of the deductive-nomological model in case of a forecast?
10. What is the formal notation of the inductive-statistical model in case of an explanation?
11. What is the formal notation of the inductive-statistical model in case of a forecast?
12. What is the advantage of the deductive-nomological model?
13. What is the disadvantage of the deductive-nomological model?
14. What is the advantage of the inductive-statistical model?
15. What is the disadvantage of the inductive-statistical model?
16. Why are explanations or forecasts with the inductive-statistical model often logically incomplete?
17. Why is time stability relevant in the inductive-statistical model?
18. What is the formal notation of modus ponens?
19. What is the formal notation of modus tollens?
20. What is falsification?
21. What is verification?
22. What is falsifiability?
23. Why are tautological and meaningless statements non-falsifiable?
24. Which type of propositions is falsifiable?
25. Which type of propositions is not falsifiable?
26. Which type of propositions is verifiable?
27. Which type of propositions is not verifiable?
28. How can a hypothesis be falsified with modus tollens?
29. What is an indicator hypothesis?
30. What is a causal hypothesis?
31. What are the advantage and disadvantage of empirical-statistical methods?
32. What are the advantage and disadvantage of logical-deductive methods?

3.5.3 Problems

3.5.3.1 Penicillin

Analysis

Learning target

Being able to understand different ways of reasoning

Instruction

Please research the history of penicillin on the Internet.

Question

Which type of academic reasoning took place while discovering the effects of this antibiotic?

3.5.3.2 Economies of scale

Analysis

Learning target

Being able to understand different ways of reasoning

Instruction

Please research the term "economies of scale" on the Internet.

Question

Is this concept based on inductive or deductive logic?

3.5.4 Additional reading

Hempel, C. G., & Oppenheim, P. (1948). Studies in the Logic of Explanation. *Philosophy of Science, 15*(2), 135–175. doi:10-1086/286983

Okasha, S. (2002). *Philosophy of Science. A Very Short Introduction* [Kindle edition]. New York, NY: Oxford University Press.

Priest, G. (2000). *Logic: A Very Short Introduction* [Kindle edition]. New York, NY: Oxford University Press.

4 Research process

Abstract

Chapter 4 introduces the reader to the research process and its cornerstones. Every research project starts with an open-ended indirect research question, which is implicitly or explicitly accompanied by a research hypothesis. Often a research problem is substantiated by an ad-hoc hypothesis, which advances to a working hypothesis and ultimately will be developed into a scientific hypothesis. The logic and quality of hypotheses can differ and determine the success of the research process. Depending on their inner logic, scientific hypotheses can be formulated as cause-effect hypotheses, distribution hypotheses, correlation hypotheses and difference hypotheses. Based on their quality, scientific hypotheses can be differentiated into nomological hypotheses, quasi-nomological hypotheses and statistical hypotheses. The research approach has to match the research problem to be investigated. Literature-based research, theoretical research, developmental research, quantitative research, qualitative research, or a mixture of the aforementioned approaches provide means to tackle a research problem at hand. Different academic disciplines favour different scientific styles that predetermine the applicable research approaches. Three general types of scientific styles are introduced and critically reflected: the theoretical solution-driven style, the empirical solution-driven style and the hypothesis-driven style.

Keywords

Research question, thesis, hypothesis, ad-hoc hypothesis, working hypothesis, scientific hypothesis, nomological hypothesis, quasi-nomological hypothesis, statistical hypothesis, philosophical research, literature-based research, theoretical research, developmental research, empirical research, quantitative research, qualitative research, scientific styles

4.1 Context and relevance

4.1.1 Context of chapter 4

In the previous chapters, the nature of academic research and writing, the implied academic principles, and the underlying research logic were discussed; the next step is to elaborate on the research process.

Figure 4.1 shows how chapter 4 is embedded within the setting of a research project.

4 Research process

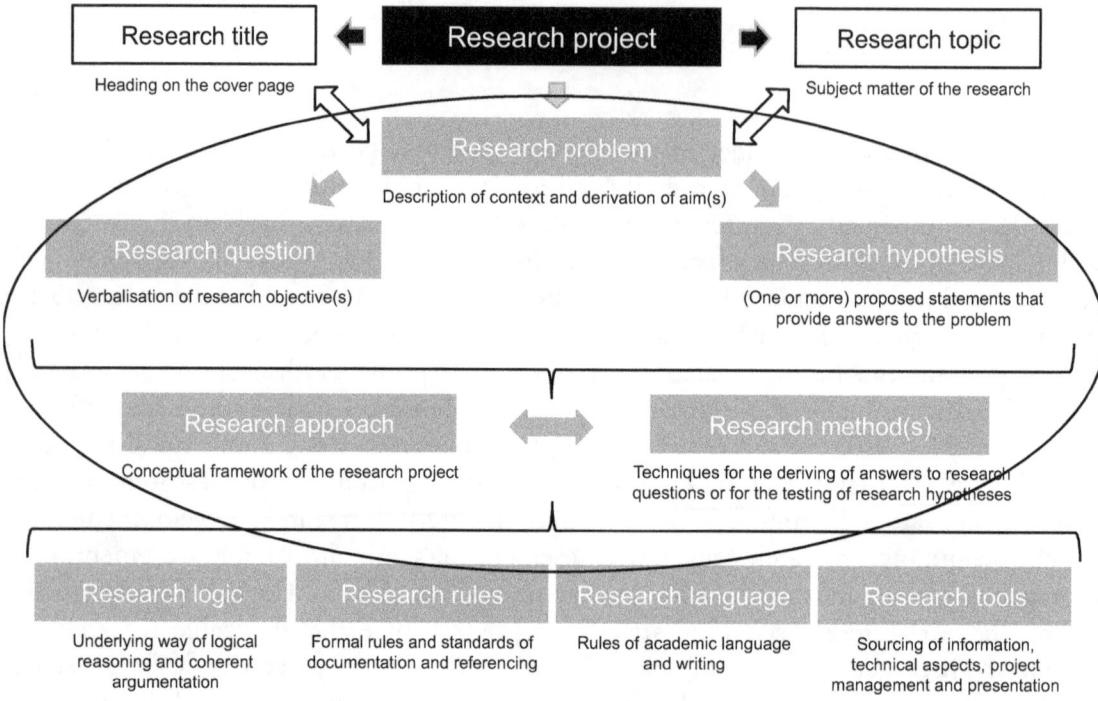

Figure 4.1: Context of chapter 4

Different aspects of academic research are touched upon:

- the research problem
- the research question
- the research hypothesis
- the research approach
- the research methods

4.1.2 Relevance of chapter 4

Different research problems require different research approaches and methods. Therefore, the careful selection of an appropriate research approach and one or more corresponding methods determines the structure and the style of research.

4.1.3 Learning objectives of chapter 4

After having studied this chapter, the reader should be able to:

- understand differences and similarities of a research question and a research hypothesis
- define and apply terminology related to the formulation of research questions
- differentiate research approaches and corresponding methods
- characterise scientific styles and understand their impact on the research process

4.2 Research question and the research hypothesis

4.2.1 Differentiation of questions

There are different ways of posing a question (Figure 4.2).

Firstly, the questions can be differentiated according to the type of the expected answer:

- Closed-ended questions are questions that permit a limited choice of responses. Closed-ended questions with two possible answers are called dichotomous questions or "yes-no-questions". The answer to these closed-ended questions is either a simple "yes" or "no" or a choice between two possibilities such as "true" or "false", "male" or "female" etc. A closed-ended question is for example: "Have you read the book?" This question is answered by either "yes" or "no".
- In comparison, open-ended questions are questions that require an individually formulated answer. An open-ended question is for example: "What is the book about?"

Furthermore, questions can differ in the syntax of the interrogative sentence.

- Direct questions are posed in a main clause that ends with a question mark. For example, both "Have you read the book?" and "What is the book about?" are direct questions.
- Indirect questions are posed in a subordinate clause that ends with a period. Examples of an indirect question are "He asked her if she has read the book." or "He wanted to know what the book is about."

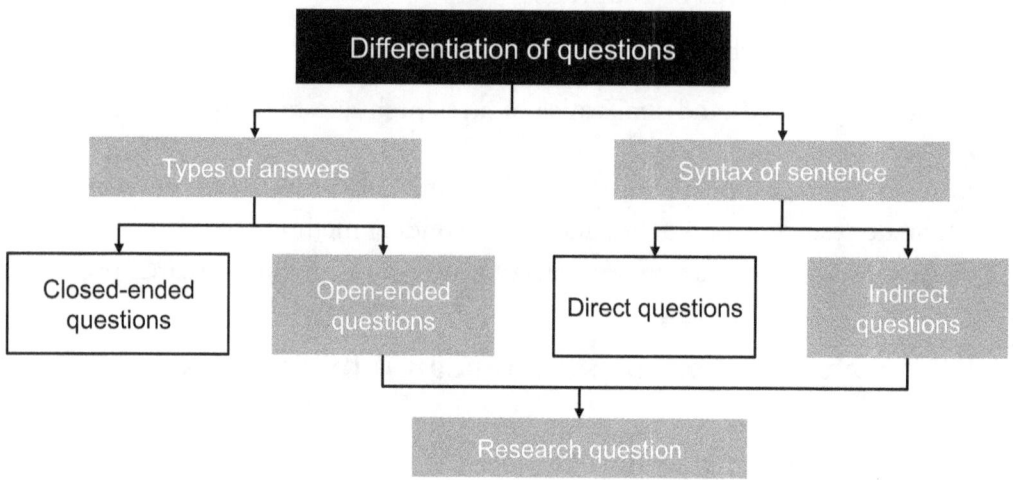

Figure 4.2: Differentiation of questions

In a research paper, the research question is always posed as an open-ended indirect question.

> Examples
> The aim of this research paper is to study how price risks can be managed with container freight derivatives.
> The aim of this research paper is to test whether the fragrance of the shampoo is responsible for the poor sales figures.
> The aim of this research paper is to investigate what the intention of the ECB money tenders is in the context of the sovereign debt crisis.
> The aim of this research paper is to analyse how the German renewable energy act (EEG) and the financial feasibility of windmill farm project financings influence each other.
> The aim of this research paper is to evaluate whether the Societas Europaea suits the objectives of a multinational enterprise.

4.2.2 Types of questions

Different interrogative words are used in order to formulate research questions (Figure 4.3).

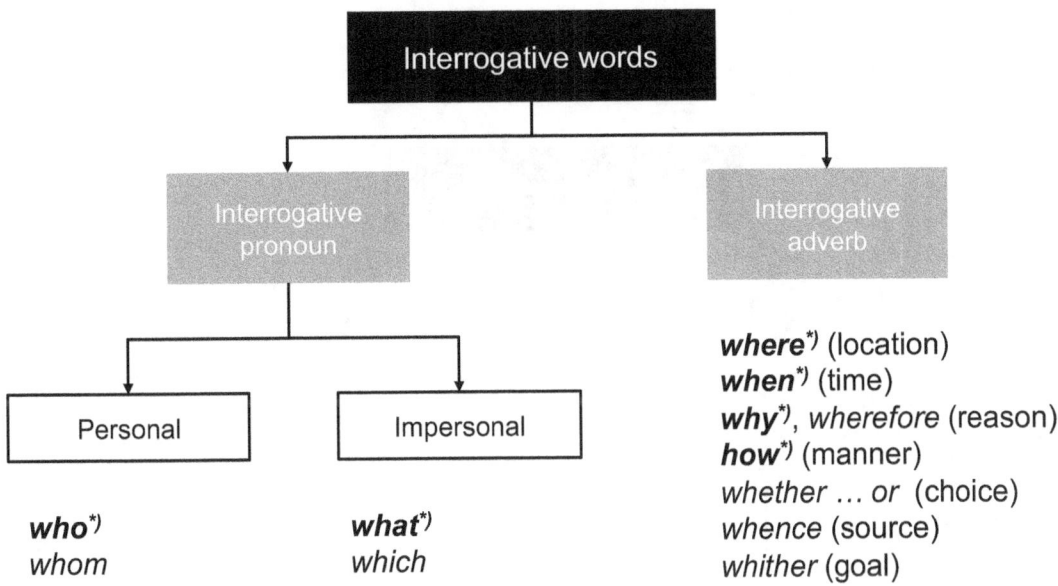

Figure 4.3: Interrogative words

More precisely, interrogative pronouns and interrogative adverbs can be distinguished from each other:

- Personal interrogative pronouns are "**who**" and "**whom**".
- Impersonal interrogative pronouns are "**what**" and "**which**".
- Interrogative adverbs are …
    o "**where**" in the case of a question that is related to a location
    o "**when**" in the case of a question that is related to time
    o "**why**" and "wherefore" in the case of a question that is related to a reason
    o "**how**" in the case of a question that is related to a manner
    o "**whether … or**" in the case of a question that is related to a choice
    o "**whence**" in the case of a question that is related to a source
    o "**whither**" in the case of a question that is related to a goal

Questions beginning with "**who**", "**what**", "**where**", "**when**", "**why**", and "**how**" are sometimes referred to as "The five Ws and one H" or "The six Ws". They are considered to be essential for information sourcing.

4.2.3 Types of hypothesis

In the following, it will be pointed out how hypotheses can be differentiated (Figure 4.4).

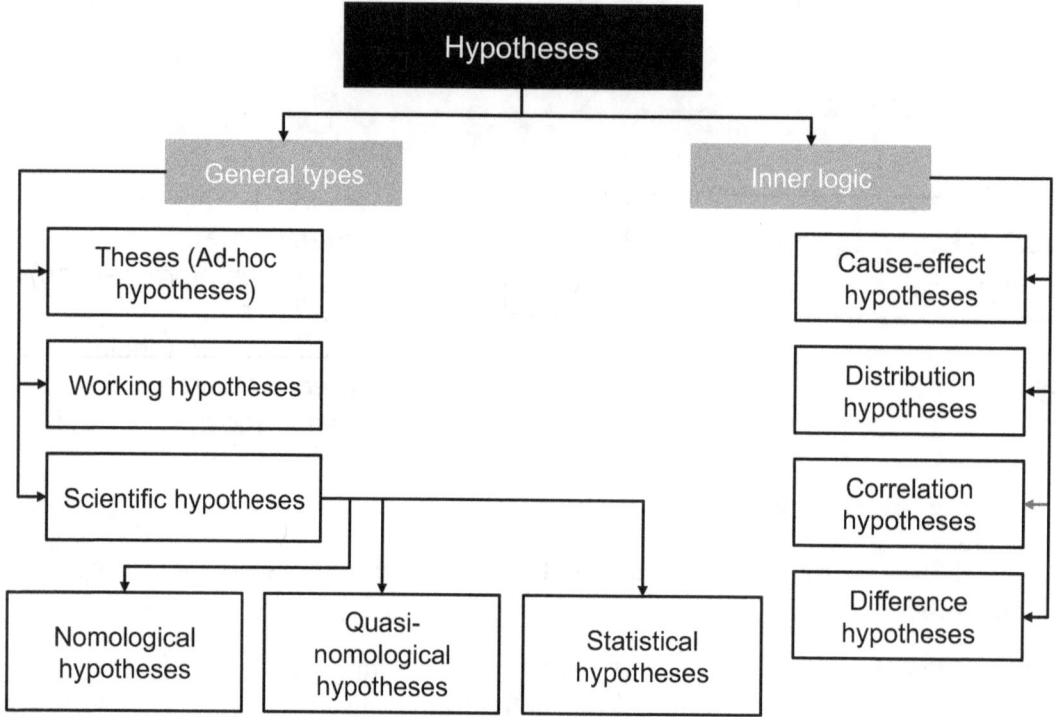

Figure 4.4: Types of hypothesis – overview

As pointed out, the term "hypothesis" stems from the Greek "hypotithenai" meaning "to put under, to suppose". The following general types of hypothesis can be differentiated:

- Theses/ad-hoc hypotheses
- Working hypotheses
- Scientific hypotheses

Scientific hypotheses can be nomological hypotheses, quasi-nomological hypotheses, or statistical hypotheses.

Furthermore, hypotheses can be viewed from a different perspective based on their inner logic. With regard to the inner logic approach, one can distinguish between cause-effect hypotheses, distribution hypotheses, correlation hypotheses and difference hypotheses.

4.2.4 Depth of hypotheses

The three general types of hypothesis differ in the depth of the hypothesis:

- Theses or ad-hoc hypotheses are first thoughts that remain to be developed and substantiated.

    Example
    Subsidy schemes have a positive impact on financings of windmill farms.

- Working hypotheses consist of a first draft of an assumed cause-effect relationship that has to be further reflected.

    Example
    If a windmill project financing is financed under the German renewable energy act, then it has a positive impact on the financial feasibility.

- Scientific hypotheses contain a fully formulated, substantiated, reflected and specified (assumed) cause-effect relationship (if-then) that can be empirically tested.

    Example
    If a windmill farm project financing is realised under the German renewable energy act (EEG), then the market risk will be reduced by a guaranteed compensation for electricity fed into the grid, and thereby the financial feasibility will be increased.

4.2.5 Inner logic of hypotheses

The following examples describe the differentiation of hypotheses according to their inner logic.

- A cause-effect hypothesis would be:

    Bank employees with university degrees tend to have a higher income.

- A distribution hypothesis would be:

    Shoe sizes of human beings follow a bell-shaped Gaussian distribution.

- A correlation hypothesis would be:

    The inflation rate is negatively correlated with the unemployment rate.

- A difference hypothesis would be:

    There are more male students than female students who study engineering sciences.

4.2.6 Scientific hypotheses

Different forms of scientific hypotheses are applied in different fields:

- **Nomological hypothesis**

    A scientific hypothesis can have the form of a nomological hypothesis. The term nomological stems from the Greek "nomos" for "law". A nomological hypothesis can be defined as an empirically proved cause-effect relationship (or mechanism) without a space-time restriction and without a probabilistic character, i.e. it is always valid and true. It is characterised by "time stability". Nomological hypotheses are typical for natural sciences.

    > Example
    > If the temperature is less than or equal to zero degrees Celsius, then pure water is (will be) frozen.

- **Quasi-nomological hypothesis**

    A scientific hypothesis can have the form of a quasi-nomological hypothesis. The term "quasi" is the Latin word meaning "almost" or "as it were". A quasi-nomological hypothesis can be defined as an empirically proved cause-effect relationship (or mechanism) with a space-time restriction and without a probabilistic character, i.e. it is valid and true only temporarily and/or for specified situations. It is characterised by limited "time stability". Quasi-nomological hypotheses are typical for business and social sciences.

    > Example
    > If a company uses the German legal form of a limited liability company (GmbH), then the liability of the shareholders is (will be) restricted to their signed equity participations.

- **Statistical hypothesis**

    A scientific hypothesis can be a statistical hypothesis. A statistical hypothesis is defined as an empirically identified, assumed, cause-effect relationship (or mechanism) with a space-time restriction and with a probabilistic character. Statistical hypotheses are typical for natural sciences as well as business and social sciences.

    > Example
    > If a customer has ordered from our home shopping TV channel and he or she lives in postal code area 60323, then he or she pays (will pay) the invoice with a probability of 95% within 10 days after delivery.

4.2.7 Interdependence of research question and hypothesis

The interdependence of the research question and the hypothesis is shown on the basis of an example. The topic of a research paper could be:

> Project finance of windmill farms under the German renewable energy act (EEG)

The research question, posed as a direct question, could be as follows:

> How do the German renewable energy act (EEG) and the financial feasibility of windmill farm project financing influence each other?

In the research paper, the research question is posed as an open-ended indirect question:

> The aim of this research paper is to analyse how the German renewable energy act (EEG) and the financial feasibility of windmill farm project financing influence each other.

Finally, the research hypotheses state a relationship corresponding with the research question:

> Hypothesis 1
> If a windmill farm project financing is realised under the German renewable energy act (EEG), then the market risk will be reduced, and thereby the financial feasibility will be increased.
>
> Hypothesis 2
> If the financial feasibility of windmill project financing increases with a reduced market risk, then the lawmaker has to adjust the tariff in the German renewable energy act (EEG) accordingly in order to support the realisation of windmill projects.

As it will be pointed out in subchapter 4.4, depending upon the applicable scientific style and chosen structural design of research, one or more hypotheses can be stated (developed) either at the beginning, in the middle or at the end of a research paper (project).

4.2.8 Why a thesis is called a thesis

In a research paper, a research question is raised. At the end of a research paper one has to provide a conclusion or, in other words, a potential answer for a given research question. It is a possible explanation for a problem and not a final or definite solution to a problem at hand. In other words: The conclusion is only a (new) hypothesis that can be supported or falsified by further research work. Hence, a research paper is called a "thesis".

4.3 Research approaches and methods

4.3.1 Overview of approaches

In academic research, there are different research approaches (Figure 4.5).

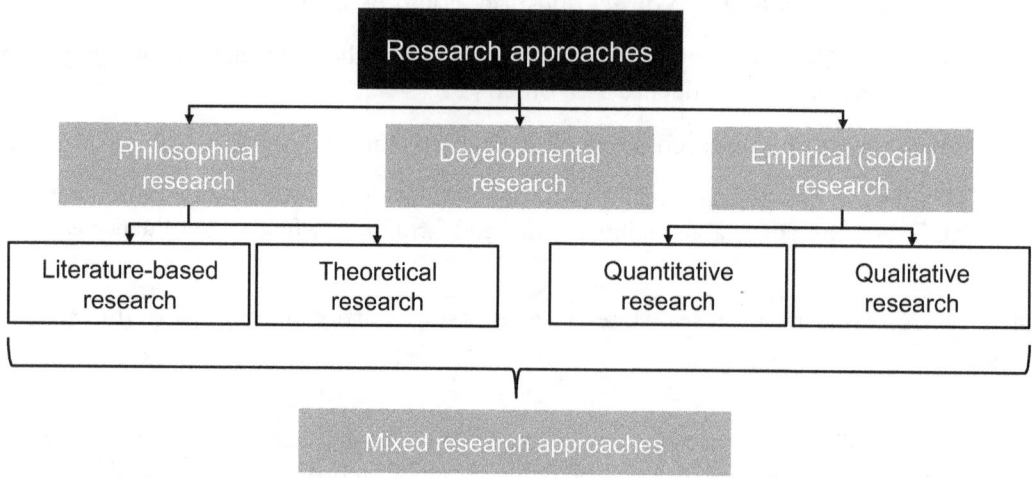

Figure 4.5: Research approaches – overview

At a glance, it can be distinguished between three main research approaches:

- Philosophical research
- Developmental research
- Empirical (or social) research

Philosophical research can be specified as literature-based research and theoretical research, whereas empirical research can be divided into quantitative and qualitative research.

In academic research, a clear distinction of research approaches is not always possible. On the contrary, mixed research approaches can be used to achieve a scientific aim.

4.3.2 Philosophical research

As pointed out, philosophical research can either be specified as literature-based research or as theoretical research (Figure 4.6).

4.3 Research approaches and methods

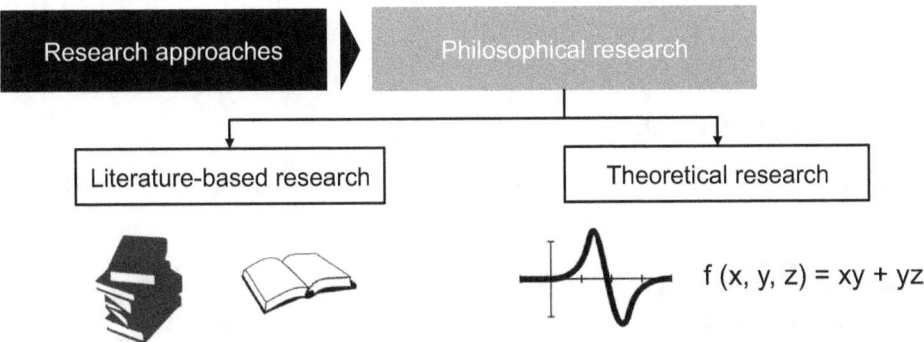

Figure 4.6: Philosophical research

Literature-based research can be defined as a critical reflection (or analysis) of the state of knowledge. Theoretical research can imply the generation of new theories or evaluation of existing theories.

4.3.3 Developmental research

Developmental research is an approach used in the field of engineering or design and, in some cases, of business and social sciences research (Figure 4.7).

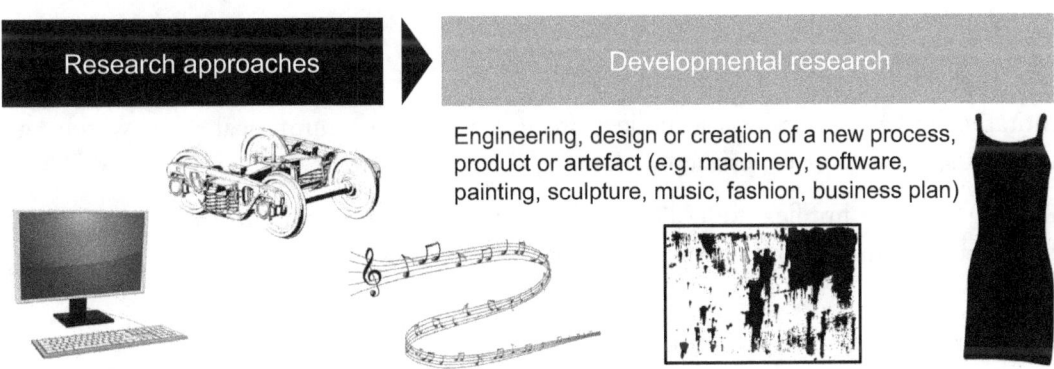

Figure 4.7: Developmental research

Although, in some cases, developmental research might be perceived as unscientific, one has to realise that disciplines such as engineering or fine arts are predominantly built on this research approach. Furthermore, disciplines as for example pedagogy have incorporated developmental research designs ("design-based research") into their research programmes.

4.3.4 Empirical (social) research

Empirical research appears as quantitative research or qualitative research (Figure 4.8).

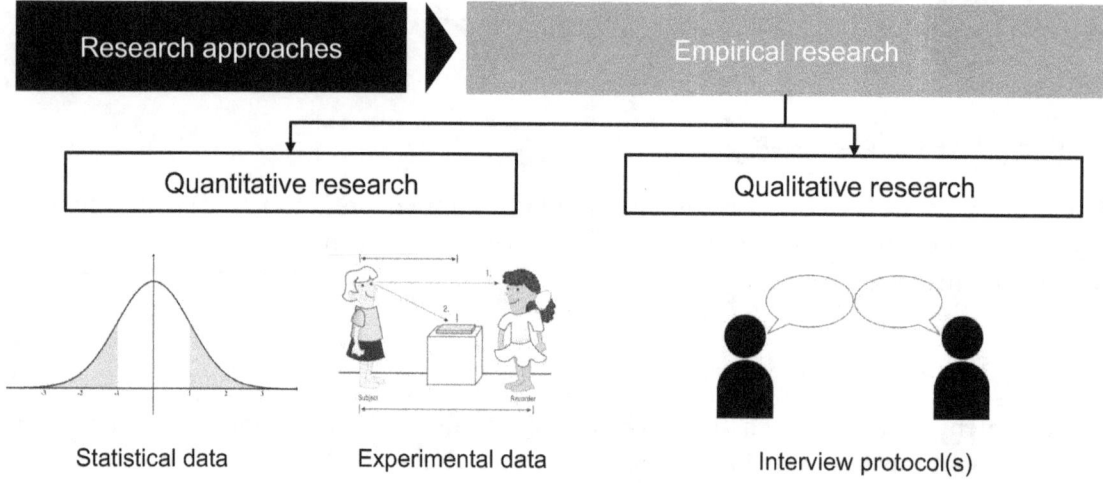

Figure 4.8: Empirical research

Quantitative research implies the collection and analysis of numerical data, which can include statistical data or experimental data.

Qualitative research implies the collection and analysis of non-standardised data that can be derived for example from interview protocols.

4.3.5 Mixed research approaches

In order to solve a problem in the context of an academic project, it can be advantageous to use mixed research approaches. Hereby, various approaches are combined as demonstrated in the following example (Figure 4.9).

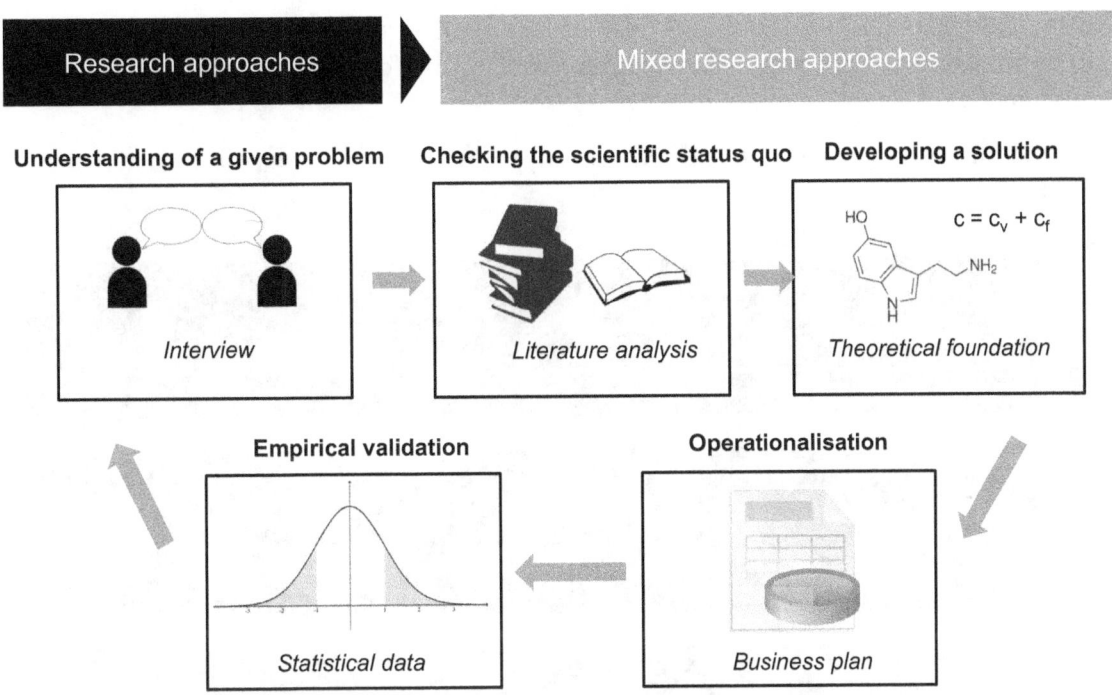

Figure 4.9: Mixed research approach – example

A general understanding of a given problem can be developed by means of qualitative interviews. In this case, it might be advisable to check the scientific status quo by a thorough literature analysis. While developing a solution for the problem, it may be necessary to build a theoretical foundation. The results might lead to the operationalisation, for example, by developing a business plan. In the next step, an empirical validation based on statistical data could follow. This, in turn, can be integrated into a further understanding of the initial problem.

4.4 Scientific styles and structural designs

4.4.1 Overview of scientific styles

While identifying a scientific style, one has to consider that there is a wide span of sciences including but not limited to the natural sciences, computer sciences, business sciences, legal sciences, social sciences and humanities. The nature of a discipline determines its academic character. Scientific styles are based upon specific research requirements as well as the particular research traditions of a science. This explains why different instructors or thesis advisors may apply different approaches and/or ask for different formal requirements.

For the purpose of this chapter, three major types of scientific style will be distinguished (Figure 4.10).

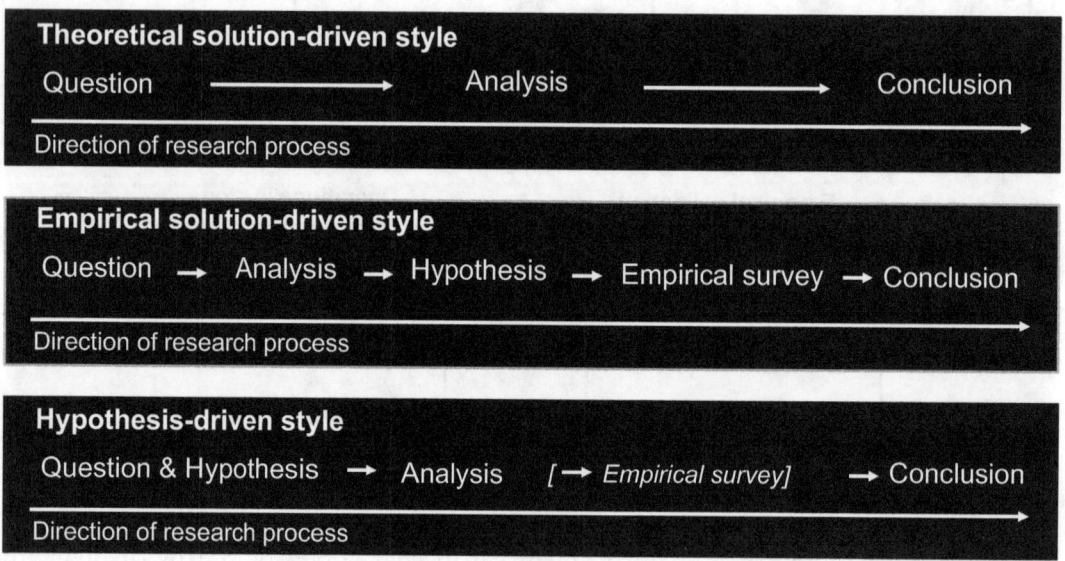

Figure 4.10: Three types of scientific style

In the field of business and social sciences, student research projects are often based on a **theoretical solution-driven style**. Viewing at the direction of the research process, one would start with a given problem, which has been derived from the topic of the project. As explained above, a research question has to be isolated as a starting point for the analysis that should lead to a conclusion.

An **empirical solution-driven style** is required for some advanced research projects. Here, the direction of the research process would encompass additional steps. Again, a given problem would lead to a research question that has to be analysed from a theoretical perspective. The theoretical analysis would lead to the deduction of one or more hypotheses. Thereafter, an empirical survey would be conducted in order to test the hypothesis and to derive a conclusion by way of inductive reasoning.

Furthermore, it should be mentioned that, in some cases, a pure **hypothesis-driven style** may be applied. Here, the direction of the research process would again start with a given problem. Instead of restricting the initial process to the verbalisation of a research question, simultaneously a research hypothesis would be formulated. Thereafter, a theoretical analysis and, in some cases, an additional empirical survey would follow. Finally, a conclusion would be derived.

4.4.2 Theoretical solution-driven style

As pointed out, the theoretical solution-driven style is frequently used in business and social sciences, particularly for student assignments and student research projects. The theoretical solution-driven style does not require a profound skillset with respect to empirical research methods (Figure 4.11).

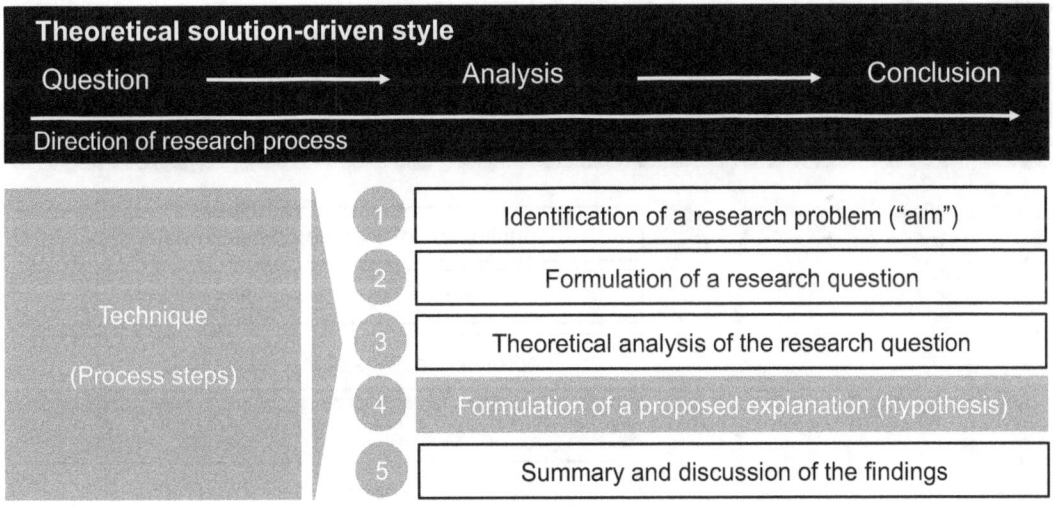

Figure 4.11: Theoretical solution-driven style – technique

The technique with its process steps can be laid out in detail as follows:

1. A research problem has to be identified.
2. A research question has to be derived from the topic and formulated for the analysis to be undertaken.

3. The theoretical analysis of the research question will take place. In business sciences, the analysis will often require a literature-based research approach. Only in rare cases, a pure theoretical research approach will be applied.
4. The objective of the theoretical analysis of the research problem is to derive a proposed explanation, which, in other words, could be interpreted as a hypothesis.
5. The analysis will be concluded with a summary and a discussion of the findings.

4.4.3 Empirical solution-driven style

The empirical solution-driven style is used for some more advanced research projects in business and social sciences. In particular research projects that require a reflection of the empirical environment are based on this style. A certain skillset is necessary with respect to empirical research methods (Figure 4.12).

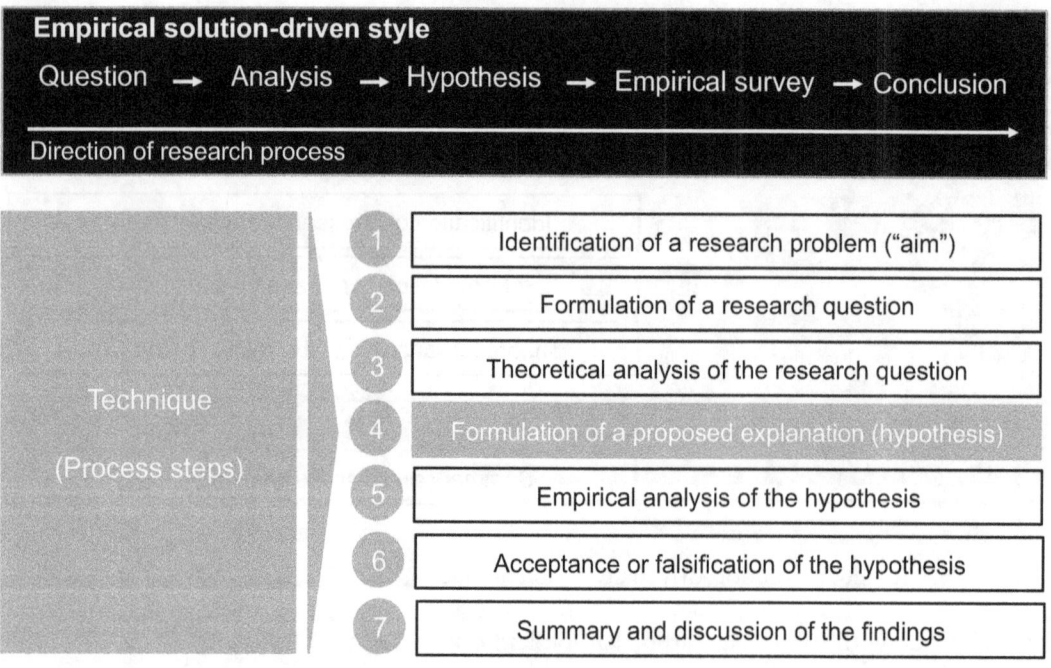

Figure 4.12: Empirical solution-driven style – technique

The technique with its process steps can be laid out in detail as follows:

1. A research problem has to be identified.

2. A research question has to be derived from the topic and formulated for the analysis to be undertaken.
3. Thereafter, the theoretical analysis of the research question will take place.
4. The objective of the theoretical analysis of the research problem is to derive a proposed explanation, or, in other words, a hypothesis by way of deduction.
5. While applying the empirical solution-driven style, an empirical analysis of the hypothesis will take place.
6. The purpose of the empirical analysis is to derive evidence that leads to the acceptance or falsification of the hypothesis by way of induction.
7. The analysis will be concluded with a summary and a discussion of the findings.

4.4.4 Hypothesis-driven style

Only in rare cases, a pure hypothesis-driven style is used in business and social sciences. Frequently, it is used in humanities (Figure 4.13).

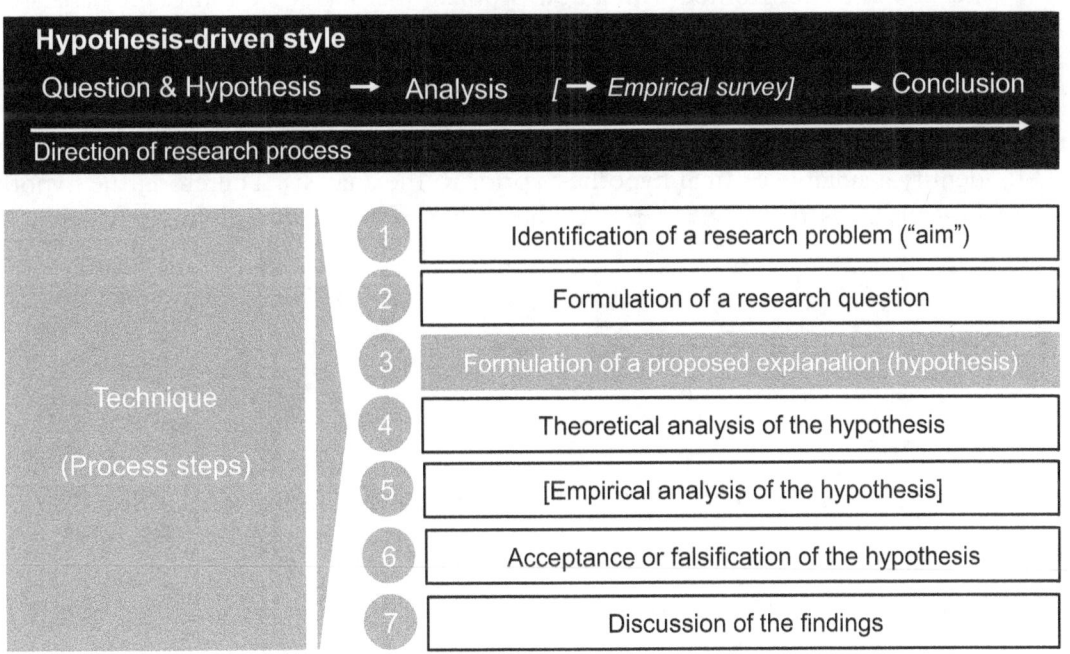

Figure 4.13: Hypothesis-driven style

The technique with its process steps can be laid out in detail as follows:

1. A research problem has to be identified.
2. A research question has to be derived from the topic and formulated for the analysis to be undertaken.
3. Simultaneously, or shortly after having formulated the research question, a research hypothesis would be formulated.
4. Thereafter, the theoretical analysis of the hypothesis will take place.
5. Optionally, as an additional process step, an empirical analysis of the hypothesis could be performed.
6. In both cases, the purpose of the theoretical analysis as well as of the optional empirical analysis is to derive evidence that leads to the acceptance or falsification of the hypothesis.
7. The analysis will be concluded with a summary and a discussion of the findings.

Particularly in business and social sciences, the following problem might occur while applying the pure hypothesis-driven style: How can one produce a hypothesis at the starting point of a research project that is prior to the analysis? Typically, at this point in time, the researcher will be confronted with a new problem that has to be thoroughly analysed. The formulation of a hypothesis requires more information with respect to the problem, and relying on available knowledge and/or existing experience might not be sufficient. Generally, in business and social sciences, the sourcing and processing of information are prerequisites for the formulation of a hypothesis. Thus, it is unlikely that a researcher is able to identify a suitable or final hypothesis prior to the analysis. Therefore, the hypothesis-driven style does typically not reflect the reality of business and social sciences research.

4.5 Summary and exercises

4.5.1 Synopsis

In chapter 4, the research process and different research approaches were addressed.

The research question and the hypothesis are closely related.

Questions have certain characteristics. In a research paper, the research question is an open-ended and indirect question.

The research question and the hypothesis are interdependent. That is, the research hypothesis (or hypotheses) formulates (or formulate) the answer(s) to a research question.

Typical research approaches are the philosophical research approach in the form of a literature-based approach or in the form of a theoretical approach, the developmental research approach, and the empirical research approach that might be a quantitative or qualitative approach.

In the field of business and social sciences, the majority of term paper projects require a theoretical solution-driven approach whereas some research projects require an empirical solution-driven approach. A pure hypothesis-driven approach is rarely used.

4.5.2 Questions

Knowledge

1. What types of questions can be distinguished?
2. What is the formal nature of a research question?
3. What are the interrogative words used in research questions?
4. What are the general types of hypothesis listed in the text?
5. Which types of hypothesis can be distinguished according to their inner logic?
6. What is an ad-hoc thesis?
7. What is a working hypothesis?
8. What is a scientific hypothesis?
9. What is a nomological hypothesis? What is a quasi-nomological hypothesis?
10. What is a statistical hypothesis?
11. What is literature-based research?
12. What is theoretical research?
13. What is developmental research?
14. What is quantitative research? What is qualitative research?
15. What are mixed research approaches?
16. What are the process steps of the theoretical solution-driven style?
17. What are the process steps of the empirical solution-driven style?
18. What are the process steps of the hypothesis-driven style?
19. Which problems might occur while applying a pure hypothesis-driven style?

4.5.3 Problem

Synthesis

Learning targets

    Understanding the nature of a topic

Formulating a topic

Formulating open-ended direct and indirect research questions as well as an underlying hypothesis

Identifying an appropriate research approach

Deciding for an appropriate structural design

Instructions

Please read the following article:

Anonymous (2009, January 23). Lip service: What lipstick sales tell you about the economy. *The Economist*.

Retrieved from http://www.economist.com

Questions

1. What could be a topic for a research paper that analyses the lipstick effect?
2. What could be an open-ended direct question?
3. What could be an open-ended indirect question?
4. What could be an ad-hoc hypothesis?
5. What could be a working hypothesis?
6. What could be a scientific hypothesis?
7. What type of hypothesis is assumed according to the inner logic of the lipstick index?
8. What could be a suitable research approach for the research paper?
9. Is the theoretical solution-driven style a suitable structural design for the research paper?
10. Is the empirical solution-driven style a suitable structural design for the research paper?
11. Is the hypothesis-driven style a suitable structural design for the research paper?

4.5.4 Additional reading

Anonymous (2009, July 16). Financial Economics: Efficiency and beyond. *The Economist*. Retrieved from http://www.economist.com

5 Identification of a topic

Abstract

Every research project addresses an underlying research problem that has to be expressed in the topic. The research topic is the subject matter of the research to be performed. All researchers need to be able to translate their research problems into appropriate research topics. The motivation and qualification of a (student) researcher play a major role while identifying a suitable research topic. Moreover, potential problems of limited information access have to be considered before choosing a research topic. The aim of a research project can be of an abstract or a problem-based nature. Both types of aim have different characteristics in terms of practicality, independence, creativity and inherent challenges. A number of proved techniques can be applied in order to identify a potential aim and ultimately a research topic. Six idealised process steps with corresponding actions can help to refine the chosen research topic. The differences between research topic and research title and possible forms of their interaction have to be kept in mind. Clarity while verbalising a research topic can be achieved by following the principles of clearness and proper composition.

Keywords

Abstract aim, problem-based aim, motivation, qualification, information access, topic, title

5.1 Context and relevance

5.1.1 Context of chapter 5

In previous chapters, a basic understanding of the principles, the logic, and the process of research has been developed. The next step is to look at the identification of a topic for a research project. This helps to understand the requirements while formulating a research proposal. Accordingly, the context of this chapter is linked to the fact that professional researchers are constantly confronted with research problems that need to be captured and specified by a relevant research topic. Furthermore, if not provided with a defined research topic, students might be required to identify a research topic on their own.

Figure 5.1 shows how chapter 5 is embedded within the setting of a research project.

5 Identification of a topic

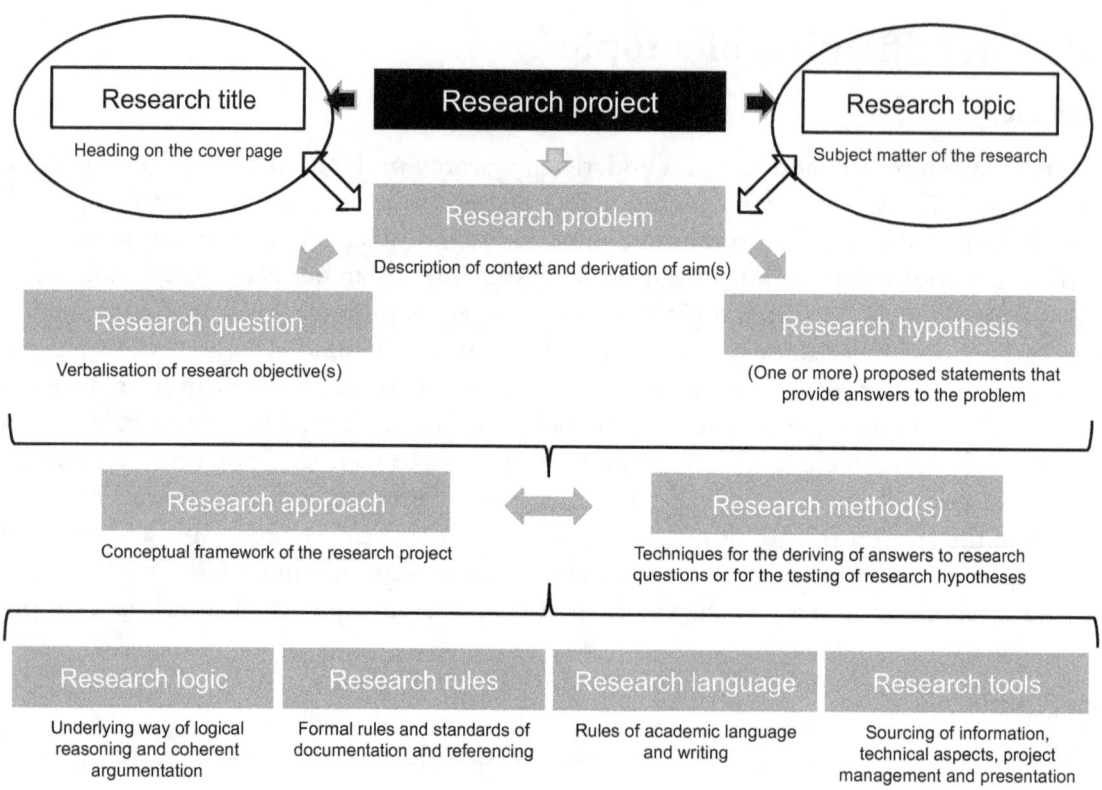

Figure 5.1: Context of chapter 5

In this chapter, the identification of a research topic is addressed.

5.1.2 Relevance of chapter 5

A well-defined research topic is fundamental for the successful execution of the research project. Consequently, it is advisable to apply certain proved criteria while identifying and formulating a research topic.

5.1.3 Learning objectives of chapter 5

After having studied this chapter, the reader should be able to:

- understand personal implications and restrictions with regard to identifying a topic
- differentiate between abstract and problem-based aims

- understand the identification process and corresponding techniques
- understand the implications of verbalising a topic

5.2 Candidate

5.2.1 Motivation

Motivation plays a vital role for the selection of a topic for a research project. There are two aspects that need to be considered:

- A personal interest in a special subject supports the successful completion of a research project. If there is a certain degree of freedom while selecting a topic, one should always opt for a topic that arouses one's own interest.
- A research project might help to acquire a special qualification for accessing a specific career field and/or employer. Therefore, candidates with carefully chosen topics might stick out from the crowd in highly competitive job markets.

5.2.2 Qualification

In the context of this chapter, the term qualification refers to the candidate's profile regarding the required abilities to work on a potential topic. A number of potential problems need to be considered:

- A research topic may require the application of a certain advanced quantitative or qualitative **methodical skillset** yet unknown to the candidate.
- A research topic may require the sourcing of information in a **foreign language**, and the candidate does not have a good command of the language.
- A research topic may require **knowledge from disciplines** unfamiliar to the candidate. Examples are business or social research topics that have a strong link to either psychology or neurology.
- A research topic may require a **level of sophistication** that is not aligned with the current qualification of a candidate. Obviously, a master's thesis should demonstrate a higher level of intellectual sophistication than a bachelor's thesis.

5.2.3 Information access

In the context of this chapter, the term information access refers to the possibility to gain access to information needed to generate a meaningful answer to a research problem. A number of potential problems need to be considered:

- The candidate might not be able to access the **literature** needed in order to perform a proper literature review.
- The candidate might not be able to access or gather the **data** needed in order to perform a proper analysis.
- The candidate might not be able to access information due to its **proprietary nature**.
- The candidate might be able to access **protected information**, but is not allowed to use it due to legal restrictions.

5.3 Abstract and problem-based aims

5.3.1 Definition

An aim is the purpose or intention of a research project or the desired outcome in terms of an answer to a question. In this chapter, abstract aims and problem-based aims are distinguished.

For an abstract aim, the purpose or intention of a research project is of an abstract (theoretical) nature.

> Sample context
> Modigliani and Miller postulated their theorem on the irrelevance of the capital structure under strict assumptions in 1958.
> Here, the aim of a research student could be to remove a set of assumptions in order to advance the theorem.

For a problem-based aim, the purpose or intention of a research project is derived from a (practical) problem.

> Sample context
> A company wants to analyse the effect of an increased debt level in its capital structure on its tax burden.
> Here, the aim of a research student could be to analyse the specific situation in order to generate a recommendation for the company.

Both examples describe problems linked to the capital structure of corporations. The first example addresses the problem from an abstract perspective whereas the second example addresses a company-specific issue from an applied perspective.

5.3.2 Characteristics

Academic research projects may be based on an abstract aim or on a problem-based aim. It is important to understand that abstract aims and problem-based aims have different characteristics (Table 5.1).

Characteristics	Abstract aim	Problem-based aim
Practicality	Coordination with instructor (as academic advisor)	Coordination with instructor and partnering institution (e.g. company)
Independence	Identification and interpretation of topic	Provided topic and predetermined interpretation
Creativity	Extended room for own creativity	Limited room for own creativity
Challenges	Satisfying instructor's expectations	Aligning instructor's and company's expectations

Table 5.1: Characteristics of abstract and problem-based aims – overview

It might seem that problem-based aims imply certain negative characteristics. All the more important it is to point out that working on practical problems can be highly rewarding due of the student researcher's exposure to real world problems.

5.4 Process and techniques

5.4.1 Idealised process

There are a number of techniques and tools that can be used in order to identify and refine a topic for a research project.

Table 5.2 describes the steps of an idealised process.

Process step	Action	Chapter
Inspire yourself	Gather information with respect to potential topics	Sourcing of information
Extend your research	Gather information with respect to short-listed topics	Sourcing of information
Phrase a topic	Verbalise a more refined draft of your topic	Academic language and writing style
Develop an interpretation (aim)	Identify possible aims and decide for one aim	Interpretation of a topic
Select a suitable research approach	Identify an appropriate methodological approach	Research process
Refine the research problem	Write a (draft) outline and a (draft) entitled "Research problem"	Structuring technique

Table 5.2: Idealised process of identifying and refining a topic

As shown above, the identification of a topic is strongly interlinked with various aspects of academic research and writing that are addressed in different chapters of this book.

5.4.2 Techniques

What happens if one is absolutely free in identifying a topic and does not know where to start?

Here are some techniques and actions for junior researchers that can be taken in order to identify a potential topic:

- **Brainstorming**

    (Student) researchers should reflect upon issues that were able to arouse their interest during the course of their studies.

- **Newspaper and magazines**

  High-class newspapers and magazines can be screened for latest topics being discussed in the media.

- **Web search**

  The Internet may be searched for information on current, up-to-date topics and related keywords, technical terms and jargon.

- **Literature research**

  With potential topics in mind, a literature research using the search engines of different library catalogues can be conducted.

- **Contact instructors**

  Student researchers may ask their instructors whether they offer potential topics for thesis projects and what individual requirements are applicable.

- **Institutional contacts**

  Student researchers may ask people they know from internships and student jobs for ideas on potential research projects.

5.5 Verbalisation

5.5.1 Topic and title

The topic is the subject matter of a research project.

However, it has to be differentiated between the "topic" and the "title" of a research paper (Figure 5.2).

5 Identification of a topic

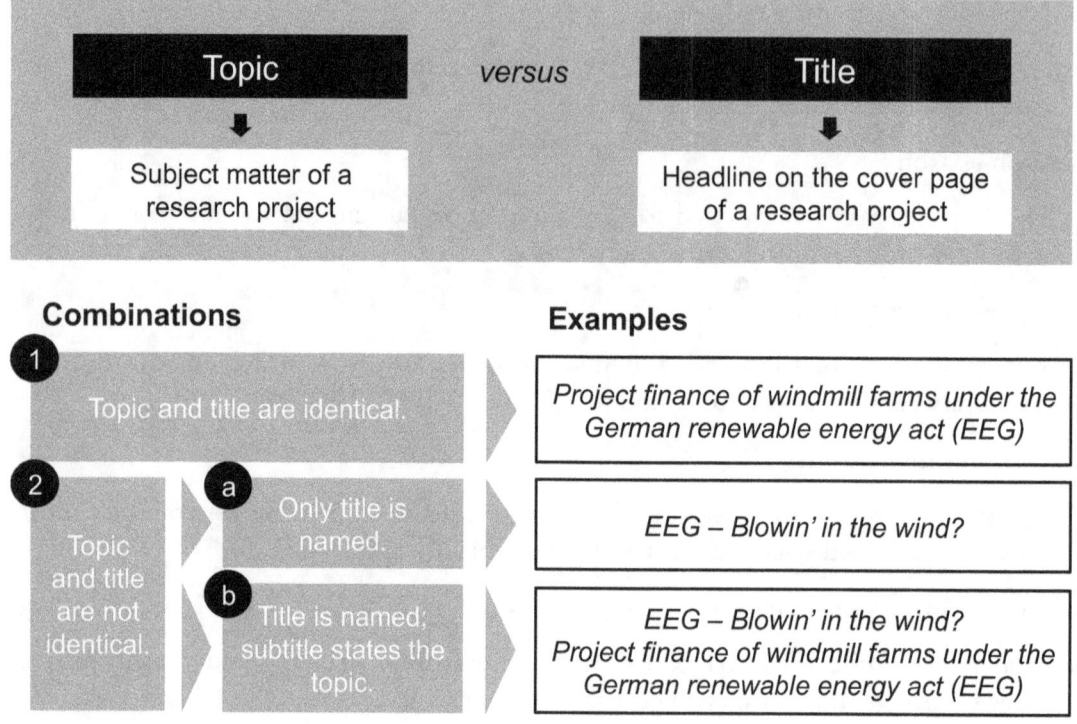

Figure 5.2: Combinations of topic and title

The title is the heading that appears on the cover page or at the top of the written documentation of a research project. As shown in Figure 5.2, topic and title can interact in a number of ways:

- **Combination 1: Topic and title are identical**

    Example of a topic/title:
    "Project finance of windmill farms under the German renewable energy act (EEG)" could be simultaneously the title and the topic of a research project.

- **Combination 2 a: Only title is named without stating the topic**

    Example of a title:
    "EEG – Blowin' in the wind?"

    Here, the recipient is not informed about the topic. It should be noted that titles for published research output might be formulated in a provoking or an entertaining way. One possible reason for this is that the authors want to stick out of the bulk of publications. This is not common or advisable for student research projects.

- **Combination 2 b: Title is named, and subtitle states the topic**

    Example of a title:
    "EEG – Blowin' in the wind?"
    Example of a subtitle stating the topic:
    "Project finance of windmill farms under the German renewable energy act (EEG)"

5.5.2 Qualitative aspects

Among the academic principles that have to be obeyed in academic research, the principle of clarity becomes especially important while verbalising a topic (Figure 5.3).

One aspect of clarity is **clearness**, which demands accurate and academic language or more precisely a clear terminological and linguistic application while formulating a topic. Another aspect of clarity is **proper composition**, which demands a focus on the topic or more precisely a strict focus on the topic to be addressed without any excursions. In other words: Clearness implies a careful selection of the terminology while verbalising a topic; proper composition implies a careful phrasing of the topic.

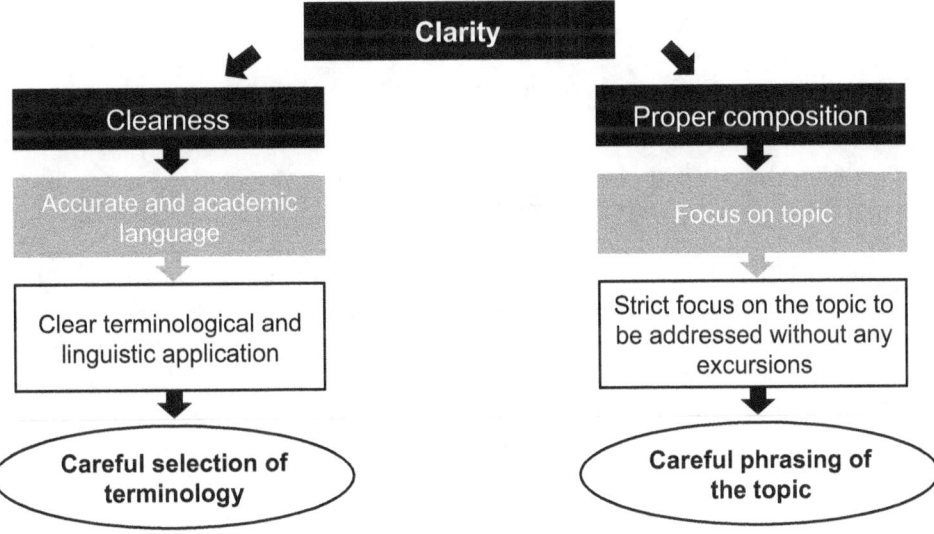

Figure 5.3: Clarity while verbalising a topic

5 Identification of a topic

The aspects of clarity in academic language are addressed in detail in chapter 11.

5.5.3 Examples of refining a topic

The pyramid in Figure 5.4 demonstrates how a topic in an **academic setting** can be refined in order to develop its final shape.

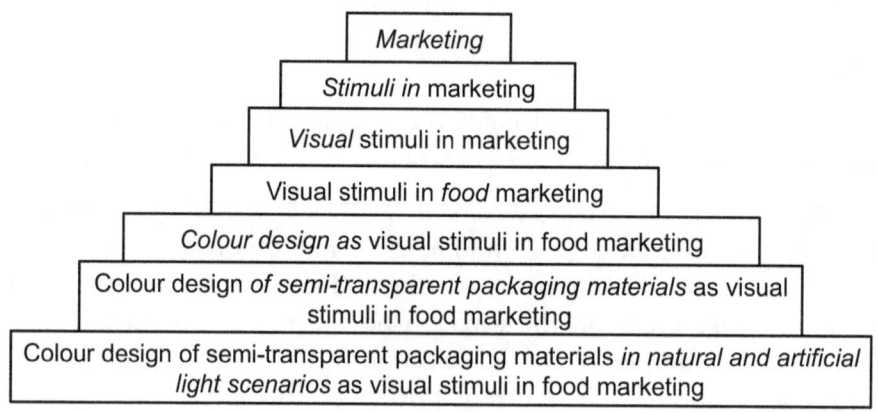

Figure 5.4: Refining a topic – example 1

The process of verbalising and refining a topic can be as follows:

> A student who has a strong interest in "Marketing" decides to submit a proposal for a bachelor's thesis. An article in a newspaper directs her interest towards sensory stimuli. She phrases the topic "Stimuli in marketing". After having given some thoughts about the sensory stimuli, she decides to focus on "Visual stimuli in marketing". Considering her latest internship in the food industry, she changes the topic of the project to "Visual stimuli in food marketing". She starts her preliminary research on visual stimuli and adjusts the topic to "Colour design as visual stimuli in food marketing". Since colour design can be applied to a variety of product features, she narrows the topic down to "Colour design of semi-transparent packaging materials as visual stimuli in food marketing". The student decides to conduct a number of experiments with test persons in different environments. Therefore, she adjusts the topic to "Colour design of semi-transparent packaging materials in natural and artificial light scenarios as visual stimuli in food marketing".

The pyramid in Figure 5.5 demonstrates how a topic in a **professional setting** can be refined in order to develop its final shape.

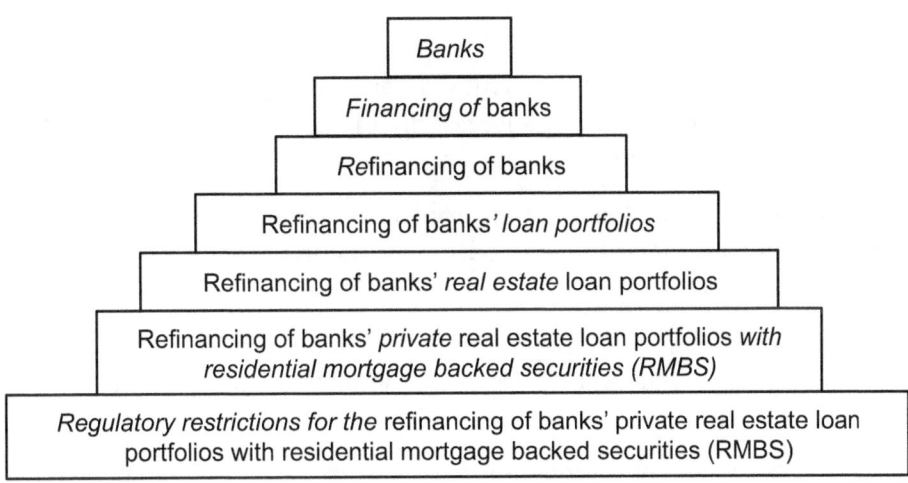

Figure 5.5: Refining a topic – example 2

The process of verbalising and refining a topic can be as follows:

> A staff member of a publicly sponsored think tank is in charge of preparing research reports with respect to "Banks". His team focuses on the "Financing of banks". More precisely, the "Refinancing of banks" is analysed by the researchers. Lately, the "Refinancing of banks' loan portfolios" has become a research priority. Our staff member is responsible for the "Refinancing of banks' real estate loan portfolios". After having discovered a common technique that can be used by banks, the staff member narrows his focus down to "Refinancing of banks' private real estate loan portfolios with residential mortgage backed securities (RMBS)". Since the emphasis of a publicly sponsored think tank is on actual and potential governmental activities, the topic is changed to "Regulatory restrictions for the refinancing of banks' private real estate loan portfolios with residential mortgage backed securities (RMBS)".

The process of refining a topic should be continued as long as an additional benefit in terms of clarity can be achieved.

5 Identification of a topic

5.6 Summary and exercises

5.6.1 Synopsis

In chapter 5, the identification of a topic was addressed.

Motivation plays a major role for the identification of a topic. Even more important are the qualifications needed in order to successfully master a topic. Moreover, information access has to be considered while deciding on a topic.

The differentiation between abstract and problem-based aims helps to identify potential topics. While doing so, different characteristics of theoretical and practical research projects have to be considered.

Following the steps of an idealised process can help to identify a topic. A number of techniques ranging from brainstorming to utilising institutional contacts may inspire the search for a topic.

While verbalising a topic, a differentiation between topic and title is necessary. The academic principles of clearness and proper composition have to be obeyed.

5.6.2 Questions

Knowledge

1. What are implications of motivation while selecting a topic?
2. What are examples of potential problems of qualification while researching a topic?
3. What are examples of potential problems of information access while researching a topic?
4. What is an aim? What is an abstract aim? What is a problem-based aim?
5. What are characteristics of abstract aims?
6. What are characteristics of problem-based aims?
7. What are the six idealised process steps and their corresponding actions for refining a topic?
8. What are actions that can be taken in order to identify a potential problem?
9. What is a topic?
10. What is a title?
11. What are the possibilities of interaction between topic and title?
12. Why is clarity important for the verbalisation of a topic?

5.6.3 Problem

Synthesis

Learning target

Being able to develop and phrase a topic from a given area

Instructions

Search the Internet for a potential research project. Develop and verbalise a matching topic. Document and organise your results according to the following structure:

1. Given area and corresponding keywords
2. Topic derived from keywords
3. Title derived from the topic
4. Character of aim (abstract or problem-based)
5. Assumed qualification of candidate required to handle the chosen topic
6. Expected access to information (literature, data, proprietary knowledge, protected knowledge)
7. List of techniques (brainstorming, web search etc.) that have been applied while working with the keywords

5.6.4 Additional reading

Coyne, K. P., & Coyne, S. T. (2011, March). Seven steps to better brainstorming. *McKinsey Quarterly*. Retrieved from http://www.mckinsey.com

6 Sourcing of information

Abstract

Every research project requires the sourcing of information in the form of literature and/or empirical data. Different types of literature, each with individual characteristics, can be used in academic research. It is important to understand the specific categories of literature, such as monographs and textbooks, articles in academic journals, concise dictionaries, edited works, working papers, conference proceedings, white papers and green papers, technical papers, consultation papers, manuals as well as legal sources and documents. Given the variety of literature sources, an academic appraisal of references with respect to their citability and credibility is essential. The existence of a peer review process can signify the academic quality of journal articles. Furthermore, the consultation of citation indices and journal rankings may help to identify acceptable references. Grey literature in particular, which is literature that is not commercially published and distributed, needs to be appraised with respect to its citability. Information access and retrieval can take place via the Internet or in a library. Library catalogues and databases allow for a literature search that uses individual search logic in order to identify adequate references.

Keywords

Literature search, references, information sources, monographs, textbooks, academic journals, concise dictionaries, edited works, working papers, conference proceedings, white papers, green papers, technical papers, consultation papers, manuals, legal sources, legal documents, appraisal techniques, citability, credibility, peer review, journal rankings, grey literature, Internet search, libraries, information access, information retrieval, search strategies, headwords, keywords, thesaurus, search logic, truncation, Boolean operations, phrase searching

6.1 Context and relevance

6.1.1 Context of chapter 6

A research project has to be based on existing and available information. Thus, the sourcing and processing of information determine the quality of a research project.

Figure 6.1 shows how chapter 6 is embedded within the setting of a research project.

6 Sourcing of information

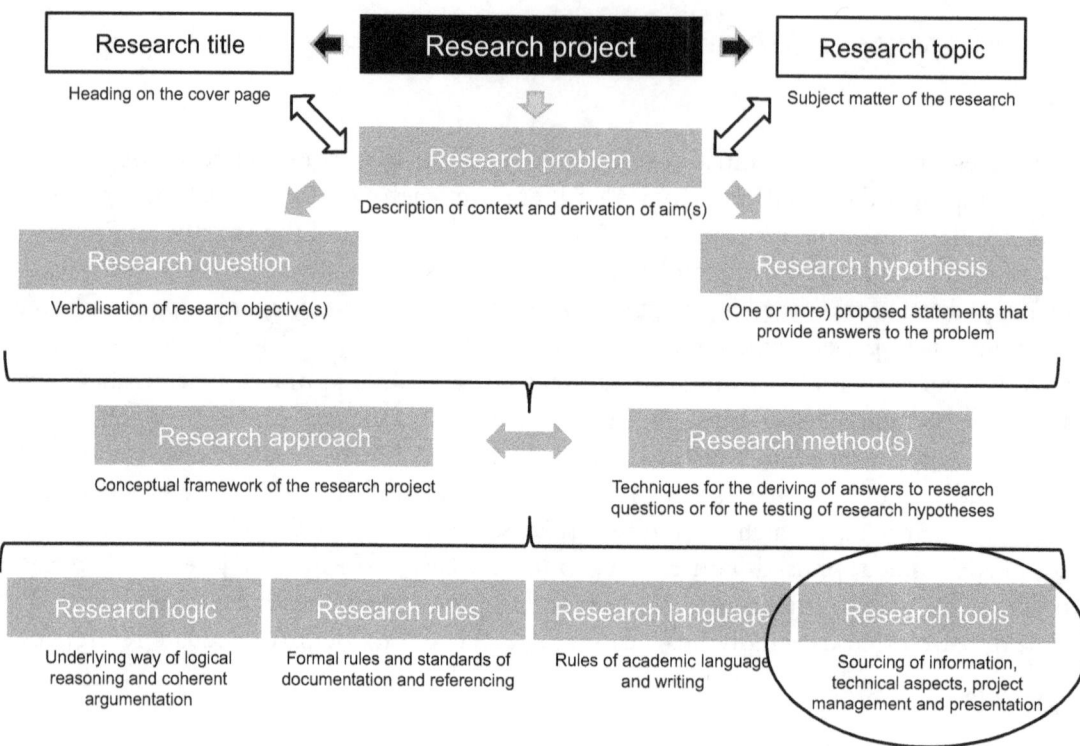

Figure 6.1: Context of chapter 6

In this chapter, the sourcing of information is addressed.

6.1.2 Relevance of chapter 6

The academic principle of qualitative completeness implies the consideration of all relevant information sources. Furthermore, the principle of comparability requires that the research work reflect the status quo of the relevant discipline or topic. Last but not least, the lack of information might lead to incomplete, false or misleading conclusions.

6.1.3 Learning objectives of chapter 6

After having studied this chapter, the reader should be able to:

- understand the character of different information sources
- distinguish between different types of literature

- appraise different types of information
- apply different ways of conducting an appropriate literature search

6.2 Information sources

6.2.1 Literature

In chapter 4, a differentiation has been made between philosophical research and empirical research. In both areas of research, literature is essential for the research process (Figure 6.2).

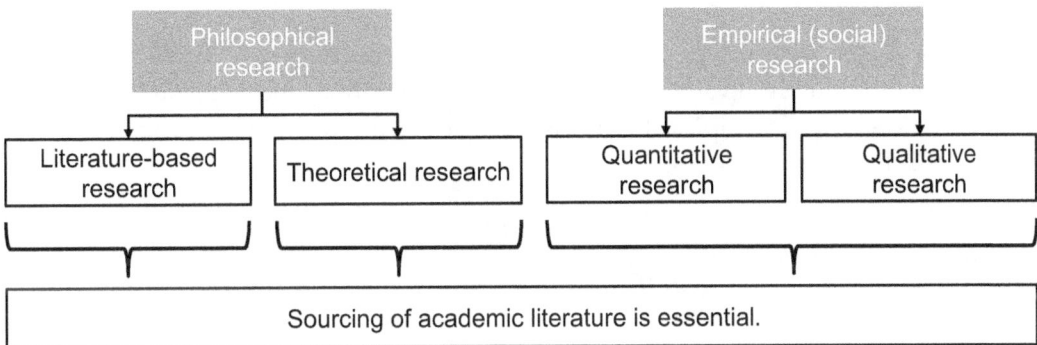

Figure 6.2: Relevance of academic literature

Philosophical research can be divided into literature-based research and theoretical research. Evidently, literature-based research depends on academic literature. (Pure) theoretical research has to reference academic literature that documents existing theories to be modified or advanced. Empirical (social) research can be divided into quantitative research and qualitative research. Both quantitative and qualitative research projects have to start with a review of the existing academic literature.

6.2.2 Empirical data

In addition to academic literature, information can be sourced in the form of empirical data. However, empirical data are not relevant in all areas of research (Figure 6.3).

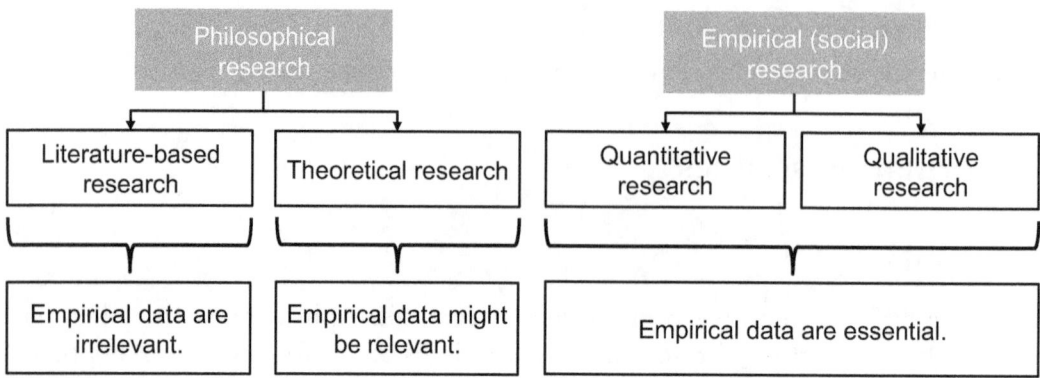

Figure 6.3: Relevance of empirical data

(Pure) literature-based research never builds upon empirical data. In some cases, (pure) theoretical research builds upon empirical data. Quantitative and qualitative research projects always build upon empirical data. In this book, the techniques of sourcing and processing empirical data are not addressed.

6.3 Types of literature

6.3.1 Monographs and textbooks

A **monograph** is a single piece of work that deals with a single subject or a single research problem. In the context of academic research, scientific or scholarly monographs are relevant.

Typically, there is one author who has written the monograph. In some cases, two or more authors have written the monograph in cooperation. Still, the monograph would deal with a single subject and would be self-contained, i.e. complete in itself. This differs from works of literature in which several authors have written on multiple subjects or topics. Therefore, anthologies and encyclopaedia are not viewed as monographs.

Examples of academic monographs are as follows:

- a professorial thesis
- a doctoral thesis
- a specialised book
- a master's thesis

- a bachelor's thesis

Generally, a professorial thesis is regarded as the monograph with the highest academic quality and credibility. In contrast, a bachelor's thesis has the lowest academic standing. It should be noted that, due to quality uncertainty, one should cautiously and selectively use bachelor's theses or master's theses as information sources in a student research project.

In some cases, **textbooks** are referred to as monographs as well. However, a textbook can be distinguished from a monograph in terms of its audience. The target group of textbooks are students or beginners in a field of study. In contrast, a monograph aims predominantly at experienced academics and researchers as well as advanced practitioners.

Due to their audience and their mostly introductory character, textbooks are typically not considered suitable as references in a research project. However, some advanced textbooks are considered as generally accepted reference sources and may be deemed to be credible and citable references in their discipline.

For students, distinguishing between monographs and textbooks can be a challenge. If a book contains questions, problems and exercises, this could indicate that it is a textbook. An indicator of whether or not a textbook is suitable as a reference within a research paper may be its title. Table 6.1 shows how monograph titles and textbook titles might differ.

Introductory textbook titles	**Advanced textbook titles**	**Monograph titles**
Fundamentals of financial markets	Principles of financial engineering	Securitisation of multi-seller mortgage loan portfolios
Marketing: An introduction	Marketing: Analysis, planning, and control	Relevance of product naming in brand management
Introduction to managerial accounting	Managerial accounting	Treatment of corporate taxes in managerial accounting

Table 6.1: Sample titles of textbooks, advanced textbooks, and monographs

As indicated in Table 6.1, textbook titles have the tendency to signal an introductory character such as "Introduction to managerial accounting". However, some textbook titles may indicate a more advanced nature. For example the title "Managerial accounting" suggests a more advanced and comprehensive approach to the subject, rather than a mere introduction. In contrast to introductory and advanced textbooks, monograph titles signal more depth and sophistication. This is exemplified with the title "Treatment of corporate taxes in managerial accounting" that indicates a detailed, specific, and in-depth work on one subject area in the field of managerial accounting.

In addition to evaluating the title of a publication in terms of its introductory or more advanced character, one should skim the content of the publication in order to clarify its level of sophistication.

6.3.2 Articles in academic journals

In essence, an article is a nonfictional text that deals with a specific subject and is self-contained. Articles are published in print or in electronic format.

Academic articles are published in academic journals. Academic journals are periodicals targeting specific academic disciplines. An editorial board sets academic standards for articles to be published. Typically, an institutionalised review process ensures compliance with these academic standards. The rigour of the review process determines inter alia the quality level of the journal.

Informally one refers to academic journals with the highest quality as "A-journals". In this sense, also B-journals, C-journals etc. are distinguished.

6.3.3 Concise dictionaries

Concise information is a piece of communication providing the essence of a subject or topic in a condensed but comprehensive way.

A concise dictionary is an academic, professional or technical encyclopaedia that encompasses the generally accepted and substantiated state of knowledge of a discipline. Typically, it is organised in dictionary entries or concise articles addressing terms or subject matters of a specific field (e.g. marketing, economics, finance).

6.3.4 Edited works

A common type of literature is the edited work. It contains a collection of self-contained works. Typically, the book chapters of an academic edited work resemble journal articles and contain non-fictional text.

The term "edited" implies that there are one or more editors. The editors are responsible for setting the stage for the edited work and select the contributing authors. Edited work can be published in print or electronic format.

There are different terms for edited work that may be used as synonyms or may describe types of edited work more precisely.

- The basic form of an edited work is the "edited book".
- The term "edited volume" might be used as a synonym for edited book or, in some cases, refers to the fact that the work consists of more than one volume.
- "Anthology" is another synonym for edited work. Although typically used for collections of poetry and fiction, the term anthology, in some cases, stands for a collection of academic articles.
- The term "reader" might refer to a published edited work or, in other cases, to a collection of articles and papers that have been distributed on an informal basis, e.g. in the context of a course at a university.
- The expression "collected work" is used for an edited book in which all or the most important works of a single person have been collected and published. In many cases, the collected work serves to honour a famous and/or deceased author by making her or his ideas available to a broader audience.

6.3.5 Working papers

A working paper is a non-fictional text that deals with a specific subject and is self-contained. Working papers are published in print or in electronic format. Other names for a working paper are "discussion paper" or "research paper".

Working papers can be published on a stand-alone basis or in a working paper series. Editions of a working paper series appear on an irregular basis. The function of editor can be filled by an institution such as a university or an organisation or a group of persons. Although a formal review process with respect to the submitted text does not exist in many cases, compliance with academic standards is expected.

In contrast to journal articles, working papers are a fast way of publishing research results. Furthermore, working papers are an option to receive a feedback from one's own research community. At a later point in time, a revised version of a working paper's text might be published as an article in an academic journal or as a book chapter.

6.3.6 Conference proceedings

Academic conferences are means of exchanging research results in the form of oral presentations, poster presentations and/or conference papers.

An academic conference paper is a non-fictional self-contained text that deals with a specific subject. Conference papers can be refereed or not refereed by conference hosts and selected experts. Typically, the purpose of a conference paper is to present research activities and/or results not yet published. Its presentation may be accompanied by an oral presentation and/or a poster presentation to the audience of an academic conference.

Normally, academic conference papers are published as conference proceedings, a special type of an edited book.

Editors of the conference proceedings may be a group of persons that have organised the academic conference and/or external experts. The publication may or may not be accompanied by a formal review process. Conference papers are made available in printed or electronic form.

6.3.7 White papers and green papers

White papers and green papers are denominations for a special type of literature.

The term "white paper", also referred to as "white book", is used in two areas:

1. White papers are issued by institutions or governments in order to announce a political or regulatory position. Whether a white paper states a final version of an intended policy or is merely an intermediate process step prior to legislation depends upon the legislatory circumstances of the country where it is published.
2. The term white paper is used in business-to-business marketing for documents that are intended to support the marketing of products and services.

A green paper is a preliminary proposal made by an institution or a government. The major purpose of a green paper is the announcement of intended policy action in order to receive feedback from interested parties. Green papers are often predecessors of white papers.

6.3.8 Consultation papers, technical papers, manuals

Other types of literature applied in academic research are consultation papers, technical papers and manuals.

Similar to a white paper or a green paper, a consultation paper states a proposal by an institution or a government. The major purpose of a consultation paper is to announce intended policy action in order to receive feedback from interested parties via an institutionalised consultation process.

A technical paper is issued by a governmental or supranational institution. The document describes and/or prescribes technical standards and procedures to be applied in a given field. In many cases, it has a legal or quasi-legal character.

A manual, also referred to as "user guide", is a technical documentation of software, hardware or other technical equipment and machinery.

6.3.9 Legal sources and documents

Legal sources and legal documents are types of literature not only applied in legal research but likewise in other fields of academic research. Examples of legal sources and documents are:

- Bodies of laws in the form of constitutions, acts, bills, statutes, decrees, regulations etc.
- Legal commentaries in the form of comments on laws and relevant court decisions
- Contracts in the form of agreements, treaties, conventions, deeds and model contracts etc.
- Court decisions in the form of judicial rulings and other legally binding decisions made by entrusted institutions as for example chambers of commerce
- Court reviews such as commentaries on court decisions written by scholars or legal practitioners

6.4 Appraisal of references

6.4.1 Citability

Citability is a consequence of the academic principle of traceability. The principle of traceability requires that research output be presented in a documented way allowing for the reproduction of conclusions by third parties. Citability means that a reference is citable in a scholarly context. Accordingly, a reference has to meet each of the following three criteria in order to be citable:

1. A reference is citable if it has been **published**.
   - Typically, publication takes place via a publishing company.
   - In some cases, the publisher can be a credible institution, for example a university or an organisation such as the United Nations, the World Bank, the European Central Bank etc.
   - Self-published literature is citable if its identifiability and checkability (as explicated by the following two criteria) have been verified.

2. A reference is citable if it is **identifiable**. Identification can take place via ISBN, ISSN, or DOI.
   - ISBN stands for "International Standard Book Number" and is used for the identification of books.
   - ISSN stands for "International Standard Serial Number" and is used for the identification of journals and serials.
   - DOI stands for "Digital Object Identifier" and is used for the identification of electronic documents.

   Alternatively, identifiability can be achieved by describing a reference with distinct information such as name of author, title of reference, name and address of publisher, place of publication, date of publication etc.

3. A reference is citable if it is **checkable**. Checking can take place by accessing the document in a library, in a database, or as attachment.
   - Libraries provide access to references in print and/or electronic form.
   - Public or commercial databases provide access to references in print and/or electronic form.
   - References can also be attached to research papers in print and/or electronic form (data carrier or other storage media).

6.4.2 Credibility

Credibility means that a reference has a certain reputation or trustworthiness. There are a number of criteria and corresponding indicators that help to form an opinion about the credibility of a reference.

- **Target group**

    If a publication aims at the academic community as its target audience, it signals academic credibility. In contrast, publications addressing target groups such as practitioners or the general public are not considered credible in an academic sense. Accordingly, publications such as daily newspapers, news magazines, or popular scientific literature miss the rigour and intersubjective comprehensibility of academic references.

- **Publishing context**

    The reputation of the publisher and/or the standing of the book series or academic journal where a reference has been published may help to identify the quality of a reference.

- **Quality certainty**

    The existence and composition of an editorial board as well as the type and extent of an editorial process may assist with determining the quality of a reference. In particular, the existence of a peer review process signals credibility.

- **Author's background**

    The function, position, education, degrees and institutional background of the author of a publication may act as indicators for the academic credibility of the reference.

6.4.3 Peer review

As pointed out, the existence of a peer review process signals quality of an academic journal (Figure 6.4).

6 Sourcing of information

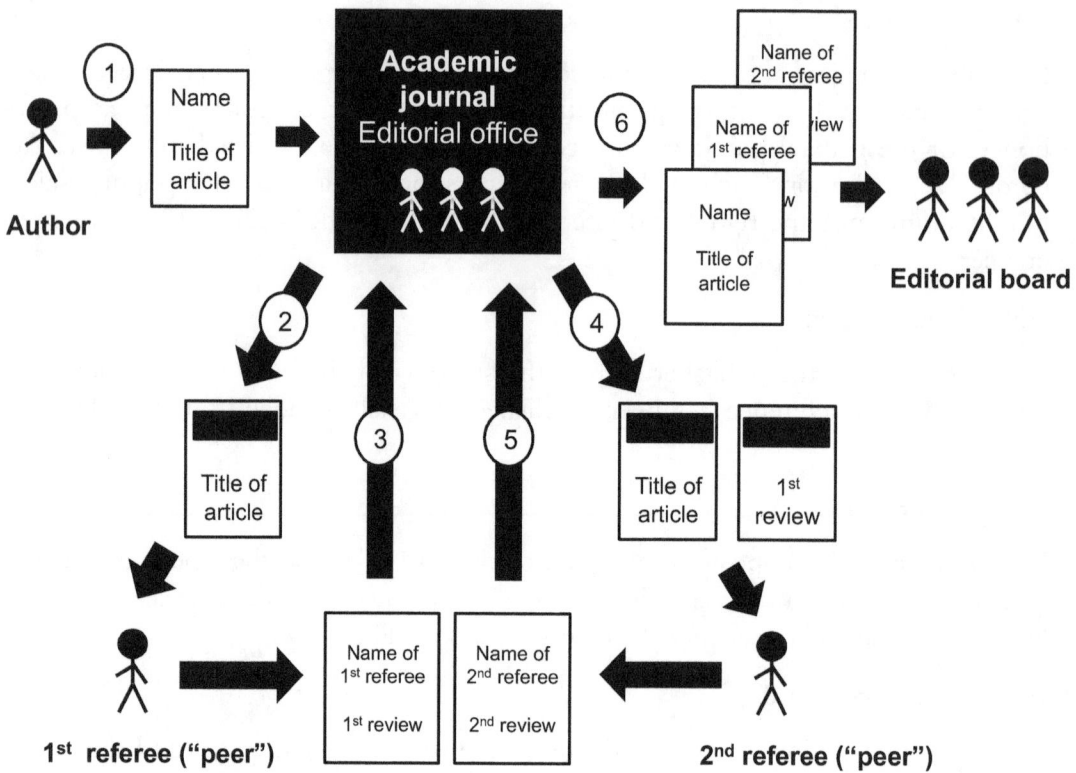

Figure 6.4: Double-blind peer review

A typical peer review process could be organised as follows:

1. An **author** submits an article to the **editorial office of an academic journal** for publication.

2. The editorial office sends an anonymised version of the article to a **first referee**, a **"peer"**, who is an accredited scholar in the field of knowledge addressed in the article.

3. The first referee appraises the article and sends a **first review** to the editorial office of the academic journal.

4. If the first review is positive, the editorial office of the academic journal sends the anonymised article, together with an anonymised version of the first review, to a **second referee**. Again, the second referee is an accredited scholar in the field of knowledge addressed in the article.

5. The second referee appraises the article and the first review in order to write a **second review** for the editorial office of the academic journal.

6. If the second review is positive, the editorial office of the academic journal forwards the article, the first review and the second review to the **editorial board**, which decides whether and when the article will be published in one of the upcoming issues of the journal.

Due to the fact that the names of the author and the first referee are anonymous, the process is called a **double-blind peer review**.

The intention of the process is to achieve a high degree of impartiality. However, in some fields of knowledge, specific orientations of research are associated with particular authors, who are typically known to the referees. Hence, the anonymity of the process and impartiality of the referees might be questionable.

Furthermore, the complexity of the appraisal procedure is time consuming and slows down the overall publication process, which, in some cases, may take months or even years. This is one reason why some researchers initially publish their findings as working papers. Again, the existence of a working paper similar to the submitted article may contradict the intention of a double-blind peer review.

6.4.4 Citation indices

A citation index is an index based on a database that collects and processes citations of authors in order to provide information regarding the importance of authors in a discipline. Examples of citation indices are Social Science Citation Index, i10-index, h-index and g-index (Table 6.2).

Index	Description
Social Science Citation Index (SCCI)	Bibliometric measure in the field of social sciences
i10-index	Bibliometric measure applied by Google Scholar
h-index	Bibliometric measure developed by Jorge E. Hirsch
g-index	Bibliometric measure developed by Leo Egghe

Table 6.2: Examples of citation indices

Whether these and other citation indices provide an additional benefit for the appraisal of references is questionable. Particularly, authors with few articles and few citations as well as authors with new articles, which have not spread yet, might be discriminated.

Citation indices are academic phenomena, which may be important to scholars who compete for research grants and third-party funds and/or academic prestige.

6.4.5 Journal rankings

An option of appraising the quality of a journal article may be the use of journal rankings. A journal ranking is a table that lists academic journals according to their perceived importance. A well-known example of a journal ranking is the Journal Impact Factor (JIF), also referred to as "Impact Factor". In its basic form it is defined as the number of citations in a given year that reference articles of the preceding two years divided by the number of articles of the preceding two years. The JIF can only be calculated for closed calendar years. The sample calculation in Figure 6.5 illustrates the logic of the JIF.

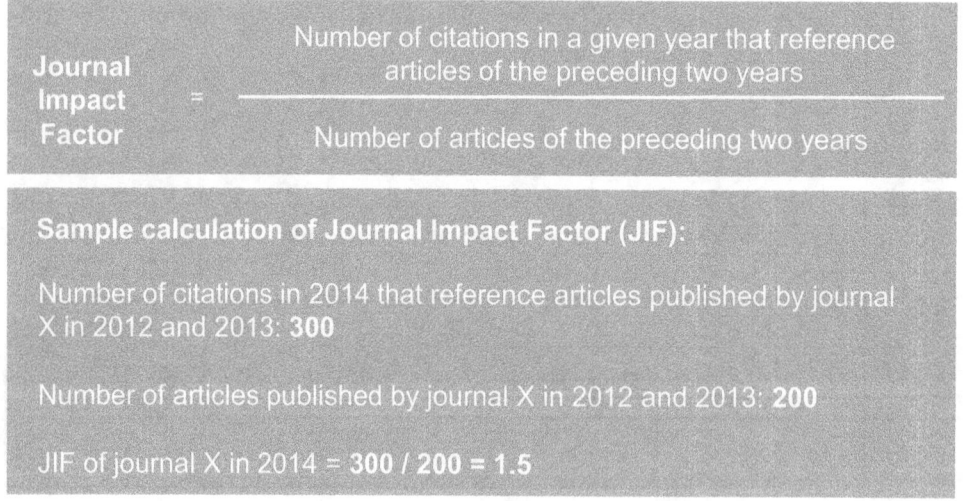

Figure 6.5: Journal Impact Factor (JIF) – sample calculation

> 🎓 **Tip**
>
> It has to be noted that one should use journal rankings carefully as their validity and reliability have been questioned by academia.

6.4.6 Grey literature

Grey literature is a commonly used term, which, generally speaking, refers to literature that is not commercially published and distributed. Metaphorically speaking, "white literature" could refer to literature that is credible and "black literature" could refer to literature that is not credible. However, some types of literature cannot unambiguously be characterised. This literature is referred to as "grey literature".

Typical originators of grey literature are governmental and non-governmental bodies and organisations, academic and research institutions as well as companies and business associations.

Examples of grey literature are working papers, conference proceedings, technical papers, consultation papers, white papers, green papers, manuals, legal documents, leaflets, brochures, financial statements and business reports.

However, the prerequisite for referencing grey literature is that the three criteria of citability are satisfied. This implies that the references are identifiable as well as checkable and have been made publicly accessible.

6.5 Literature search

6.5.1 Information access and retrieval

Generally, information can be accessed and retrieved via the Internet and in libraries (Figure 6.6).

The term "Internet" needs to be clarified from the perspective of academic literature search. "Internet" is often used as a synonym for content accessed or distributed via the World Wide Web. However, the term refers to a global network of interconnected computer networks and devices used for information exchange and related services.

The term "libraries" refers to research libraries and/or reference libraries that provide physical and/or digital access to literature.

6 Sourcing of information

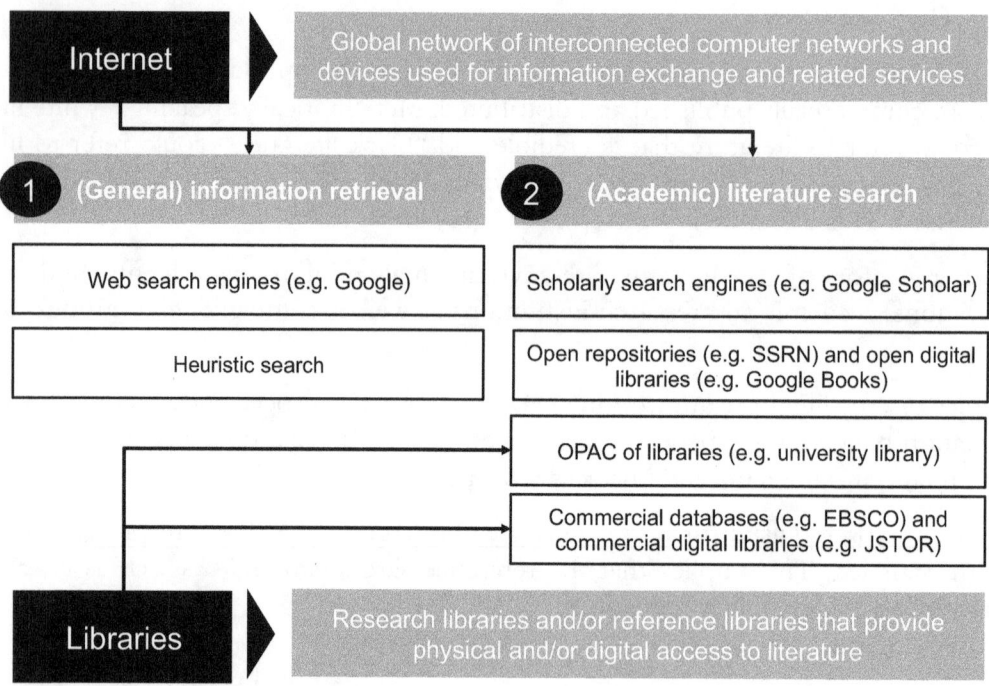

Figure 6.6: Information access and retrieval

Broadly speaking, two manifestations of information access and information retrieval via the Internet can be distinguished.

First, the process of general information retrieval might be applied:

- **Web search engines**, such as Google, Bing etc., can be used during the search process. However, the results might be disappointing and have to be carefully evaluated. There are several aspects diminishing the credibility of information retrieved via web search engines:
    o The quantity of findings complicates the processing of information.
    o The ranking of findings is determined by unknown search algorithms.
    o The quality of findings might be impaired by non-academic search results.
    o The outcome leads to distorted conclusions because the state of the discipline is not adequately reflected by search results.
- Besides the use of web search engines, a **heuristic web search** can be undertaken. Here, websites of organisations, companies and institutions are directly accessed and

analysed for relevant information. Conducting a heuristic search, one might encounter the following problems:
- Previous knowledge is needed in order to have an idea where to look for information.
- The search process might not lead to successful or sufficient results.
- The search process may require an excessive amount of time.

In spite of its aforementioned disadvantages, general information retrieval might assist in forming an idea about a research topic. However, it can only support more efficient ways of academic information retrieval.

The second way of retrieving information about a research project is the academic literature search. There are a number of possible search methods:

- **Scholarly search engines**, for example Google Scholar, allow searching for academic articles and, in some cases, redirect the user to free or paid services in order to access these articles.
- **Open repositories**, for example the Social Sciences Research Network, as well as **open digital libraries**, for example Google Books, provide the free search, access and retrieval of literature.
- An **open access public catalogue (OPAC)** is a web-based library catalogue, for example of a university library, that allows searching for literature. Some information might be retrievable in an electronic format; other literature can exclusively be accessed in physical form in the library.
- **Commercial databases**, for example EBSCO, and **commercial digital libraries**, for example JSTOR, provide paid access to literature. Additionally, some references might be for free. Some libraries have subscribed to the digital services of commercial databases and commercial digital libraries. Library users can access the content from terminals within the libraries or as the case may be from their own computers.

Evidently, the use of libraries is often a prerequisite for accessing digital resources. Furthermore, libraries allow the direct access to their non-lending collections, which is helpful in order to develop a preliminary understanding of the topic at hand.

A common question asked by students is whether they can use references retrieved from the Internet for their research projects. The answer is: it depends. All references have to satisfy the criteria of citability and credibility.

6.5.2 Search strategies

The starting point for literature research is a library catalogue (Figure 6.7). The majority of libraries can be accessed via an open public access catalogue or OPAC for short. As pointed out, OPACs are web-based and allow users to search for literature via the Internet from remote locations, e.g. from home.

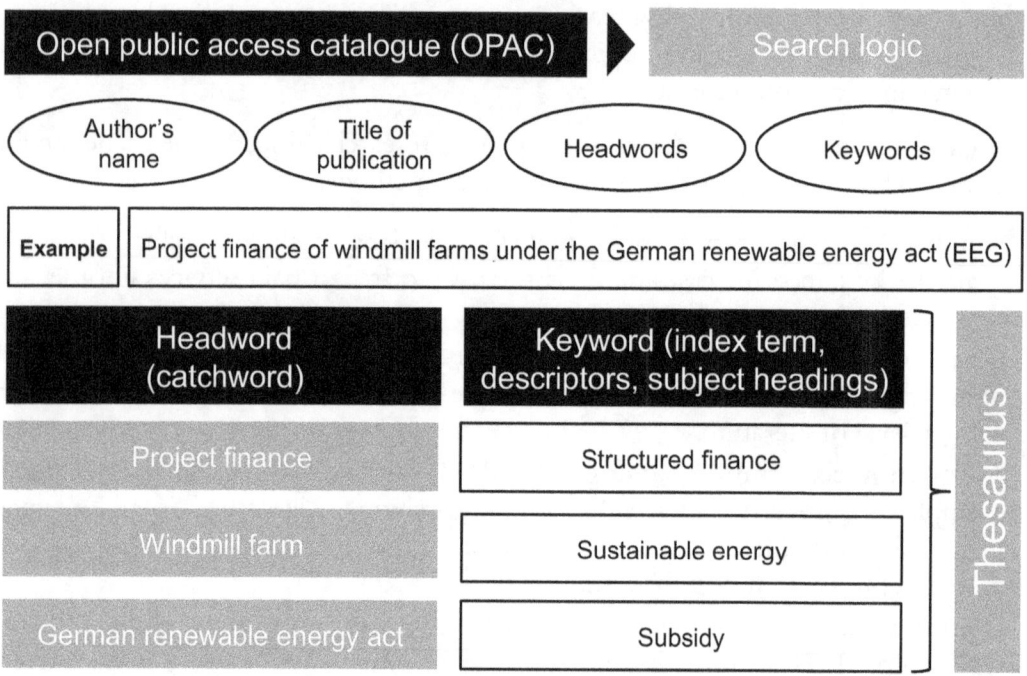

Figure 6.7: OPAC search logic – example

OPACs use a search logic that enables the use of intelligent search requests. The underlying logic varies from catalogue to catalogue. It is advisable to inform oneself about the search logic before starting a literature search process.

Typically, OPACs provide different search option criteria such as author's name, title of publication, headwords or keywords. In particular, searching for headwords and keywords are powerful options. The difference between headwords and keywords can be demonstrated by the sample topic "Project finance of windmill farms under the German renewable energy act (EEG)":

- Headwords are catchwords that can be extracted directly from the topic. Accordingly, headwords of the sample topic could be "project finance", "windmill farm", "German renewable energy act".
- Keywords are terms that are linked to the index of the OPAC. Keywords corresponding to the sample topic could be "structured finance", "sustainable energy", "subsidy" etc.

Whereas it is easy to isolate headwords from the topic, it requires some background knowledge about the topic in order to identify suitable keywords. Therefore, some libraries offer a thesaurus that assists in the search for keywords. A thesaurus is a structured list of index terms, also referred to as descriptors, that allows for the identification of keywords related to scholarly disciplines.

In the case of new topics, there may be no literature available at first sight. One should not expect to find literature that fully covers one's topic or exactly matches the title of one's research paper project. Instead, it is necessary to use literature that has been written with respect to adjacent fields of research. This can be explained on the basis of the sample topic "Project finance of windmill farms under the German renewable energy act (EEG)" (Table 6.3).

Example	Project finance of windmill farms under the German renewable energy act (EEG)
Literature titles directly related to the topic	"Project finance under the EEG"
	"Financing of renewables"
	"How to develop windmill farms"
Literature titles indirectly related to the topic	"Energy politics"
	"Sustainable energy – Utopia or reality?"
	"Handbook of energy law"

Table 6.3: Sample literature search

First, there may be literature that is directly related to the title/topic of the research paper project.

6 Sourcing of information

Additionally, there may be literature that is indirectly related to the title/topic of the research paper project.

The deeper the understanding with respect to the field of research, the easier it becomes to identify references that are indirectly related to the topic.

6.5.3 Thesaurus

As explained earlier, in a bibliographic context a thesaurus is a structured list of index terms (descriptors) that enables the identification of keywords related to scholarly disciplines.

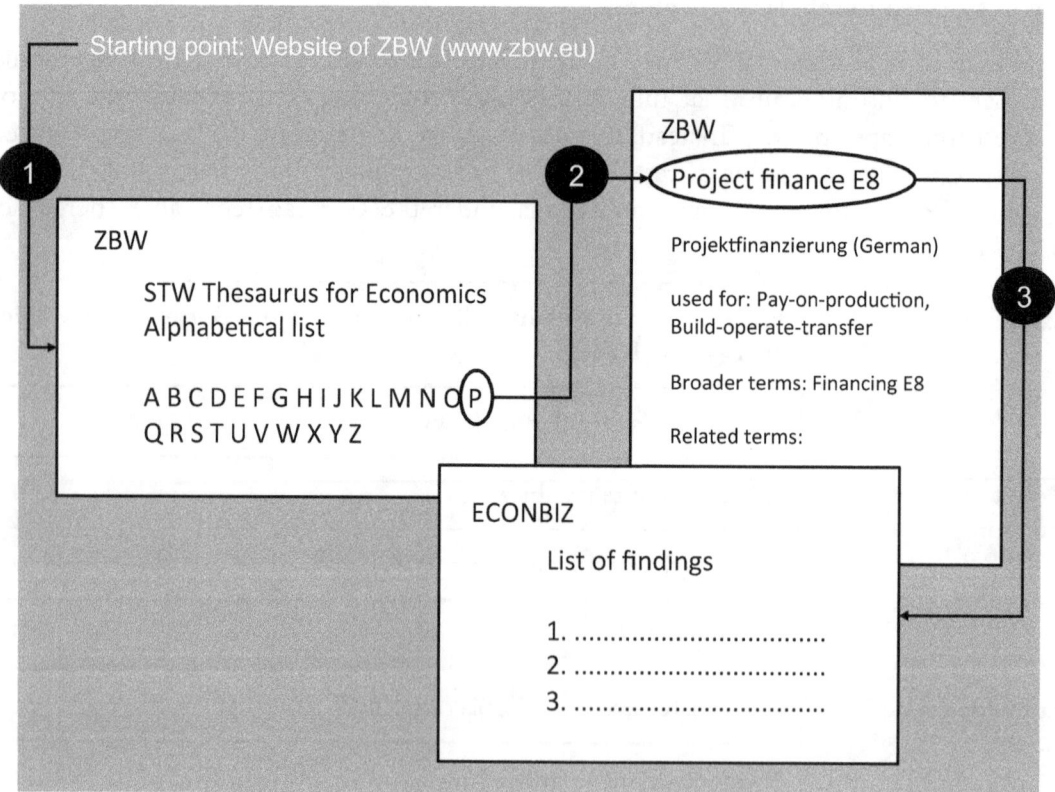

Figure 6.8: Thesaurus – example

The example in Figure 6.8 uses the STW Thesaurus for Economics of ZBW Leibniz Information Centre for Economics:

1. An alphabetical list of standardised descriptors of the STW Thesaurus for Economics can be accessed via the Internet.
2. Headwords from the sample topic are "project finance". In the alphabetical list, a corresponding descriptor entitled "project finance" can be found. In this case, the headwords "project finance" are simultaneously keywords.
3. By clicking on the symbol on the right hand-side of the descriptor "project finance", a window is opened that shows the virtual library catalogue of the ZBW Leibniz Information Centre for Economics. The virtual library catalogue lists literature sources related to the descriptor.

It should be noted that other thesauruses might use other alphabetical lists with different descriptors.

6.5.4 Search logic

6.5.4.1 Truncation

A common technique applied in literature research is truncation (Table 6.4). A placeholder, also referred to as "wildcard" or "joker", is used in search fields of OPACs or databases in order increase the flexibility of the search request and the quantity of the search results.

Techniques	Examples	
Right-sided truncation	market*	market**ability**, market**able**, market**eer**, market**er**, market**ing**, market**place**, market**s**
Left-sided truncation	*market	**super**market, **hyper**market, **grey-**market, **mark-to-**market
Multiple character truncation	mode*ing	mode**ll**ing, mode**l**ing, mo**de**rat**ing
Single character truncation	mode?ing	modeling

Table 6.4: Truncation – examples

Depending upon the syntax prescribed by the software, symbols to be used in order to formulate a search request may vary. Common symbols are asterisk (*), exclamation mark (!), question mark (?), dollar sign ($), and hash or number sign (#).

There are different techniques of applying truncation:

- **Right-sided truncation**

    The example *market** retrieves literature titles that contain words with the word component *market* on the left side of the word. Potential retrievals are titles that contain words such as *marketability, marketable, marketeer, marketer, marketing, marketplace, markets*.

- **Left-sided truncation**

    The example **market* retrieves literature titles that contain words with the word component *market* on the right side of the word. Potential retrievals are titles that contain words such as *supermarket, hypermarket, grey-market, mark-to-market*. Whether compound words with hyphen such as *grey-market* are included in the findings depends upon the syntax prescribed by the applied software.

- **Multiple character truncation**

    The example *mode*ing* retrieves literature titles that contain words such as *modelling, modeling, moderating*. The advantage of multiple character truncation is that it allows to search for different spellings of a word. However, the disadvantage is that meaningless words might be included in the search results. The word *moderating* for example would be out of context while searching for literature about *financial modelling* or *financial modeling*.

- **Single character truncation**

    The example *mode?ing* retrieves literature titles that contain the words *modeling*. The advantage is that one can avoid meaningless results. The disadvantage is that it does not include findings with different spelling such as *modelling*. In the example, the single character truncation would be helpful to identify literature titles in American English.

Prior to starting the literature search, one should consult the instructions for use of the OPAC or database at hand.

6.5.4.2 Boolean operations

Another technique applied in literature research is the use of Boolean operations (Figure 6.9).

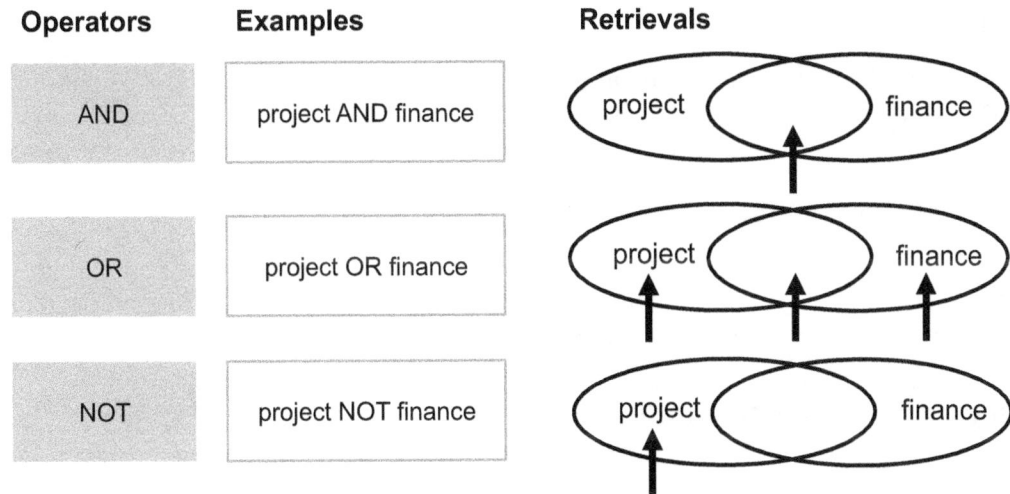

Figure 6.9: Boolean operations

Boolean operations are logical connectives used in OPAC or database search. Operators such as AND, OR, NOT can be used in order to connect search words. This can be demonstrated by the following examples using the search words *project finance*:

- AND

    The operator AND is used in order to combine search words retrieving literature sources that include both search words. The combination *project AND finance* retrieves literature titles that contain the word *project* as well as the word *finance*.

- OR

    The operator OR is used in order to combine search words retrieving literature sources that include either one or both search words. The combination *project OR finance* retrieves literature titles that contain (i) the word *project* or (ii) the word *finance* as well as (iii) the word *project* and the word *finance*.

6 Sourcing of information

- NOT

    The operator NOT is used in order to combine search words retrieving literature sources that include some search words but exclude other words. The combination *project NOT finance* retrieves literature titles that contain the word *project* but not the word *finance*.

Again, one should consult the instructions for use of the OPAC or database at hand for further Boolean operators.

6.5.4.3 Phrase searching

In a phrase search, phrases or sentences composed of adjacent words enclosed with quotation marks or other symbols such as parentheses are used for OPAC or database search. This is demonstrated by the example in Figure 6.10.

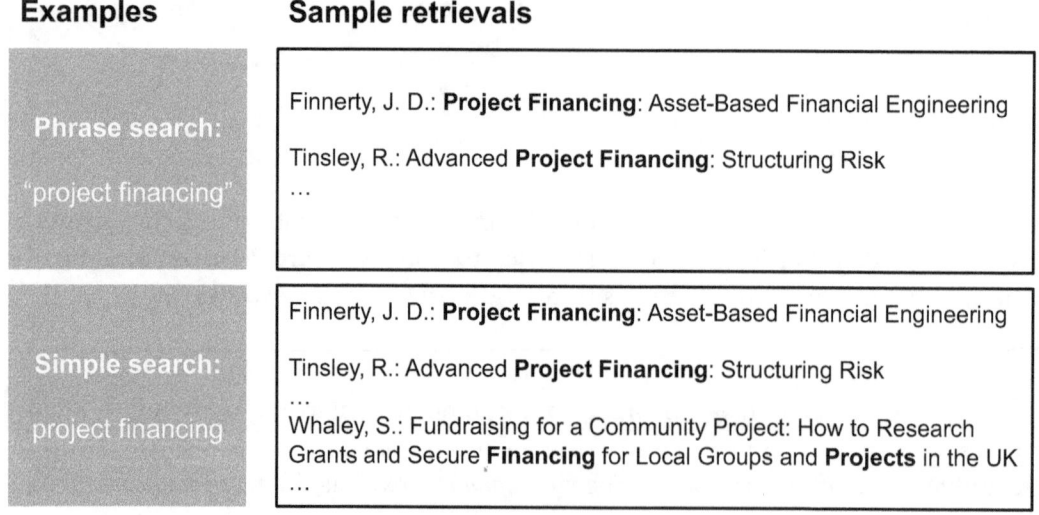

Figure 6.10: Phrase searching – example

The phrase search *"project financing"* retrieves literature titles that contain the exact word combination *project financing*. In contrast, the simple search *project financing* additionally retrieves literature titles that contain the words *project* and *financing* in a random order.

6.6 Summary and Exercises

6.6.1 Synopsis

Chapter 6 provided an introduction to the sourcing of information.

Generally, two information sources have to be distinguished:

- Literature
- Empirical data

Furthermore, different types of literature can be differentiated and explained:

- Monographs and textbooks
- Articles in academic journals
- Concise dictionaries
- Edited works
- Working papers
- Conference proceedings
- White papers and green papers
- Consultation papers, technical papers, manuals
- Legal sources and documents

Special emphasis has to be given to the appraisal of references:

- The aspects of citability and credibility need to be verified.
- Peer review processes, citation indices and journal rankings are aspects of qualitative appraisal.
- Grey literature needs special attention with respect to its citability and credibility.

The search for literature can be assisted in different ways:

- A differentiated information access and retrieval
- Applying intelligent search strategies and corresponding techniques:
    - Using a thesaurus
    - Truncation
    - Boolean operations
    - Phrase searching

6.6.2 Questions

Knowledge

1. What is a monograph?
2. What is a textbook?
3. What is an academic journal?
4. What is a concise dictionary?
5. What is an edited work?
6. What is a working paper?
7. What is the difference between an article in an academic journal and a working paper?
8. What are conference proceedings?
9. What are white papers and green papers?
10. What are technical papers?
11. What are consultation papers?
12. What are manuals?
13. What types of legal sources and documents can be distinguished?
14. What is citability of a reference?
15. What are the three criteria of citability?
16. What is credibility of a reference?
17. What are the four criteria of credibility?
18. What is a double-blind peer review?
19. What is a citation index?
20. What are examples of citation indices?
21. What is a journal ranking?
22. How is the Journal Impact Factor (JIF) calculated?
23. What is grey literature?
24. Who are potential originators of grey literature?
25. What are potential examples of grey literature?
26. What is the Internet?
27. What are potential problems while using web search engines?
28. What is a heuristic search?
29. What are potential problems while applying a heuristic search strategy?
30. What are options for an academic literature search?
31. What is an OPAC?
32. What is an advantage of research libraries and/or reference libraries?
33. What is the difference between headwords and keywords?
34. What is a thesaurus?

35. What is truncation?
36. What are Boolean operations?
37. What is phrase searching?

6.6.3 Problems

6.6.3.1 Citation indices

Application

Learning target

Being able to analyse the quality of references with the help of citation indices

Instructions

1. Please identify five Nobel laureates in one of the seven Nobel Prize disciplines.

    http://www.nobelprize.org/

2. Please look-up the profiles of the Nobel laureates in Google Scholar and compare citations, h-index and i10-index.

6.6.3.2 Peer review

Analysis

Learning target

Being able to understand implications and limitations of peer review processes

Instructions

1. Please read the article *Writing the "The Market for 'Lemons'": A Personal and Interpretive Essay* and particularly the section *Rejections and acceptance* written by Nobel laureate George A. Akerlof:

    http://www.nobelprize.org/nobel_prizes/economic-sciences/laureates/2001/akerlof-article.html

2. What were the limitations of the peer review processes in this particular case?

6.6.4 Additional reading

Briotta Paroloa, P. D., Pan, R. K., Ghoshb, R., Hubermanc, B. A., Kaskia, K., & Fortunato, S. (2015, March 9). *Attention decay in science*. Preprint. Retrieved from http://arxiv.org/pdf/1503.01881v1.pdf

7 Elements of a research paper

Abstract

The structural elements to be applied in academic writing depend on the nature of the research project. Manifestations of academic writing range from student assignments and term papers to doctoral theses and other forms of complex research documentations. Some structural elements are always used in research papers. Other structural elements are optionally or selectively used. Technically, research papers can be divided into four sections: addments, directories, main body and annex. Each of these sections contains different structural elements that have to be applied in accordance with the formal instructions laid out in academic style guides. Although the applicable rules may vary according to the field of research, some commonalities for structural elements exist. These commonalities may be based on logical considerations or result from traditional academic conventions. Important elements to be discussed in this chapter are cover page, abstract, outline, directories, main body, bibliography and list of references, glossary and appendix, declaration of originality as well as data carrier and electronic storage media.

Keywords

Structural elements, sections, page numbering, addments, directories, main body, annex, cover page, abstract, foreword, preface, dedication, outline, decadal numbering, alpha-numerical numbering, figures, tables, abbreviations, symbols, formula, bibliography, references, glossary, appendix, data carrier, storage media, index of names, subject index

7.1 Context and relevance

7.1.1 Context of chapter 7

Even in an early stage of a research project, preliminary insights and findings will appear. Skilfully applying the elements of the research paper helps researchers to organise and document their research and writing from the start.

Figure 7.1 shows how chapter 7 is embedded within the setting of a research project.

7 Elements of a research paper

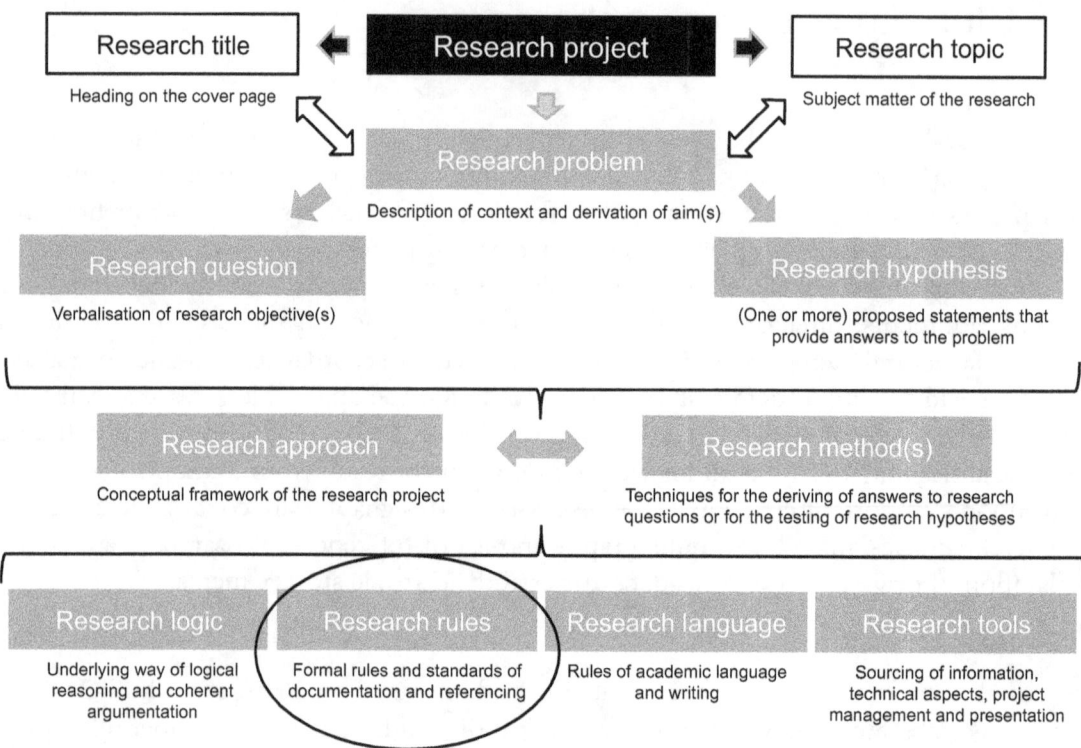

Figure 7.1: Context of chapter 7

In this chapter formal rules and standards of documentation are addressed.

7.1.2 Relevance of chapter 7

Throughout the research process, thoughts and findings have to be written down. In order to organise and guide the research and writing process, one should store information in a systematic way. For this purpose, it helps to use the proved elements of a research paper from the start. Last but not least, the proper documentation of a research project signals academic credibility. One might criticise that the substance of findings is more important than the form of the documentation and/or presentation. However, in many cases the violation of formal criteria and academic conventions is a first indicator of an inferior substance.

7.1.3 Learning objectives of chapter 7

After having studied this chapter, the reader should to be able to:

- recognise the four sections of an academic research paper
- distinguish between the three types of structural elements
- match different structural elements with different types of research papers
- apply relevant structural elements of research papers

7.2 Structural elements and their application

7.2.1 The four sections of a research paper

The formal structure of a research paper can be divided into four sections (Figure 7.2).

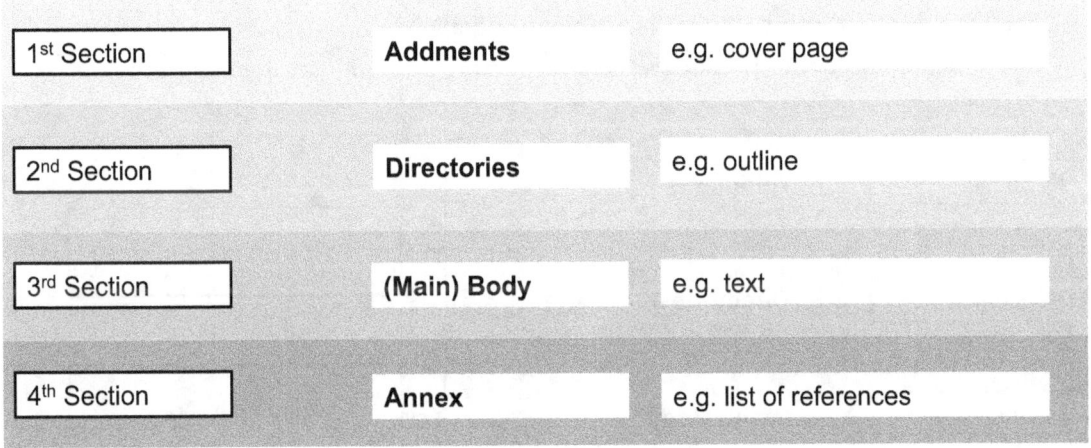

Figure 7.2: The four sections of a research paper

The first section is named "addments". It includes all parts of a research paper that are located before the directories section; for example, the cover page forms part of the addments section.

The second section is called "directories". As the name implies, it includes directories and lists of a research paper; for example, the outline (table of contents) forms part of the directories section.

The third section is the "body" or "main body". The body of a paper is the part that includes the chapters of the research paper.

The fourth section is called "annex". The annex includes everything that follows the main body; for example, the list of references forms part of the annex section.

In book design, the first and the second section are collectively referred to as "front matter"; the third section is called "body matter", and the fourth section is referred to as "back matter".

7.2.2 Page numbering of sections

In some academic disciplines, there are traditional page numbering systems that prescribe a differentiated use of Roman and Arabic numerals.

Figure 7.3 shows a traditional form of page numbering:

- The sections addments and directories are numbered with Roman numerals.
- The main body is numbered with Arabic numerals.
- The annex could either be numbered with Arabic numerals or Roman numerals.

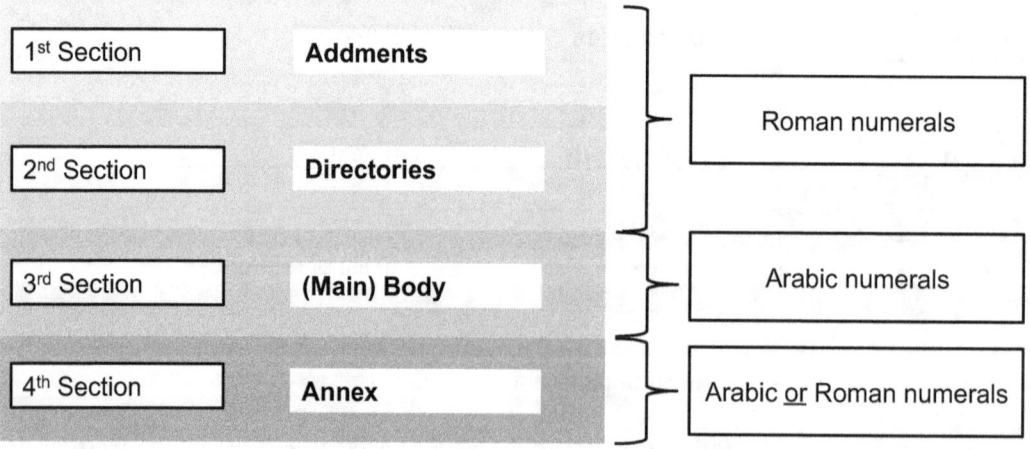

Figure 7.3: Page numbering

The advantage of the presented page numbering system is that Arabic numerals are solely used for the core of the research paper, i.e. the main body. Thus, it becomes easier for the reader to navigate the sections while flipping through the pages. Additionally, the person who reads and/or evaluates the research paper is able to notice the number of pages devoted to the core of the paper at a glance.

☞ Tip

Researchers should check whether the traditional page numbering system or a different system stemming from an individual style guide is applicable to their research project.

7.2.3 The three types of structural elements

7.2.3.1 Overview

Generalising, three types of structural elements of an academic research paper or thesis project can be distinguished:

1. Structural elements that are **always** used in research papers
2. Structural elements that are **optionally** used in research papers
3. Structural elements that are **selectively** used in published academic research (monographs, articles in journals etc.)

This differentiation is needed in order to understand different types of formal requirements for research papers.

Before the structural elements are described in greater detail, the use of each structural element in the context of the four sections of a research paper is explained in the following subchapters.

7.2.3.2 Mandatory structural elements

Figure 7.4 shows the structural elements always used in a research paper.

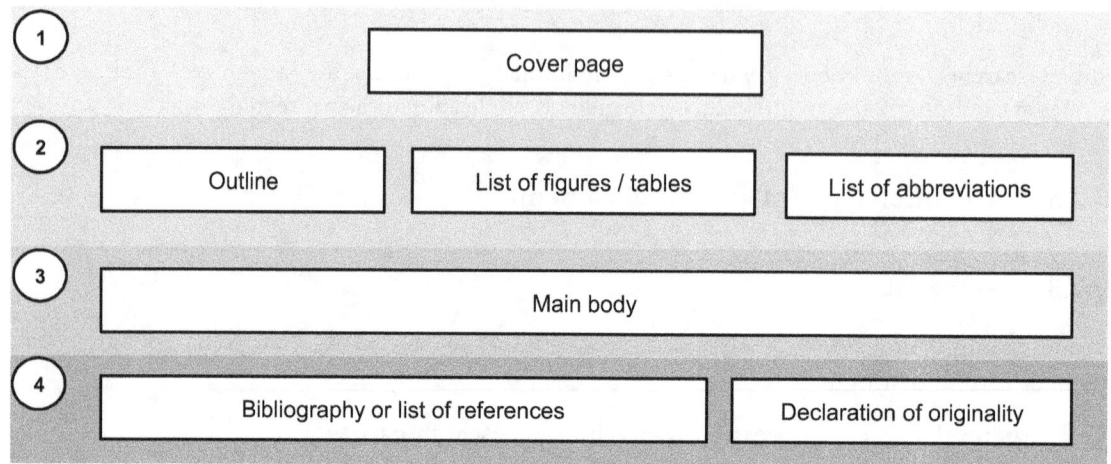

Figure 7.4: Structural elements always used in a research paper

Every research paper contains a **cover page**, which forms part of the addments section. The cover page is the front page of a research paper. Besides the title and the name of the candidate or researcher, it contains all the relevant information needed for readers or recipients.

In the directories section, there will be an **outline**, a **list of figures and tables** as well as a **list of abbreviations**. Generally speaking, an outline is the table of contents of a research paper. Nevertheless, the term table of contents is not always used in academic research papers. The list of figures and the list of tables list all figures and tables that form part of the research paper. The list of abbreviations contains and explains all abbreviations that need further explanation.

The third section of a research paper is comprised of the **main body**. The main body is the core of the research paper. It is composed of text, figures and tables.

The annex section contains the **bibliography and/or the list of references**. Furthermore, a **declaration of originality** typically forms part of the fourth section.

7.2.3.3 Optional structural elements

Figure 7.5 shows structural elements optionally used in a research paper.

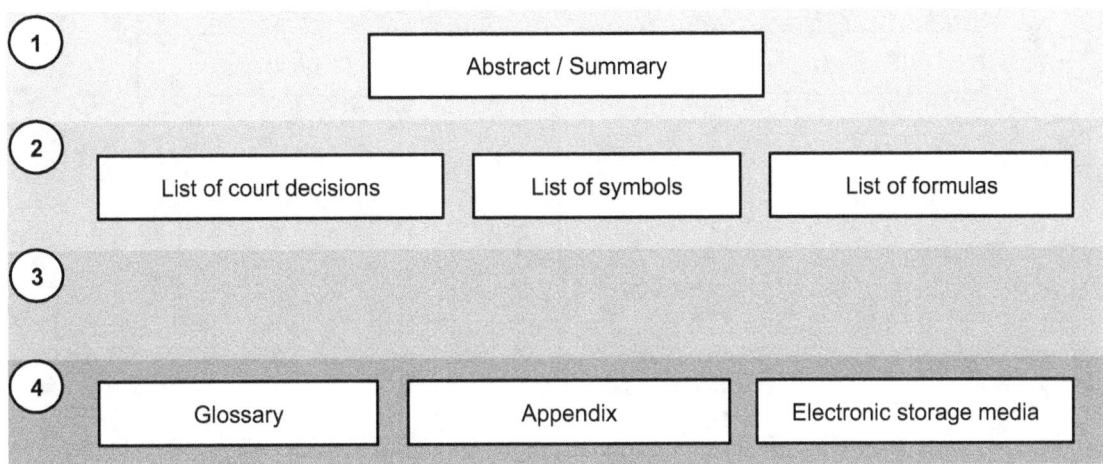

Figure 7.5: Structural elements optionally used in a research paper

The addments section can include an **abstract**. An abstract is a brief summary of the research paper. Furthermore, it may list keywords, which can be linked to a classification system.

> 🎓 **Tip**
>
> In some academic publications such as journal articles and working papers, the abstract forms part of the cover page.

The directory section can include a **list of court decisions**, a **list of symbols** and a **list of formulas**. A list of court decisions is common for research projects that deal directly or indirectly with legal topics. A list of symbols is common for quantitative and analytical research projects. In some cases, an additional list of formulas is provided.

The annex can include a **glossary**, an **appendix** and **electronic storage media**. A glossary is used in order to explain technical terms that form part of a research project. An appendix can serve the purpose of attaching relevant information used in the context of the research project that would go beyond the scope of the main body, for example extensive sets of data, drawings, and maps. Sometimes electronic storage media are needed in order to attach soft copies of spreadsheet calculations, data sets or documents.

7.2.3.4 Special structural elements

Figure 7.6 shows structural elements selectively used in a research paper.

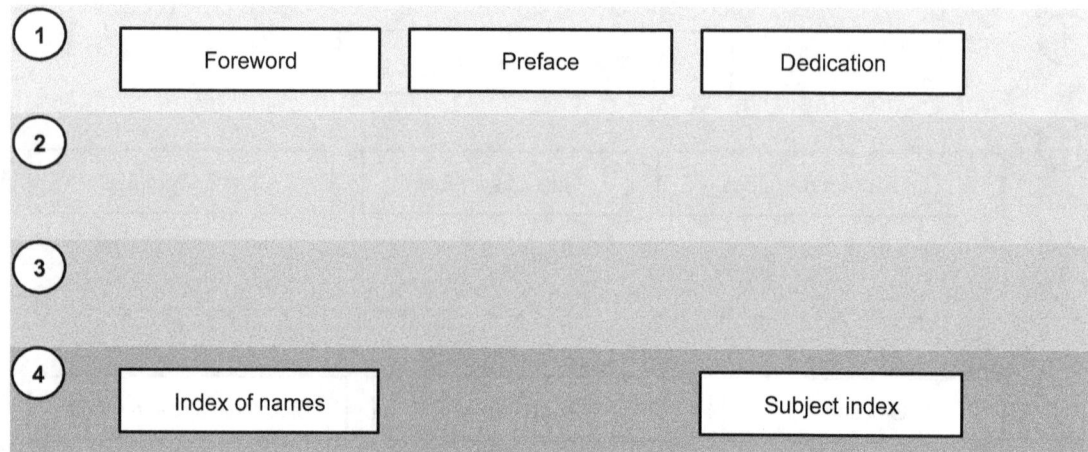

Figure 7.6: Structural elements selectively used in a research paper

The addments section can include a **foreword**, a **preface** or a **dedication**.

A foreword is an introductory text written by a third person. It introduces the reader to the research project from a subject-specific perspective. Typically, the writer of the foreword praises the research paper and the achievements of the author. A preface is an introductory text written by the author. In some cases, the preface contains an acknowledgement, where the author explains her or his thanks to colleagues, academic supervisors or her or his parents. Prefaces are common for published versions of doctoral thesis projects. Students should not incorporate prefaces in their research papers. A dedication is placed on a separate page. It contains personal statements as for example "to mum and dad" or "in memory of my grandparents". In case of doubt, students should avoid dedications.

The annex section can contain an **index of names** and a **subject index**. An index of names lists names of persons referred to or the titles of cited thesis projects in alphabetical order. The names are listed together with the corresponding pages of the main body, where the names have been mentioned. Printed versions of doctoral dissertations may in particular contain an index of names. The subject index is similar to the index of names. It lists technical terms in alphabetical order accompanied by the corresponding pages of the main body, where the terms have been used. Modern text processing software provides an automated compilation of an index of names and an index of subjects.

7.2.4 Application

Table 7.1 is intended to provide an overview of the cases in which a structural element may be considered suitable or not.

Structural elements	Term Paper	Master's thesis Bachelor's thesis	Ph. D. thesis
Cover page	Yes	Yes	Yes
Abstract/summary	If required	Optional	Optional
Outline	Yes	Yes	Yes
List of figures/tables	Yes	Yes	Yes
List of abbreviations	Yes	Yes	Yes
List of symbols	Optional	Optional	Optional
List of formulas	Optional	Optional	Optional
Main body	Yes	Yes	Yes
Bibliography/list of references	Yes	Yes	Yes
Glossary	If required	Optional	Optional
Appendix	Optional	Optional	Optional
Declaration of originality	Yes	Yes	Yes
Electronic storage media	If required	If required	If required

Table 7.1: Structural elements and their application

Generally, one should refer to the applicable institutional rules. Typically, academic institutions provide style guides containing information on structural elements as well as formatting requirements (e.g. margining, spacing, font, font size etc.) to be used in research projects.

If a research project contains sensitive data or information, one may consider adding a confidentiality clause to the research paper. Typically, it is placed on the cover page or on the second page.

7.3 Description of structural elements

7.3.1 Elements

The following elements of academic research projects will be discussed in further detail in subsequent subchapters:

- Cover page
- Abstract
- Outline
- List of figures
- List of tables
- List of abbreviations
- List of symbols
- List of formulas
- Main body
- Bibliography/list of references
- Glossary
- Appendix
- Declaration of originality
- Data carriers and storage media

7.3.2 Cover page

The cover page is the entry point of an academic research paper. It gives the reader a first impression of the accuracy to be expected from the forthcoming analysis.

Therefore, the cover page should solely contain relevant information:

- Purpose (term paper, bachelor's thesis, diploma thesis or master's thesis)
- Title of paper/thesis
- Name of institution, faculty and department
- First name and family name
- Date and place of birth
- Matriculation number (student number)
- Address, telephone, e-mail
- Date of submission
- Name of degree programme
- Term papers contain: course title, name of instructor, semester (for example summer term [YEAR])
- Thesis projects contain: names of referees (including academic degrees)

Moreover, the cover page should not contain unnecessary and distracting components. In the majority of the cases, a plain design is expected. Accordingly, one should avoid "fancy" designs such as graphics and photographs as they are generally not considered academic. Additionally, one should avoid coloured fonts such as coloured headings. A rule of thumb is to use a black font on white paper.

To sum it up: The cover page, which provides the first impression of the research project, should be designed in a neutral fashion.

7.3.3 Abstract

An abstract is a brief summary of the research paper. It serves as an instrument of information and documentation. Libraries may use it in order to archive the research or thesis project. Academic journals, particularly editorial boards, require an abstract for information and publication purposes.

The abstract should fit on a single page and contain the following information:

- A short summary of the research problem and the key findings of the research project
- Keywords that are derived from the topic/subject matter of the thesis
- A frequently used classification system, the JEL classification that has been developed by the Journal of Economic Literature.

Figure 7.7 exemplifies the use of keywords.

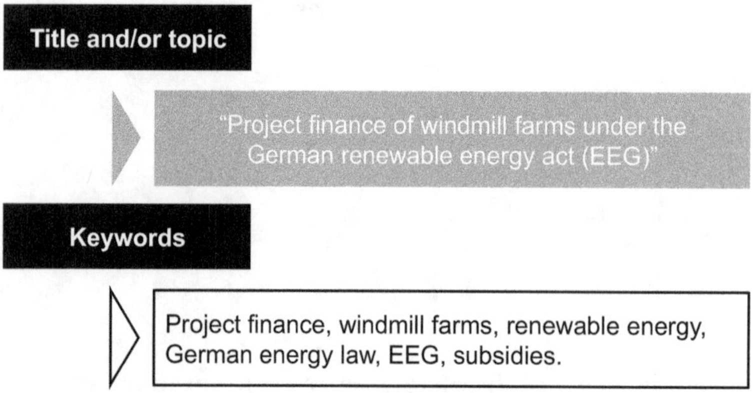

7 Elements of a research paper

Title and/or topic

▷ "Project finance of windmill farms under the German renewable energy act (EEG)"

Keywords

▷ Project finance, windmill farms, renewable energy, German energy law, EEG, subsidies.

Figure 7.7: Keywords of an abstract – example

If the title/topic is "Project finance of windmill farms under the German renewable energy act (EEG)", the keywords that can be directly extracted from the topic are "project finance", "windmill farms", "renewable energy", "German energy law", "EEG" and, implicitly, "subsidies". In many cases, however, there are more advanced keywords, which cannot be extracted from the title or the topic. A deeper understanding of the topic and the underlying research problem is needed in order to identify these keywords.

A source for identifying more keywords is the JEL classification system developed by the Journal of Economic Literature. It provides an alphanumerical classification system that can be used for classifying research papers, articles and monographs.

If the titel/topic of the research project is "Project finance of windmill farms under the German renewable energy act (EEG)" the JEL classification G21, G32, H23 and O38 could be used in order to describe the topic:

- G21 stands, amongst others, for Banks; Other Depository Institutions; Micro Finance Institutions.
- G32 stands, amongst others, for Financing Policy; Financial Risk and Risk Management.
- H23 stands, amongst others, for Externalities; Redistributive Effects; Environmental Taxes and Subsidies.
- O38 stands, amongst others, for Government Policy.

The website of the Journal of Economic Literature (http://www.aeaweb.org) provides a comprehensive overview of the JEL classification system, which helps to identify the appropriate classification for a topic.

7.3.4 Outline

Factually, the outline is the table of contents of a research paper. However, as pointed out, some academics consider the term table of contents unscholarly. Therefore, the suitability of the term table of contents in a given context should be clarified.

There are two options of numbering an outline:

- Decadal numbering system
Alphanumerical numbering system

Figure 7.8 shows an example of the **decadal numbering system**.

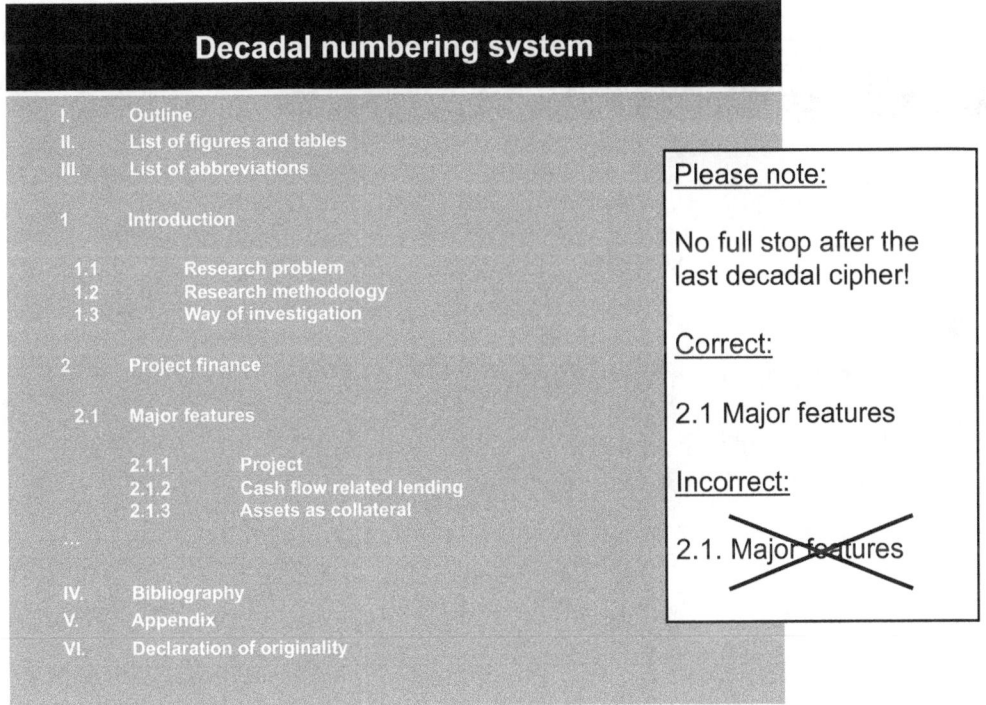

Figure 7.8: Decadal numbering system – example

The addments, directories and annex section are numbered with Roman numerals, and the main body is numbered with Arabic numerals. An advantage of the decadal numbering system is that the position of each chapter can be exactly identified due to the logic of the continuous numbering.

It has to be noted that there is no full stop after the last decadal cipher.

> Example
> Correct: 2.1 Major features
> Incorrect: 2.1. Major features

Tip

Some academic advisors require a full stop after the decadal cipher of the first level, e.g. "1. Introduction" instead of "1 Introduction". Again, it is advisable to inquire about the applicable preferences.

Figure 7.9 shows an example of the **alphanumerical numbering system**.

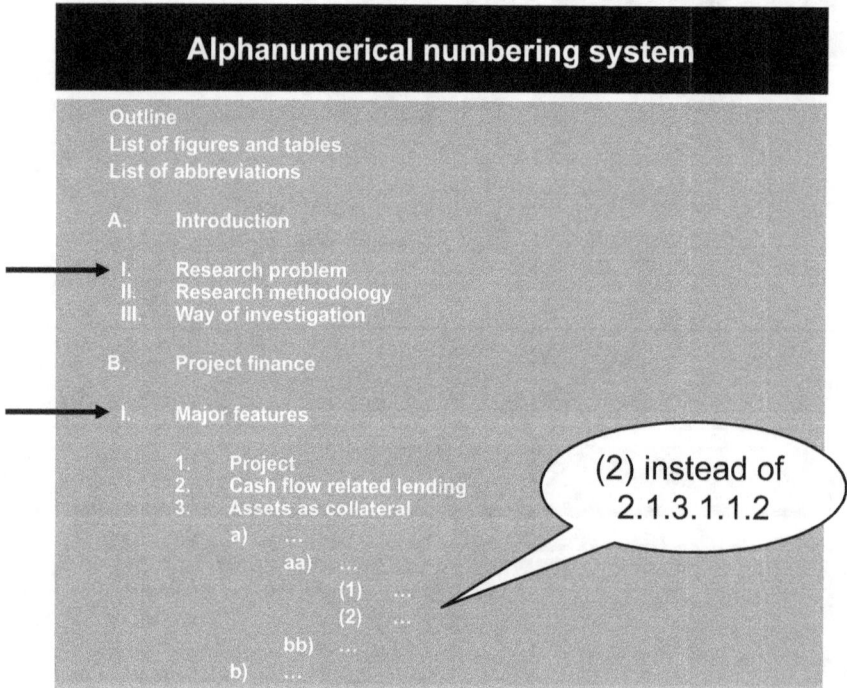

Figure 7.9: Alphanumerical numbering – example

The main advantage of the alphanumerical numbering system is that overly long numbers can be avoided. The sample outline enfolds six levels. Instead of the decadal numbering 2.1.3.1.1.2 within the sixth level, the alphanumerical numbering requires a simple (2).

The disadvantage of the alphanumerical numbering system is that subchapters of different chapters might carry the same numbers. In the sample outline, both the subchapter "Research problem" and the subchapter "Major features" are denominated with the Roman "I.". This may be considered confusing.

Tip

It has to be pointed out that alphanumerical numbering is not allowed by some examination regulations. It is advisable to check which type of numbering system is suitable for a piece of research.

7.3.5 Directories

There are two options of documenting the **list of figures and tables** (Figure 7.10):

1. All figures and tables can be included in a combined list of figures and tables.
2. If the list contains a considerable number of figures and tables, it is advisable to split it into a separate list of figures and a separate list of tables.

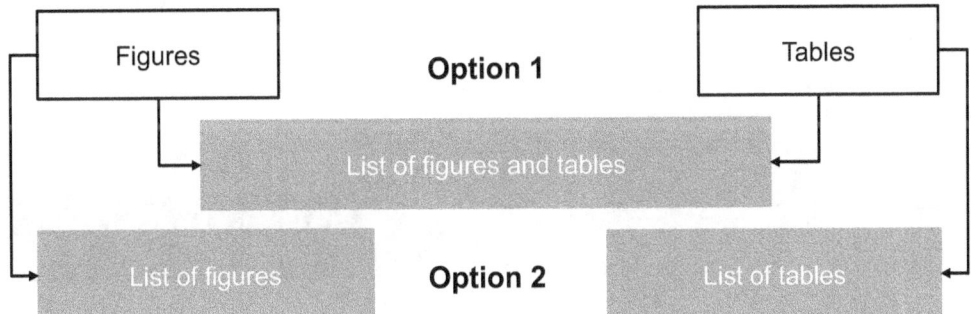

Figure 7.10: List of figures and list of tables – options

For both options the following rules apply:

- Figures and tables have to be numbered, for example "Figure 1" or "Table 1".
- Directories have to list the individual numbers of the pages where figures and tables can be found.
- Solely the captions, not the references, of figures and tables should be listed.

7 Elements of a research paper

It is considered good scientific style to explain abbreviations by specifying them in a **list of abbreviations**. Some rules of thumb apply for lists of abbreviations.

- It is recommended to:
    - introduce abbreviations and their meaning in the text and to list them in a list of abbreviations
    - list commonly used abbreviations of the field of study (e.g. ECA for Export credit agency; M&A for mergers and acquisitions)
    - amend names of institutions with legal form and location (e.g. VW for Volkswagen AG, Wolfsburg/Germany)

- In contrast, one should:
    - not list commonly known abbreviations (for example etc., cm, no.)
    - not use and list abbreviations out of convenience, which implies:
        - not to abbreviate general terminology of the field of subject (e.g. HRM for human resource management; SCM for supply chain management)
        - not to introduce self-made abbreviations (e.g. NIEF for new institutional economic framework)

Figure 7.11 illustrates the introduction of the word or expression together with its abbreviation in the text.

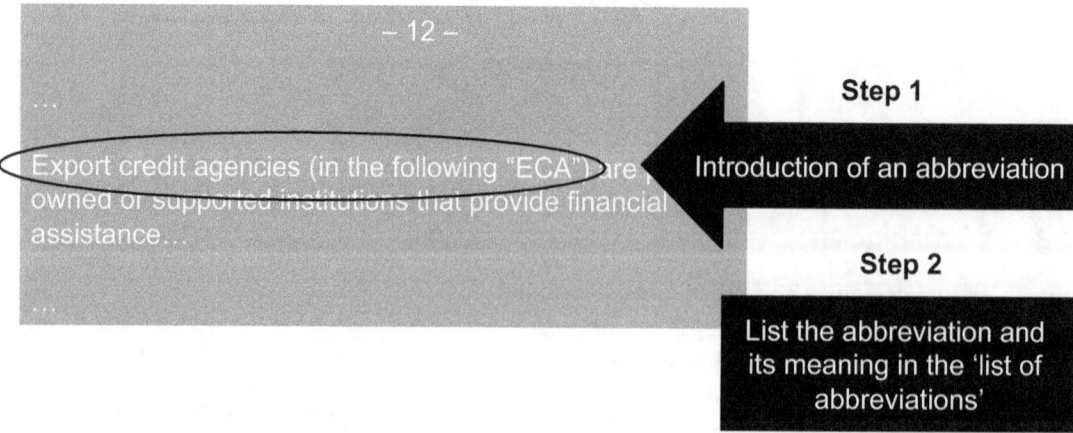

Figure 7.11: Abbreviation – example

🎓 Tip

While an abbreviation is introduced, one should consider whether the spelled-out term is followed by its abbreviation in parentheses <u>or</u> the abbreviation is followed by its meaning in parentheses. For this purpose, it is advisable to consult the applicable institutional requirements or to inquire about the preferences of the academic advisor.

After the introduction, one has to include the abbreviation and its meaning in the list of abbreviations. In the text following the introduction, only the abbreviation should be used.

Symbols and/or formulas are an integral part of many research projects. All symbols and formulas should be listed in a **list of symbols** and a **list of formulas**.

While using symbols in a research project, one should:

- explain symbols, when they are introduced in the text
- additionally specify symbols in a list of symbols

A list of formulas is common in quantitative research projects.

- Synonyms of list of formulas are list of equations or list of algorithms.
- One should number each formula within the text

    Example
    Formula 21: EL = PD * LS * EAD

🎓 Tip

It is advisable to check with the instructor or research advisor whether a separate list of formulas is required or desired.

7.3.6 Main body

7.3.6.1 Numbering and structuring

The main body is the core of a term paper or thesis project.

Generally, the following principles have to be applied:

- The headings of the chapters are numbered.
- The numbering of the chapters has to correspond (to be identical) with the numbering of the outline.

7 Elements of a research paper

- The first page of the main body starts with the page number one (– 1 –).
- There is no intermediate text outside of the numbering structure as prescribed by the outline.
- The structure has to correspond with the logic of the research question.

In the following, mistakes of numbering and structuring will be addressed. More precisely, the problems of **incomplete numbering** and **illogical structure** will be discussed.

Figure 7.12 represents the structure of a chapter that forms part of the main body. The chapter is entitled "2 Dynamic capital budgeting methods". The task is to structure this chapter.

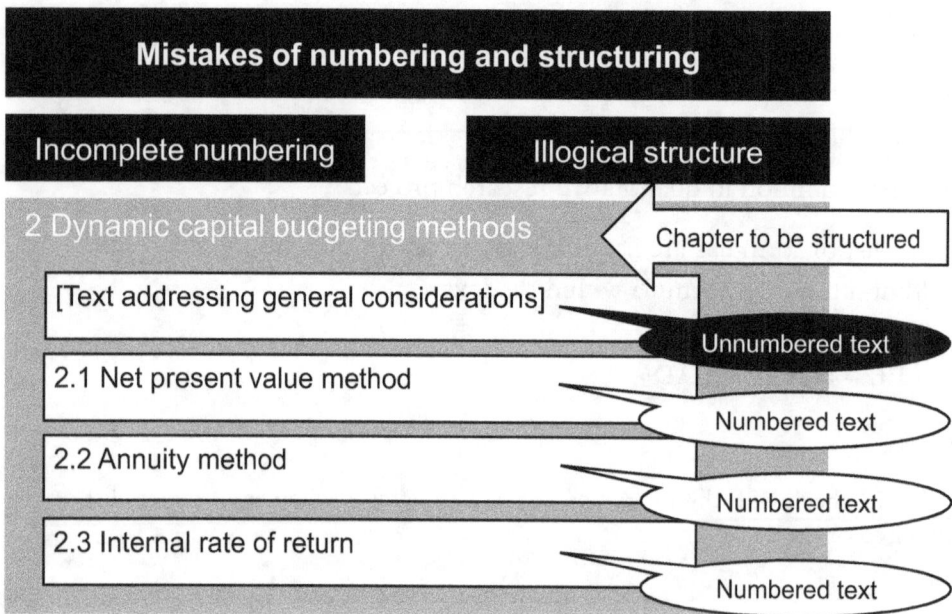

Figure 7.12: Incomplete numbering, illogical structure – example

In the example shown in Figure 7.12, the chapter is structured as follows:

- There is a text addressing general considerations regarding dynamic capital budgeting methods. There are two mistakes: The text has no heading and is not numbered.
- The first subchapter is entitled "2.1 Net present value method". It has a heading and it is numbered.

- The next subchapter is entitled "2.2 Annuity method". It has a heading and it is numbered.
- The last subchapter is entitled "2.3 Internal rate of return". It has a heading and it is numbered.

Although subchapters 2.1, 2.2 and 2.3 have headings and are numbered, the overall structure is illogical. Therefore, the structuring and numbering of the chapter and its subchapters have to be revised. In a first step, the numbering could be completed. Figure 7.13 represents the structure of the sample chapter, now with complete numbering.

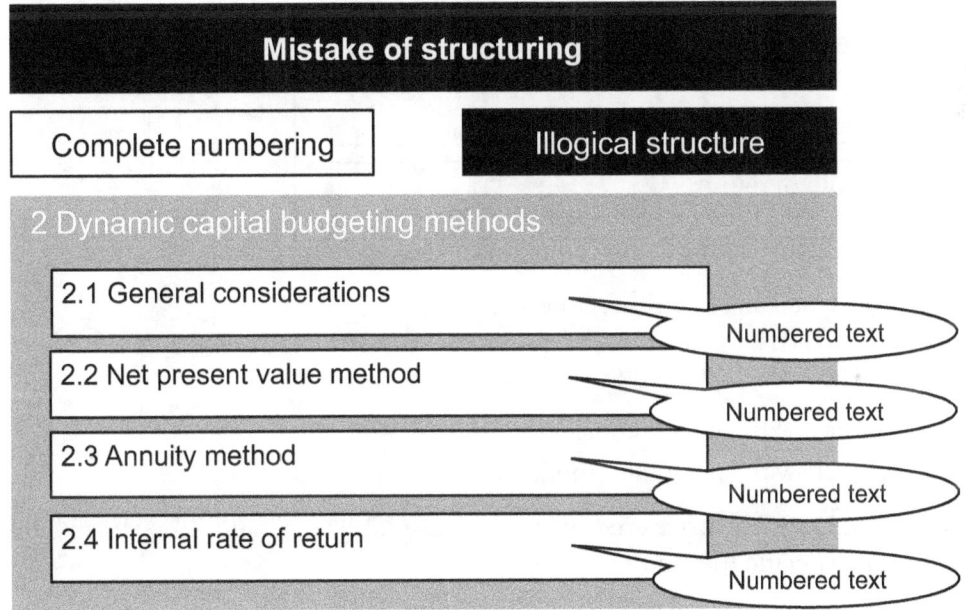

Figure 7.13: Complete numbering, illogical structure – example

Still, the chapter as presented in Figure 7.13 is structured in an illogical way:

- Subchapter 2.1 addresses general considerations.
- Subchapters 2.2, 2.3 and 2.4 address specific methods.

Therefore, the structuring has to be adjusted in a further step. Figure 7.14 represents the correct final structure of the sample chapter with a complete numbering and a logical structure.

7 Elements of a research paper

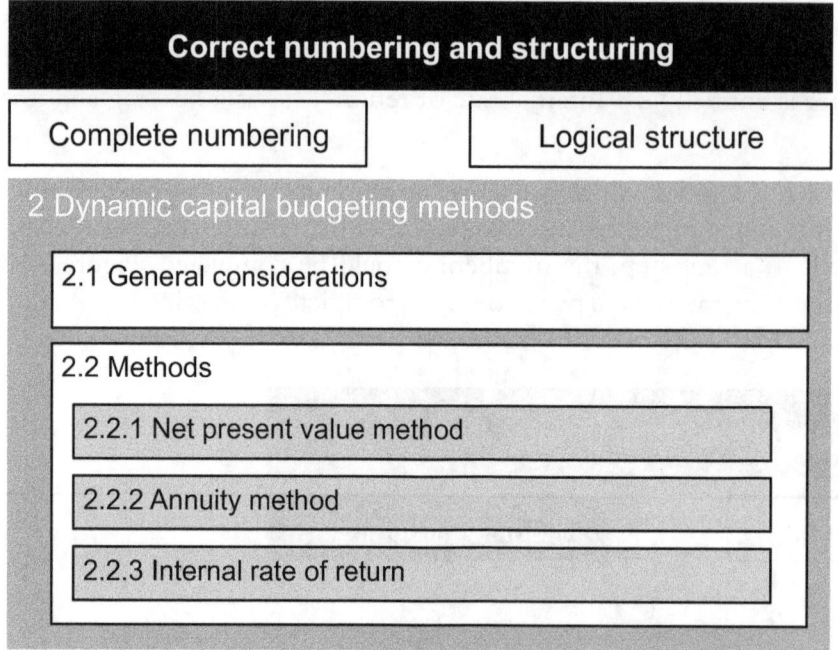

Figure 7.14: Complete numbering, logical structure – example

Chapter 2 is structured in two subchapters:

- Subchapter 2.1 deals with general considerations.
- Subchapter 2.2 deals with specific methods.

Furthermore, subchapter 2.2 is structured in subsections 2.2.1, 2.2.2 and 2.2.3. Each subsection addresses one specific method.

A further major mistake that should be mentioned here is the **incomplete structuring** of the text. This is exemplified in Figure 7.15, where subchapter 2.2 is missing.

Figure 7.15: Incomplete structuring – example

The rule is: If a chapter is subdivided, there have to be at least two subchapters.

7.3.6.2 Intermediate text

Typically, incomplete numbering mistakes are related to intermediate text. Accordingly, the problem of intermediate text is often linked to text without a proper structure. Therefore, intermediate text should be avoided (Figure 7.16).

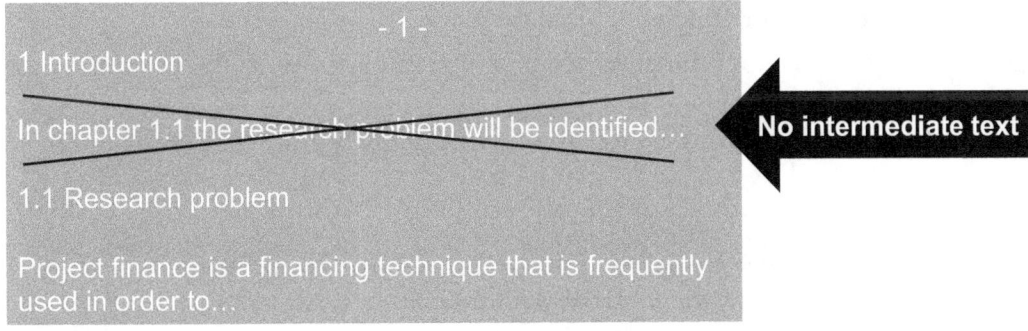

Figure 7.16: Intermediate text – example

There are arguments in favour as well as against the use of intermediate text. Some authors intend to provide a thread by using intermediate text as a means of orientation within a paper or thesis or as a recursion to the subchapter "Course of investigation". In contrast, intermediate text is considered bad academic style since it can be assumed that an educated reader is able to comprehend the outline, the research problem and the course of investigation. Furthermore, intermediate text creates redundancy and consumes space needed for focussed thoughts.

> **Tip**
>
> Some instructors and thesis advisors might emphasise, tolerate or even require the use of intermediate text ("journalistic style" or "narrative style"). Other instructors and thesis advisors will consider intermediate text to be redundant, illogical and/or non-academic ("strictly academic style"). Therefore, it is advisable to clarify the position of the instructor's or thesis advisor's position regarding intermediate text.

7.3.6.3 Figures and tables

Figures and tables are important elements of research papers or thesis projects. Some specifics of lists of figures and lists of tables were already addressed in a previous subchapter. At this point, the focus is on aligning figures and tables with the text of the main body.

There are some formal rules:

- Figures and tables need an individual and numbered caption, which is typically placed at the top of the figure or table.
- Figures and tables need a reference, which is typically located at the bottom of the figure or table.
- Figure or table, caption and reference have to be placed together on a single page.

> **Tip**
>
> It should be noted that, due to the style rules of the publisher, in printed books or e-books figures and tables might be subject to different formal rules.

Additionally, there are the following material rules:

- Figures and tables have to be logically linked to the text of the main body.
- Figures and tables have to be introduced and discussed in the text of the main body.
- A chapter should not start or end with a figure or a table.

7.3.7 Bibliography and references

In many cases, the terms "bibliography" and "list of references" are used as synonyms. However, a bibliography and a list of references can be differentiated as follows:

- The bibliography refers to information sources that have been used in the research process and may have been cited or not been cited in the text.
- The list of references, sometimes also referred to as "sources list", solely lists information sources that have been cited in the text.

As shown in Figure 7.17, the type of referencing has an effect on the type of bibliography or list of references.

7.3 Description of structural elements

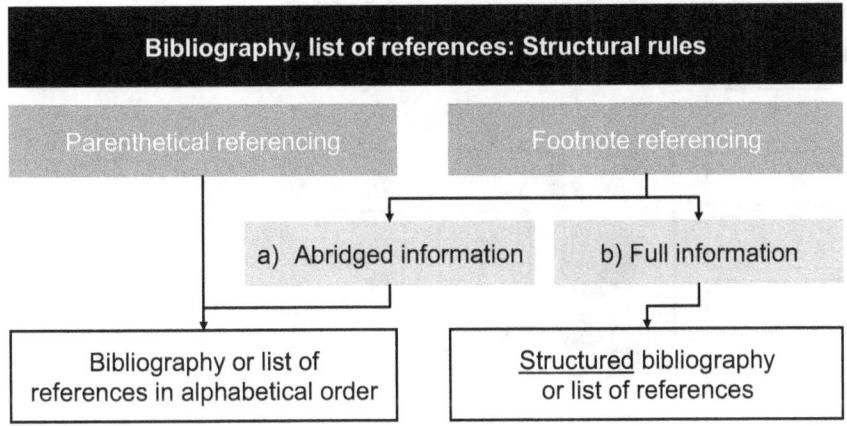

Figure 7.17: Parenthetical referencing vs. footnote referencing

Basically, there are two options of referencing:

- Parenthetical referencing
- Footnote referencing

Furthermore, there are two options of footnote referencing:

- Footnote referencing with abridged information
- Footnote referencing with full information

Further details on referencing and citation will be given in chapter 10 "Referencing".

The use of one of the above-mentioned methods has a direct impact on the way references have to be listed in a bibliography or list of reference:

- Parenthetical referencing and footnote referencing with abridged information require an unstructured bibliography or list of references in alphabetical order.
- Footnote referencing with full information allows for a structured bibliography or list of references.

The structure of a structured bibliography or list of references could be as shown in Figure 7.18:

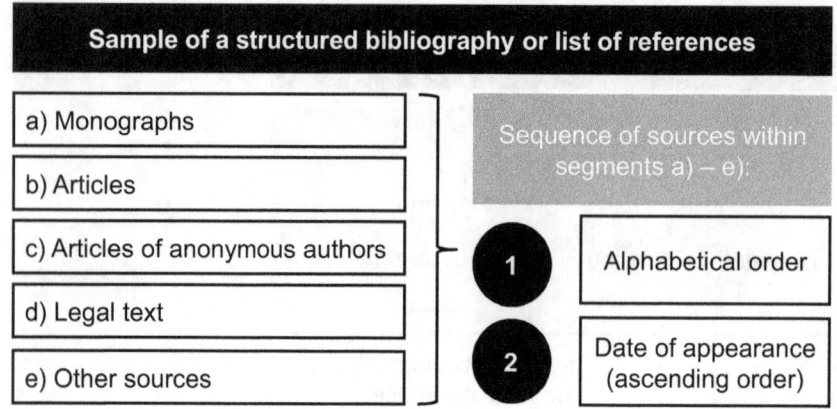

Figure 7.18: Structured bibliography or list of references – sample

The sources could be organised in the segments:

a) Monographs
b) Articles
c) Articles of anonymous authors
d) Legal text
e) Other sources

Within these segments, references are listed in alphabetical order and thereafter by the date of appearance in ascending order.

7.3.8 Glossary

Some research topics imply the use of specific terminology such as individual company terms or the jargon of a company or industry.

The following rules apply for a glossary:

- Relevant terms should be listed and explained in alphabetical order.
- Explanations should not exceed two to four sentences.
- General terms such as "finance", "loan", "cash flow" etc. should not be listed.
- A glossary should have a minimum length of one page.

If the research paper contains only a few specific terms, their explanation should be provided within the core text, for example as a footnote.

7.3.9 Appendix

The following documents should be included in an appendix instead of in the core text:

- Documents, text of a law, contracts
- Profiles and financial statements of companies
- Questionnaires
- Large amounts of data, statistics
- Protocols of interviews
- Pictures, maps, tables, figures, special graphics like flow-charts, org-charts etc.

7.3.10 Declaration of originality

Typically, examination regulations require a declaration of originality that implicitly confirms the avoidance of:

- Plagiarism, which means copying other authors without proper referencing
- Collusion, which means copying previously submitted research work or secretly co-operating with other candidates

Plagiarism and collusion will be brought to the attention of the examination board and might lead to severe consequences. One should use the text of the declaration of originality that is typically provided by the faculty or department in its citation guidelines or examination regulations.

7.3.11 Data carrier

For some thesis projects, it is required to submit soft copies of the thesis and of all sources from the bibliography or list of references (Table 7.2).

Soft copies	Submission	Purpose
Thesis (Word and PDF)	Data carrier	Archiving ("paperless office")
Sources (PDFs of references)	Upload	Plagiarism and collusion check

Table 7.2: Non-physical elements, electronic submission

The submission can be realised by providing a data carrier containing the relevant files or by uploading the files to a learning management system. The soft copy may be used for archiving the research project. Furthermore, the soft copy of the thesis and bibliography might be used for the enforcement of plagiarism and collusion rules.

7.4 Summary and exercises

7.4.1 Synopsis

A written documentation of a research project can be divided into four sections with corresponding mandatory, optional or selectively used structural elements:

- The addments section with the cover page, the abstract, the foreword, the preface and the dedication
- The directories section with the outline, list of figures and/or tables, the list of abbreviations, the list of court decisions, the list of symbols and the list of formulas
- The (main) body
- The annex section with the bibliography, the list of references, the glossary, the appendix, the declaration of originality, the index of names, the subject index and the electronic storage media

Furthermore, some specific problem areas have to receive special attention:

- The implications of decadal and alphanumerical numbering systems
- The aspects of incomplete structuring, illogical structuring and intermediate text
- Footnote referencing with full information as a prerequisite for structured bibliographies or lists of references
- Plagiarism and collusion

7.4.2 Questions

Knowledge

1. What are the three types of structural elements?
2. What are the four sections of a research paper?
3. What is a foreword?
4. What is a preface?
5. What is a dedication?

6. What is an index of names?
7. What is a subject index?
8. Which structural elements are typically used in a term paper?
9. Which information should be stated on a cover page?
10. What is an abstract?
11. What is an outline?
12. What are rules for a list of abbreviation?
13. What are principles for the design of the main body?
14. What is meant by incomplete numbering of an outline?
15. What is meant by an illogical structure of an outline?
16. What is incomplete structuring of an outline?
17. What is the problem of intermediate text?
18. What are formal and material rules for the presentation of figures and tables?
19. What is the difference between a bibliography and a list of references?
20. How is the chosen referencing style related to the structure of a bibliography or list of references?
21. What is a glossary?
22. What are the rules for a glossary?
23. What could form part of an appendix?
24. What is the rationale of a declaration of originality?
25. What is the difference between plagiarism and collusion?

7.4.3 Problem

Analysis Synthesis

Learning target

Being able to understand the relevance of a logical structure of an outline

Background

A student submits a term paper with the following topic (title) and corresponding outline (structure):

Topic: Blue-collar insourcing in the course of globalisation

Outline:

1 Introduction

2 Blue-collar

    2.1 What is blue-collar work?

    2.2 History of blue-collar work

3 Outsourcing, offshoring, insourcing

    3.1 Definition of insourcing

    3.2 History of insourcing

    3.3 Insourcing: risks

    3.4 Insourcing: chances

    3.5 Reasons for insourcing

4 Globalisation

    4.1 Insourcing and the global effects

5 Conclusion

Instructions

1. Please reflect critically upon the overall structure of the term paper as well as the internal structure of chapters 2, 3 and 4 from a logical perspective.
2. Please develop a revised outline.

8 Interpretation of a topic

Abstract

A well-thought-out interpretation of the topic is a prerequisite for the successful execution of a research project. Especially in academic settings, research candidates have not only the duty, but also the right to develop an interpretation of their topics. In some cases, the thesis advisor might assist the interpretation process. In other cases, research candidates have to derive an interpretation on their own. An ideal interpretation process starts with a negative and a positive interpretation of the topic and thereby the identification of possible aims. Once possible aims and their implications are known, the research candidate has to select one aim or a combination of aims. There are five possible aims: description, causal connection, intention, function, and comparison. The interpretation of a topic can be of an abstract (theoretical) or problem-based (applied) nature. Within the process of a problem-based interpretation, the empirical environment has to be considered. The identified aim predetermines the nature of possible research questions to be investigated.

Keywords

Interpretation, positive interpretation, negative interpretation, abstract interpretation, problem-based interpretation, aim, description, causal connection, intention, function, comparison, research question

8.1 Context and relevance

8.1.1 Context of chapter 8

In previous chapters, a basic understanding of research principles, research logic, research processes, research topics, and information sourcing has been developed. Furthermore, the elements of a research paper have been introduced and discussed. The next step is to explain the interpretation of a topic in a given research situation. The interpretation of a topic is a prerequisite for the identification of a suitable research question and the structuring of a research paper.

Figure 8.1 shows how chapter 8 is embedded within the setting of a research project.

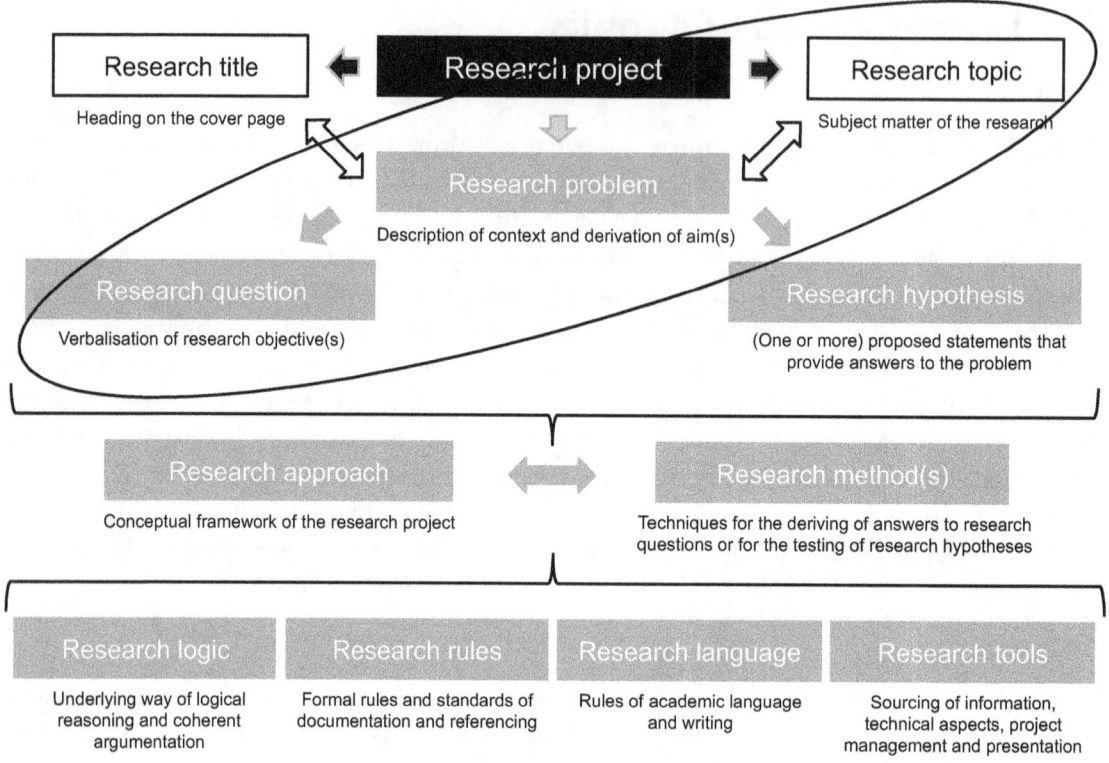

Figure 8.1: Context of chapter 8

In this chapter, the interpretation of a topic including the selection of an aim is addressed.

8.1.2 Relevance of chapter 8

Before structuring a research project, the researcher should derive an interpretation of a topic. The interpretation ensures precision while analysing a potential aim of a research project. Thus, a false approach of the research project can be avoided.

8.1.3 Learning objectives of chapter 8

After having studied this chapter, the reader should be able to:

- understand the interpretation technique and its three process steps

- differentiate the five potential aims of research projects
- comprehend different problem set-ups in the context of real life research situations
- analyse an aim in a problem setting

8.2 Interpretation technique

8.2.1 Process of interpretation

Each topic or problem needs an interpretation that determines possible aims and thereby the nature of the research project (Figure 8.2).

Each candidate has the duty as well as the right to develop an interpretation of the topic.

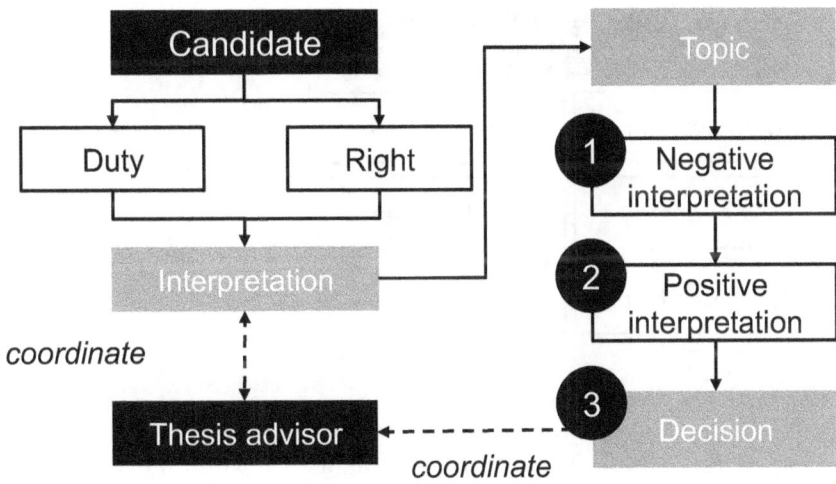

Figure 8.2: Interpretation of a topic – process steps

The technique of interpretation implies three process steps:

1. Negative interpretation
2. Positive interpretation
3. Decision on an aim

The aim is predetermined, if the topic allows only for one aim. If the topic allows for more than one aim, the candidate is free to select one aim for the research project.

8 Interpretation of a topic

▼ Tip

For thesis projects, it is advisable to coordinate the desired aim of the topic with the thesis advisor.

8.2.2 Negative interpretation

It is easier to start with a negative interpretation prior to the positive interpretation of a topic than vice versa. Negative interpretation means to identify aspects that are not covered by the topic. A definition of the terminology helps to postulate a negative interpretation, which can be demonstrated with the example shown in Figure 8.3.

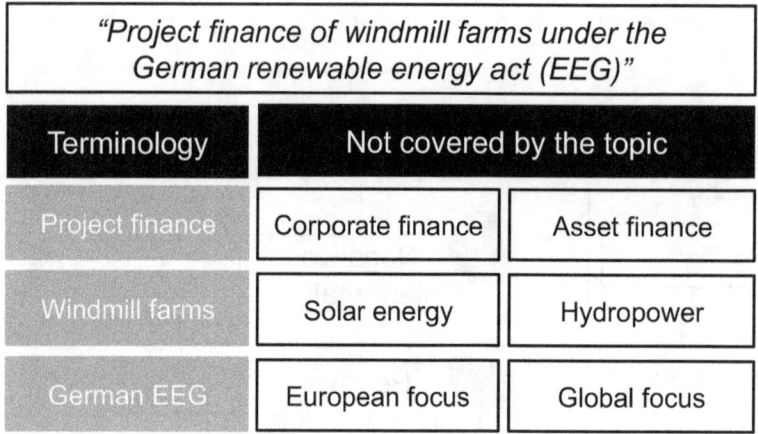

Figure 8.3: Negative interpretation – definition of terminology

A negative interpretation of the sample topic "Project finance of windmill farms under the German renewable energy act (EEG)" could reveal the following findings:

- "Project finance" has to be addressed, but not "corporate finance" or "asset finance".
- "Windmill farms" have to be addressed, but not other forms of renewable energy such as "solar energy" or "hydropower".
- "German renewable energy act (EEG)" implies a German focus, but not a European focus or a global focus.

A negative interpretation is helpful in order to sharpen the focus of the research to be undertaken.

8.2.3 Positive interpretation

The positive interpretation intends to identify possible aims of a research project (Figure 8.4).

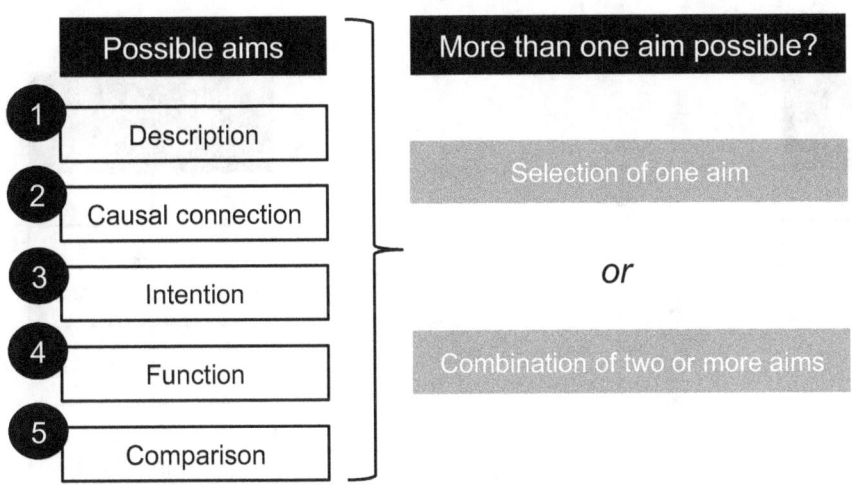

Figure 8.4: Interpretation – possible aims

Potential aims of research projects are:

1. Description
2. Causal connection
3. Intention
4. Function
5. Comparison

In many cases, more than one aim is possible. This would either require a selection of one aim or allow for a combination of two or more aims in a research or thesis project. The specifics of the five aims will be discussed in greater detail in subchapter 8.3.

8.2.4 Decision on an aim

As explained, there are three process steps in order to derive an interpretation of a topic:

1. Negative interpretation
2. Positive interpretation
3. Decision on an aim

8 Interpretation of a topic

The decision on an aim can be a challenging task, particularly, if more than one aim is possible.

In a situation where the problem setting is known, an analysis of the context might be helpful (Figure 8.5).

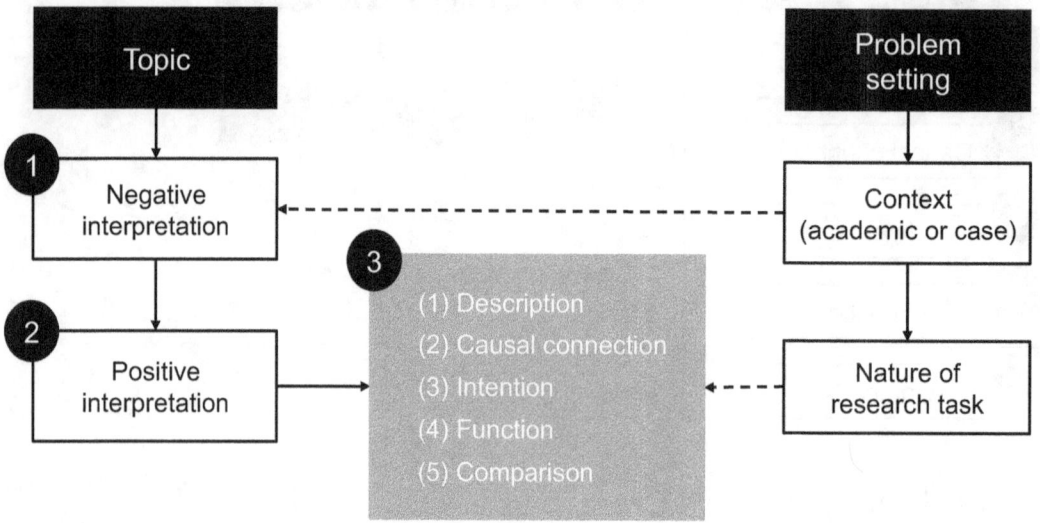

Figure 8.5: Deciding on an aim by identifying the nature of the task

The context of the problem setting can be purely academic or linked to a practical problem. It helps to identify the nature of the research task. Thus, one can narrow the options down to those aims, which serve the research purpose best.

8.2.5 Sample case "Windy decision"

In the following, the sample case introduced in chapter 1, here entitled "Windy decision", is used in order to exemplify the three process steps of interpretation:

> Sample case "Windy decision"
> A farmer who wants to erect a small windmill farm on his farmland has approached a local bank in a rural area. The farmer has funds available that will only cover up to 20% of the investment costs. Therefore, he applies for a loan that will make up for the remaining 80%. Besides the windmill and the income derived from electricity sales, he is not able to provide additional collateral or security to the bank. As a consequence, the electricity sales become a key factor for the financial feasibility (market risk). The farmer claims that

electricity sales are guaranteed by the German renewable energy act (EEG). The bank has no experience concerning windmill project financings. Therefore, the executive committee of the bank asks the credit department to provide a memorandum that analyses the interdependencies between the EEG and project financing of windmill projects in general.

The inherent topic of the sample case "Windy decision" is "Project finance of windmill farms under the German renewable energy act (EEG)" (Figure 8.6).

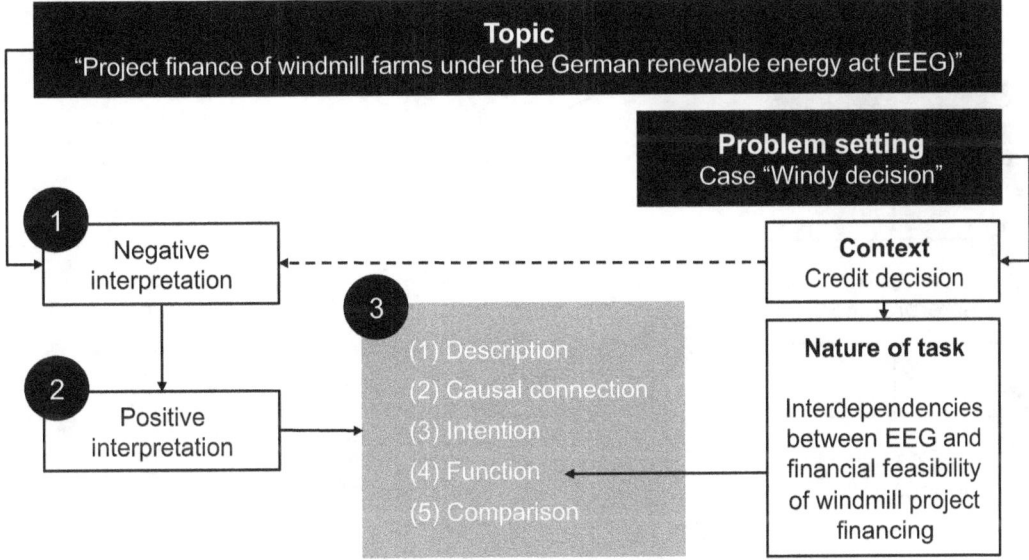

Figure 8.6: Sample case "Windy decision" – context, nature of the task, functional aim

Again, the three process steps of interpretation are laid out:

1. Negative interpretation
2. Positive interpretation
3. Decision on an aim

In the sample case "Windy decision", the problem setting is known. The text provides information with respect to the context. The context is the credit decision to be made by the local bank. In order to come up with a credit decision, the executive committee needs more information regarding the "Interdependencies between the EEG and the financial feasibility of windmill project financing". This leads to the conclusion that a functional research aim is appropriate. It analyses the functional relation between the German renewable energy act (EEG) and the financial feasibility of windmill project financing.

8.3 Abstract interpretation

8.3.1 Abstract analysis of aims

In the following, the focus will be on the abstract analysis of potential aims (Figure 8.7).

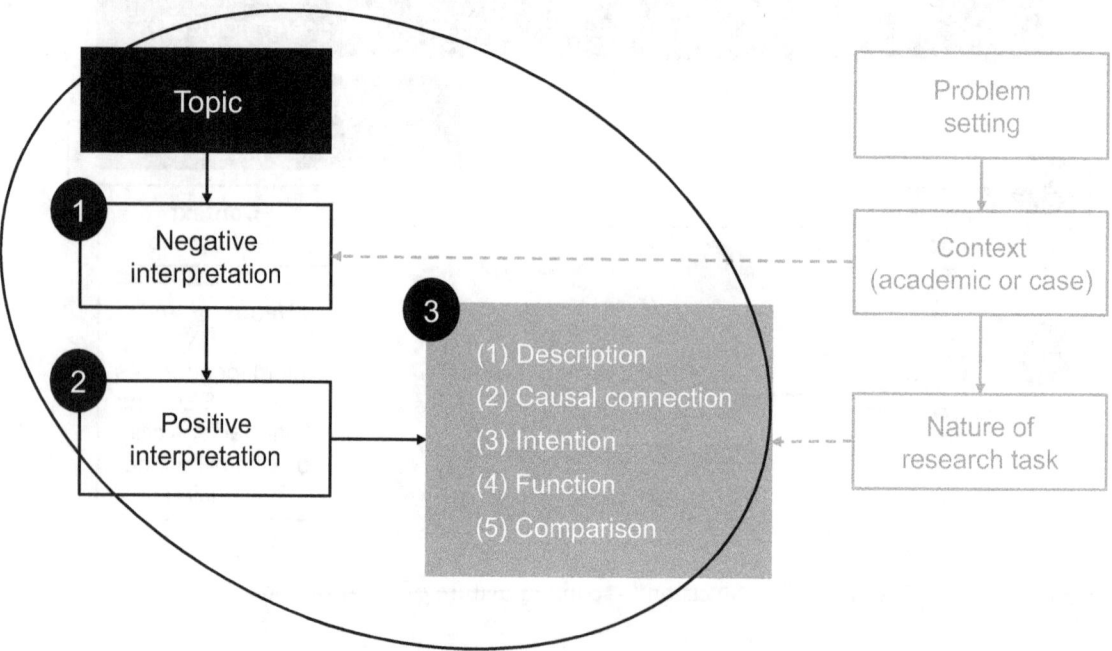

Figure 8.7: Abstract analysis of potential aims

Accordingly, the five potential aims – description, causal connection, intention, function and comparison – are explained from a theoretical perspective.

8.3.2 Description

An object of investigation (for example incident, instrument, agent, method or procedure) can be described, characterised, or explained (Figure 8.8). The description has to be restrained to facts, circumstances, structures, and processes that form part of the objects of investigation. Real cases or data can be used in order to provide additional empirical evidence.

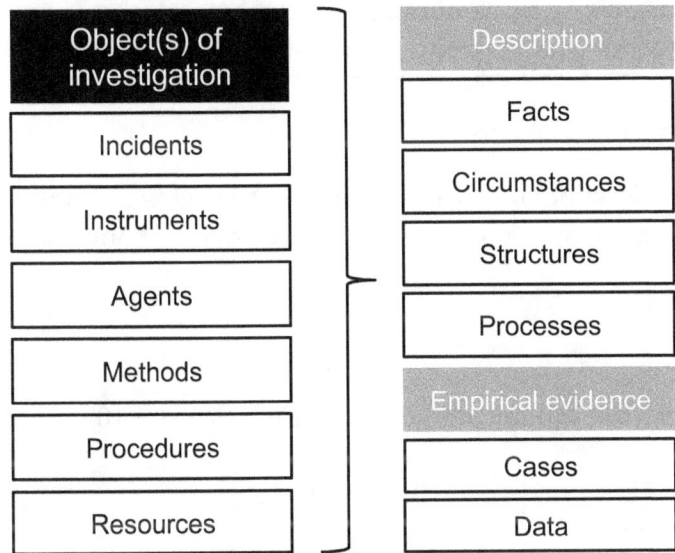

Figure 8.8: Abstract analysis – description

If a topic without a problem setting is "Project finance of windmill farms under the German renewable energy act (EEG)", one could raise different questions that address the object of investigation from a perspective, which may be for example

- technical
- institutional
- regional
- time-related

Sample research questions are formulated in Figure 8.9.

8 Interpretation of a topic

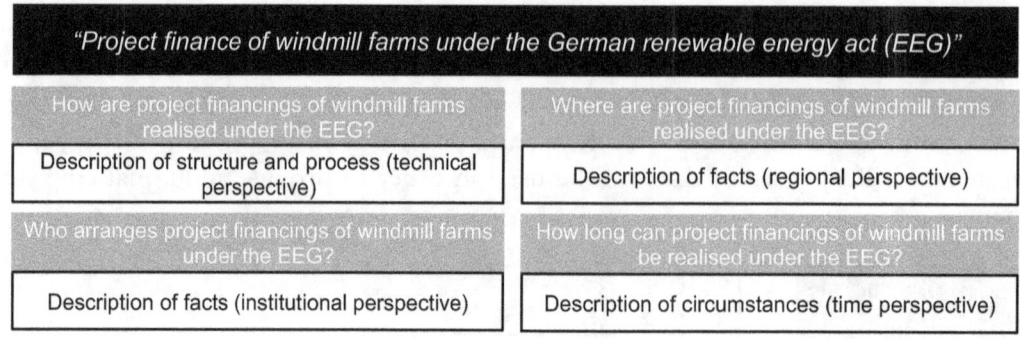

Figure 8.9: Description – examples of research questions

A common misconception is that a description is a simplistic way to deal with a topic. Actually, the description of new objects can be quite sophisticated and in some cases rather challenging.

8.3.3 Causal connection

An object of investigation can be analysed with respect to its causality (Figure 8.10).

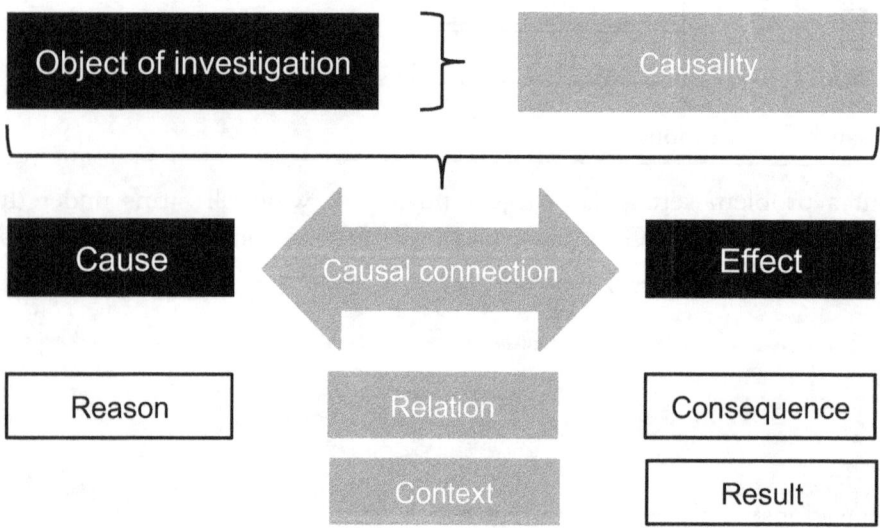

Figure 8.10: Abstract analysis – causal connection

The causal connection addresses a relation or a context. A cause, in other words a reason, leads to an effect, in other words, a consequence or a result. In some cases, there is a cause-and-effect chain, where the effect becomes the cause for the next effect and so forth.

If a topic without a problem setting is "Project finance of windmill farms under the German renewable energy act (EEG)", one could raise questions addressing causal connections as presented in Figure 8.11.

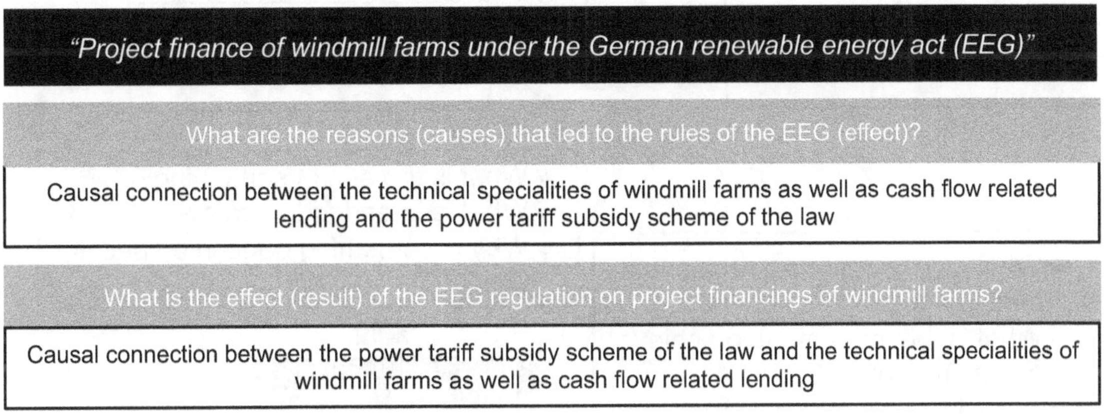

"Project finance of windmill farms under the German renewable energy act (EEG)"
What are the reasons (causes) that led to the rules of the EEG (effect)?
Causal connection between the technical specialities of windmill farms as well as cash flow related lending and the power tariff subsidy scheme of the law
What is the effect (result) of the EEG regulation on project financings of windmill farms?
Causal connection between the power tariff subsidy scheme of the law and the technical specialities of windmill farms as well as cash flow related lending

Figure 8.11: Causal connection – examples of research questions

The analysis of a causal connection requires an understanding of the underlying object of investigation. Therefore, descriptive aspects have to be incorporated into the analysis as well.

8.3.4 Intention

An object of investigation can be analysed with respect to its intention (Figure 8.12). Potential objects of investigation are means, instruments, agents, methods, and resources. Potential intentions are aims, purposes, objectives, motives, and designations.

8 Interpretation of a topic

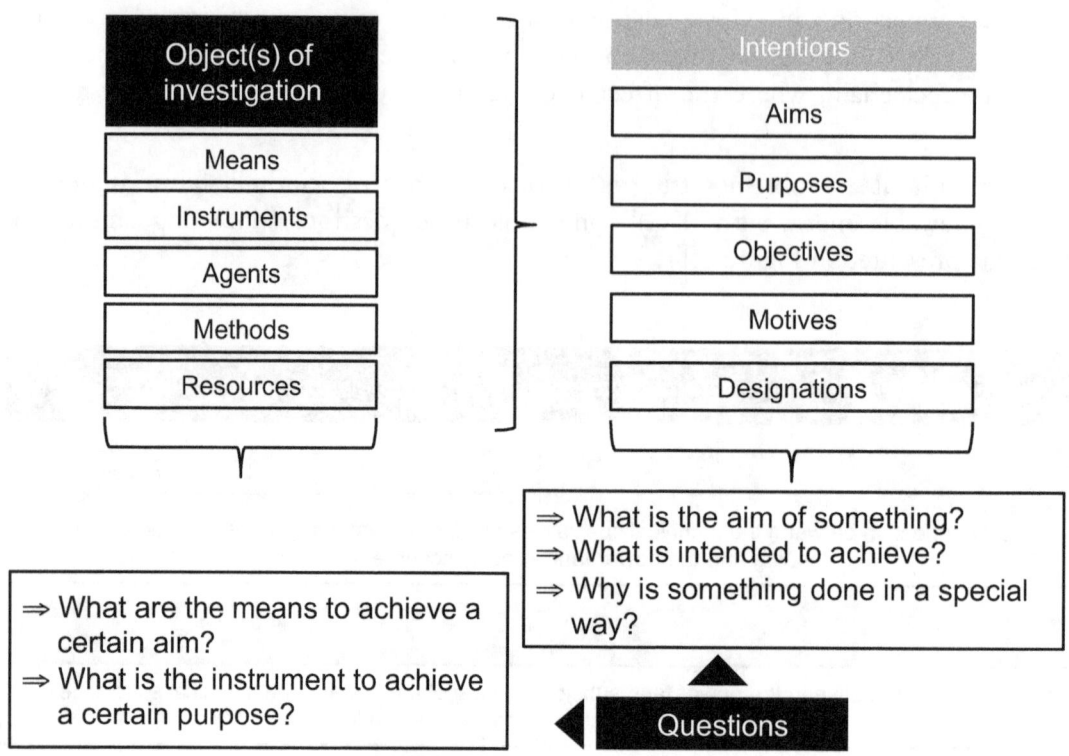

Figure 8.12: Abstract analysis – intention

As Figure 8.12 indicates, there are two ways to look at the problem:

1. If an intention is available, the task can be to investigate a matching object.

    Questions could be: What is the aim of something? What is intended to achieve? Why is something done in a special way?

2. If an object is available, the task can be to investigate its intention.

    Questions could be: What are the means to achieve a certain aim? What is the instrument to achieve a certain purpose?

If a topic without a problem setting is "Project finance of windmill farms under the German renewable energy act (EEG)", one could raise questions addressing intentional aspects as presented in Figure 8.13.

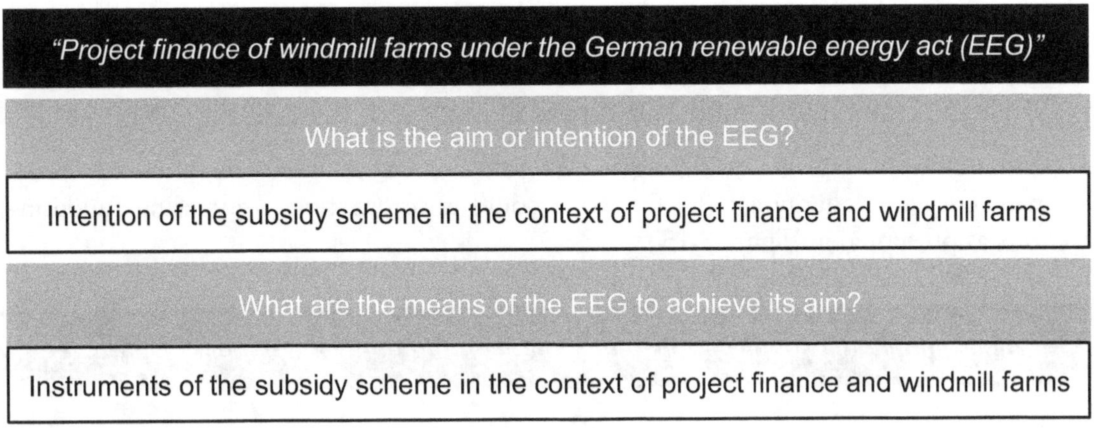

"Project finance of windmill farms under the German renewable energy act (EEG)"
What is the aim or intention of the EEG?
Intention of the subsidy scheme in the context of project finance and windmill farms
What are the means of the EEG to achieve its aim?
Instruments of the subsidy scheme in the context of project finance and windmill farms

Figure 8.13: Intention – examples of research questions

The analysis of intentions requires an understanding of the underlying object of investigation. Therefore, descriptive aspects have to be incorporated into the analysis as well.

8.3.5 Function

Objects of investigation can be analysed with respect to their inherent functional relations, i.e. interdependencies, reciprocities, correlations, relatedness, and/or connections (Figure 8.14).

Object(s) of investigation
Functional relations
Interdependencies
Reciprocities
Correlations
Relatedness
Connections

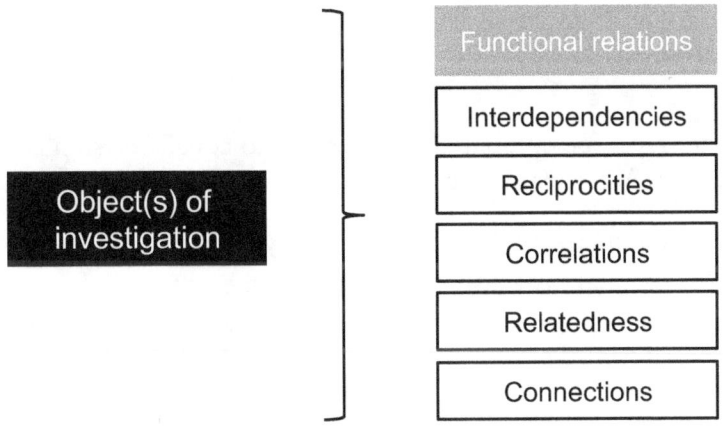

Figure 8.14: Abstract analysis – functional approach

8 Interpretation of a topic

Questions resulting from a functional approach can be:

- How is A influenced by B, and how is B influenced by A?
- What is the impact of A on B, and what is the impact of B on A?

If a topic without a problem setting is "Project finance of windmill farms under the German renewable energy act (EEG)", one could raise questions addressing functional relations as presented in Figure 8.15.

> **"Project finance of windmill farms under the German renewable energy act (EEG)"**
>
> **How** is project finance of windmill farms influenced by the German renewable energy act (EEG) **and how** was (is) the structure of the EEG influenced by the special character of project finance and windmill farms?
>
> **What** is the impact of project finance of windmill farms on the German renewable energy act (EEG) **and what** is the impact of the EEG on project finance of windmill farms?

Figure 8.15: Functional approach – examples of research questions

The analysis of functional relations requires an understanding of the underlying object of investigation. Therefore, descriptive aspects have to be incorporated into the analysis as well.

8.3.6 Comparison

One or more objects of investigation can be compared with respect to equalities, similarities, and/or differences (Figure 8.16). A comparison can be performed in different ways:

- Objects of investigation can be compared with respect to quality and quantity.
- Objects of investigation can be compared at different points in time.
- Objects of investigation can be compared with respect to different sectors, companies or countries.

Supervisions, assessments, tests, examinations, audits, controls, and certifications are typically linked to target/actual comparisons of attributes.

8.3 Abstract interpretation

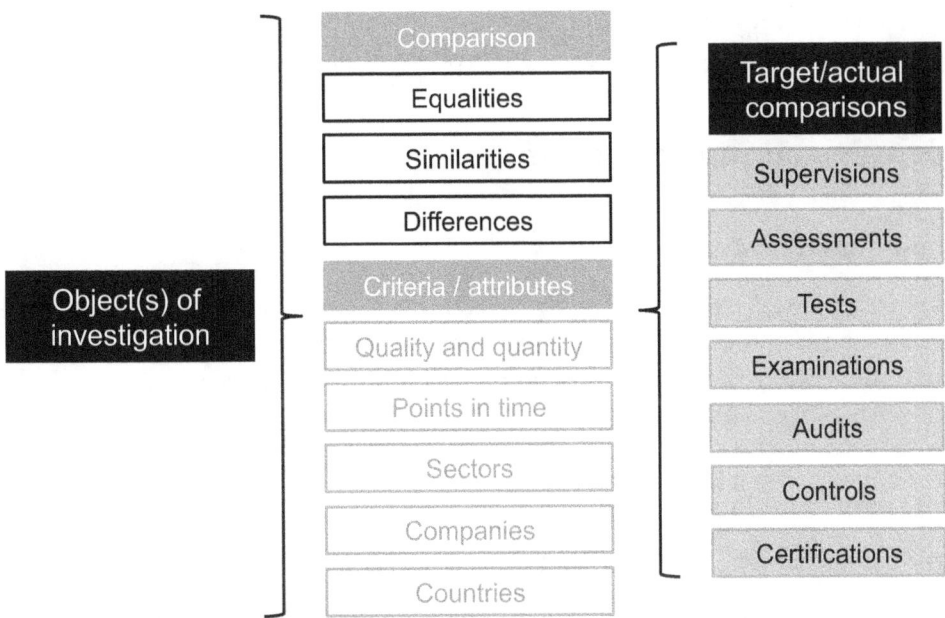

Figure 8.16: Abstract analysis – comparison

Figure 8.17 exemplifies three topics implying comparative research questions.

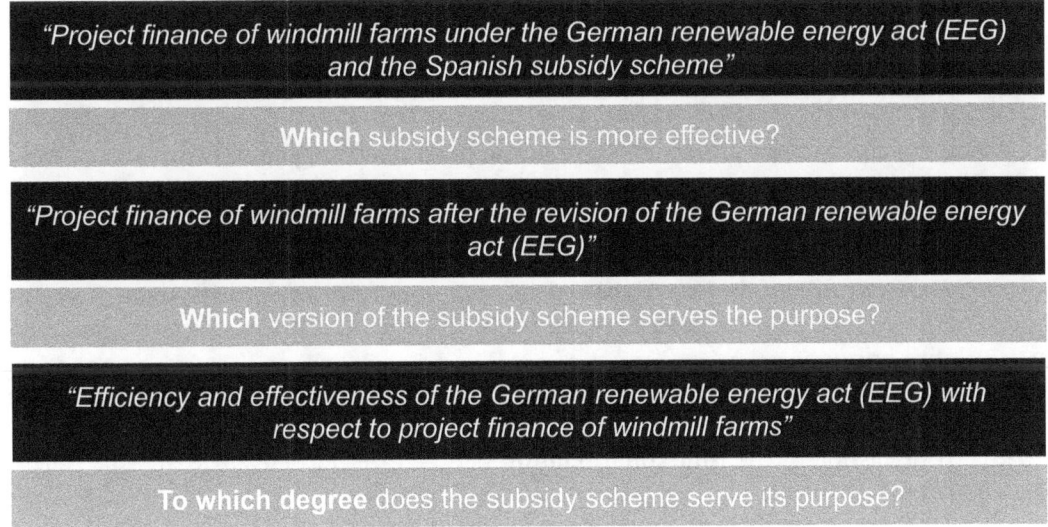

Figure 8.17: Comparison – examples of topics and research questions

The comparative analysis requires an understanding of the underlying object of investigation. Therefore, descriptive aspects have to be incorporated into the analysis as well.

8.4 Problem-based interpretation

8.4.1 Problem-based analysis of aims

In the previous subchapter, five potential aims have been explained from a theoretical perspective. Following is the analysis of the problem-based interpretation of a topic. In order to illustrate the context-driven interpretation of topics, five sample cases with individual problem settings are introduced.

8.4.2 Sample case "Sinking ships"

The first sample case is entitled "Sinking ships".

> A Hamburg based logistics service provider offers specialised transportation services for bulky, lower value goods like heavy equipment, spare parts and consumer goods. The company does not operate its own ships; it charters container transportation capacity from shipping companies. Due to an unpredictable transportation volume the company cannot arrange for long-term contracts but has to make use of the spot market. Spot market prices for container transportation are highly volatile which makes it difficult to calculate price quotations for customers as well as the profitability of a given transaction in advance. A relatively new financial product named container freight derivatives enables companies to lock in future transportation costs by concluding forward agreements and to hedge themselves against spot market price risks. Having heard about this product the managing director asks a trainee to lay out the process of hedging with container freight derivatives.

One could consider the following potential aims (nature of the task):

- a) A **description** of the process of hedging with container freight derivatives
- b) An explanation of the **causal connection** between expected freight rates and derivative pricing
- c) An analysis of the **intention** of companies that participate in the container freight derivative market
- d) A discussion of the **functional relation** between freight derivatives and the freight rates
- e) A **comparison** of situations with and without hedging

In this case, the nature of the task is to provide a **description** of the process of hedging with container freight derivatives.

A research question for the research project could be:

"How can price risks be managed with container freight derivatives?"

A research topic explicitly indicating the aim could be:

"Hedging spot market price risks for logistic service providers with container freight derivatives (CFD)"

A research topic requiring an interpretation could be:

"Risk management with container freight derivatives (CFD)"

8.4.3 Sample case "Smelly shampoo"

The following sample case is entitled "Smelly shampoo".

Recently, an Asian cosmetics corporation has entered the European market in order to sell its hair care products based on a traditional formula. The price for the product has been set at a level that is comparable to similar products. Furthermore, the company spends a relatively high amount on its advertising budget. Although the products are superior in terms of care and texture, the sales volumes are stagnating. A fashion journal has claimed in an article that European consumers, in contrast to Asians, prefer intense fragrances. Headquarters asks its international marketing division to perform an investigation whether the softness of the fragrance is responsible for low sales volumes.

One could consider the following potential aims (nature of the task):

a) A **description** of olfactory marketing strategies with fragrances
b) An explanation of the **causal connection** between the intensity of the fragrance and the sales figures
c) An analysis of the **intention** of using fragrances in hair care products
d) A discussion of the **functional relation** between the amount of fragrances and the sales volumes
e) A **comparison** of situations with and without fragrances

In this case, the nature of the task is to analyse whether there is a **causal connection** between the intensity of the fragrance and the sales figures.

A research question for the research project could be:

"Is the fragrance of the shampoo responsible for the poor sales figures?"

A research topic explicitly indicating the aim could be:

> "Impact of fragrance specification of hair care products on European sales volumes"

A research topic requiring an interpretation could be:

> "Olfactory marketing strategies for hair care products"

8.4.4 Sample case "Printing money"

The following sample case is entitled "Printing money".

> In the aftermath of the financial crisis ("subprime crisis") of 2007 – 2009, a sovereign debt crisis has unfolded in Europe. The European Central Bank (ECB) tried to intervene in the crisis in the context of its duty to conduct monetary policies. The ECB involves itself inter alia in "longer-term refinancing operations" whereby banks can borrow funds from the ECB against collateral in the form of securities (so called "repurchase agreements"). In December 2011 banks borrowed roughly EUR 500 billion with a tenor of 3 years and for an interest rate of 1% from the ECB. This action was heavily criticised and questioned by some economists, politicians and other market participants due to the risk of inflation and implicit financing of sovereign debt. Members of the German parliament ("Bundestag") were confused and asked the research and documentation services of the parliament to provide a paper that addresses the purpose of the ECB's action.

One could consider the following potential aims (nature of the task):

a) A **description** of the ECB's duty to conduct monetary policies and related instruments
b) An explanation of the **causal connection** between repurchase agreements and inflation
c) An analysis of the **intention** of the ECB's action
d) An analysis with respect to the **functional relation** between repurchase agreements and inflation
e) A **comparison** of alternative actions in the context of the European sovereign debt crisis

> In this problem setting, the nature of the task is to analyse the **intention** of the ECB's action. Furthermore, options a), b) and e) leave room for alternative or additional aims.

A research question for the research project could be:

> "What is the intention of the ECB money tenders in the context of the sovereign debt crisis?"

A research topic explicitly indicating the aim could be:

> "Purposes of ECB's long-term refinancing operations in the context of the sovereign debt crisis"

A research topic requiring an interpretation could be:

> "Monetary policies and sovereign debt crisis"

8.4.5 Sample case "Windy decision"

The sample case "Windy decision" has been introduced above. It is described as follows:

> A farmer who wants to erect a small windmill farm on his farmland has approached a local bank in a rural area. The farmer has funds available that will only cover up to 20% of the investment costs. Therefore, he applies for a loan that will make up for the remaining 80%. Besides the windmill and the income derived from electricity sales, he is not able to provide additional collateral or security to the bank. As a consequence, the electricity sales become a key factor for the financial feasibility (market risk). The farmer claims that electricity sales are guaranteed by the German renewable energy act (EEG).

One could consider the following potential aims (nature of the task):

a) A **description** of windmill farm project financing in Germany
b) An explanation of the **causal connection** between the EEG and the feasibility of windmill farm project financing
c) An analysis of the **intention** of the implicit sales guarantee provided by German renewable energy act (EEG)
d) An analysis of the **functional relation** between the EEG and the feasibility of windmill farm project financing
e) A **comparison** of a financing situation with and without the EEG

In this problem setting, the nature of the task is to analyse the **functional relation** between the EEG and the feasibility of windmill farm project financing. Moreover, options a), b), c) and e) leave room for alternative or additional aims.

A research question for the research project could be:

> "How do the German renewable energy act (EEG) and the financial feasibility of windmill farm project financing influence each other?"

A research topic explicitly indicating the aim could be:

> "Interdependencies between the German renewable energy act (EEG) and project financing of windmill projects"

8 Interpretation of a topic

A research topic requiring an interpretation could be:

"Project finance of windmill farms under the German renewable energy act (EEG)"

8.4.6 Sample case "Clara Couture"

The following sample case is entitled "Clara Couture".

> Clara started as an entrepreneur with a small shop for designer shirts in Hamburg. After ten successful years her company owns shops in 25 European cities and has an annual turnover of over EUR 500 million. The legal form of the company has to be changed in order to keep track with the aggressive cross border expansion strategy. Various legal, anti-trust, financial and taxation objectives have to be obeyed and optimised. Moreover, the interests of the current owners shall be maintained. An external law firm has already proposed the legal form of a "Societas Europaea (SE)" as the most suitable option. Clara who still acts as CEO is sceptical and asks the head of the strategy department to come up with an appraisal of the proposal.

One could consider the following potential aims (nature of the task):

a) A **description** of the proposed legal form and how it can be used for an expansion strategy
b) An analysis of the **causal connection** between the expansion strategy and the proposed legal form
c) An analysis of the **intention** of Clara Couture in the context of the expansion strategy
d) A discussion of the **functional relation** between the cross border expansion strategy and the proposed legal form
e) A **comparison** of the implications of the proposed legal form and the objectives of Clara Couture

> In this case, the nature of the task is a **comparison** of the implications of the proposal with the objectives of Clara Couture. The steps could be as follows: (i) an analysis of the implications of the SE; (ii) an explication of the company's objectives; (iii) a comparison of implications with objectives and conclusion.

A research question for the research project could be:

"Does the Societas Europaea (SE) serve the objectives of Clara Couture?"

A research topic explicitly indicating the aim could be:

"Appraisal of the suitability of the legal form "Societas Europaea (SE)" for the cross border expansion strategy of Clara Couture"

A research topic requiring an interpretation could be:

"Societas Europaea (SE) and cross border expansion strategies of fashion companies"

8.4.7 Implications of sample cases

Figure 8.18 summarises the sample cases, their aims and their research questions.

Case	Nature of task /aim	Research question
"Sinking ships"	Description	How can price risks be managed with container freight derivatives?
"Smelly shampoo"	Causal connection	Is the fragrance of the shampoo responsible for the poor sales figures?
"Printing money"	Intention	What is the intention of the ECB money tenders in the context of the sovereign debt crisis?
"Windy decision"	Function	How do the EEG and the financial feasibility of windmill farm project financings influence each other?
"Clara Couture"	Comparison	Does the Societas Europaea suit the objectives of Clara Couture?

Figure 8.18: Sample case, nature of the task, research question – examples

Typically, a problem setting provides a context that helps with the interpretation of a topic.

8.5 Summary and exercises

8.5.1 Synopsis

The three process steps of interpretation are:

- Negative interpretation
- Positive interpretation
- Decision on an aim

The five potential aims of a research project are:

- Description
- Causal connection
- Intention
- Function
- Comparison

A research candidate has to decide on one aim or a combination of more than one aim.

The interpretation can be based on an abstract-analysis or a problem-based analysis of potential aims.

8.5.2 Questions

Knowledge

1. What are the three steps of the interpretation process?
2. What is a negative interpretation?
3. What is a positive interpretation?
4. What are the five possible aims?
5. Is it possible to select more than one aim?
6. What is meant by problem setting in the context of the selection of an aim?
7. What is an abstract analysis of a potential aim?
8. What is a problem-based analysis of a potential aim?
9. What are potential objects of investigation while applying a descriptive aim?
10. What can be described?
11. What has to be addressed while analysing a causal connection?
12. What are potential objects of investigation while applying an intentional aim?
13. What are potential intentions to be analysed while applying an intentional aim?
14. What are potential objects of investigation while applying a functional aim?
15. What is the fundamental difference between the analysis of a causal connection and a functional relation?
16. What are potential objects of investigation while applying a comparative aim?
17. What are examples of criteria or attributes while applying a comparative aim?
18. What are examples of "target/actual comparisons"?

8.5.3 Problem

Synthesis

Learning target

Being able to derive an interpretation for a topic within an academic context

Background

The title/topic of a term paper project is as follows:

Intercultural communication in global supply chains

Problem setting: academic context (abstract interpretation)

Instructions

1. Please develop a negative and a positive interpretation of the topic.
2. Please analyse whether one or more of the following aims are applicable:
   - Description
   - Causal connection
   - Intention
   - Function
   - Comparison
3. Would you choose one aim or a combination of two or more aims? Please explain your decision.
4. Please develop a research question that matches your aim and the problem setting.

8.5.4 Additional reading

The following articles have inspired the case studies:

Anonymous (2010, August 19). Boxing clever: Are container derivatives poised for bumper growth? *The Economist*. Retrieved from http://www.economist.com

Anonymous (2008, April 3). German lessons: An ambitious cross-subsidy scheme has given rise to a new industry. *The Economist*. Retrieved from http://www.economist.com

Anonymous (2005, September 15). Limited appeal. One giant step across Europe may find few imitators. *The Economist*. Retrieved from http://www.economist.com

Anonymous (2012, July 14). QE, or not QE? An assessment oft the most controversial weapon in the central banker's armoury. *The Economist.* Retrieved from http://www.economist.com

Negishi, M., & Dvorak, P. (2013, December 13). In Japan, Scented Fabric Softeners Wrinkle Some Noses. *The Wall Street Journal.* Retrieved from http://www.wsj.com

9 Structuring technique

Abstract

A research problem needs to be clarified and has to be transformed into a precisely formulated research question. In a research paper, this could be done in a subchapter entitled "Research problem". A pragmatic way to structure the subchapter "Research problem" is to apply the concept of deductive reasoning. According to deduction, the writer advances from paragraphs with general information to paragraphs with a higher specificity and ends with the research question. Simultaneously, the research problem with its research question determines the overall structure of the research paper, i.e. the outline. Once an aim has been identified, its implicit logic prescribes the structure of the outline. Moreover, the outline should be aligned with the structure of the subchapter "Course of investigation" and, if applicable, with the subchapter "Research method". A research paper ends with a conclusion that can be segmented into three subchapters: summary of research findings, critical acclaim and outlook. Again, the summary of the findings should be aligned with the structure of the research problem and the outline of the main body. Finally, it is good style to critically reflect upon one's own research findings in the subchapter "Critical acclaim" and to provide an outlook regarding potential future developments in the subchapter "Outlook". Furthermore, empirical and experimental research projects may require the application of more advanced structuring techniques.

Keywords

Research problem, research question, outline, course of investigation, research method, conclusion, summary, critical acclaim, outlook, interpretation-based structuring, IMRaD, AIMRaD, AILMRaD, AILDMRaD, hourglass model

9.1 Context and relevance

9.1.1 Context of chapter 9

Structural elements of a research paper have been addressed in a previous chapter. Additionally, different options for the interpretation of a topic have been explained. At this point, the researcher may want to develop a suitable structure for the outline and the main body of the research documentation. The structure should be aligned with the research question and support the research and writing process. The context of this chapter is the development of a logical structure and a framework for the execution of the research.

Figure 9.1 shows how chapter 9 is embedded within the setting of a research project.

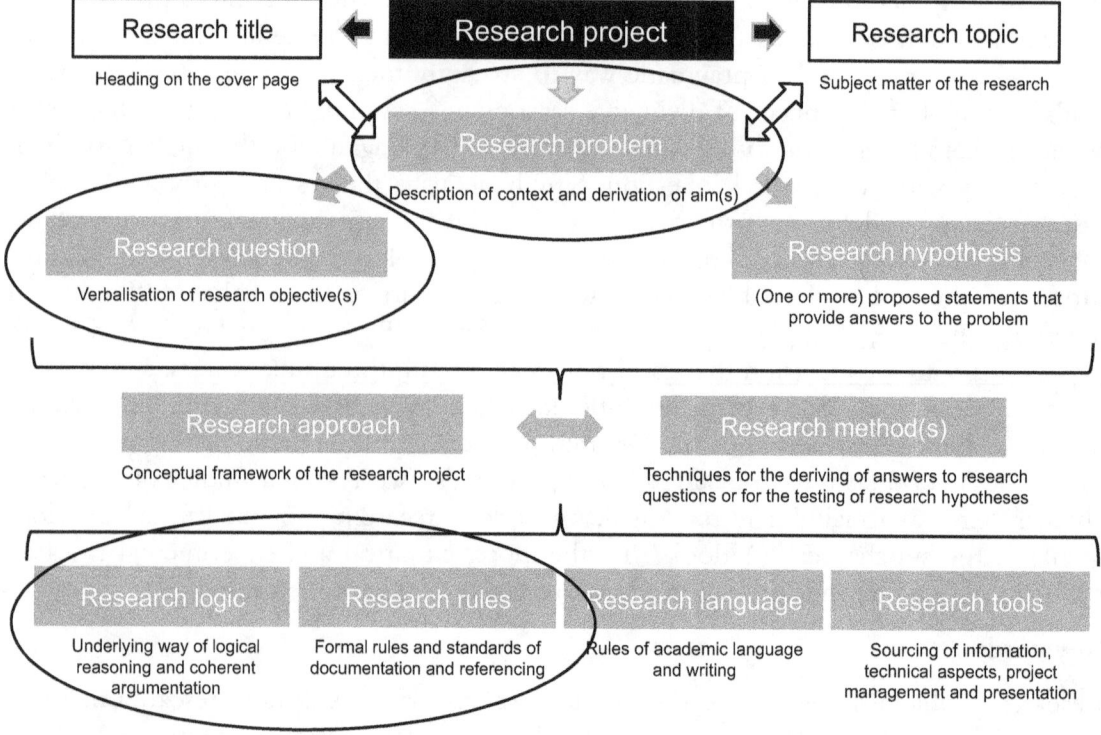

Figure 9.1: Context of chapter 9

Chapter 9 addresses common structuring techniques. Different aspects of academic research are affected: the research problem, the research question, the research logic, and the research rules. Thus, this chapter combines different aspects of academic research.

9.1.2 Relevance of chapter 9

The structuring technique allows for consistency within the research project. Thus, proper structuring raises the quality of the research output. Furthermore, as one can easily get lost in a research project, the application of a structuring technique helps to avoid disappointments.

9.1.3 Learning objectives of chapter 9

After having studied this chapter, the reader should be able to:

- understand deductive reasoning and its implications for writing research problems
- apply deductive reasoning in order to structure a research problem
- align the research problem, the outline and the course of investigation in a consistent way
- understand the structure of a conclusion and its relation to the outline and the research problem
- apply the interpretation-based structuring technique
- distinguish more advanced structuring techniques applied in empirical and experimental research approaches

9.2 Deductive reasoning and research problem

9.2.1 From title to research question

A major challenge while writing a research paper is to isolate and define a research question from the title of the research project. However, once the underlying logic is understood, the task can be successfully accomplished as visualised in Figure 9.2.

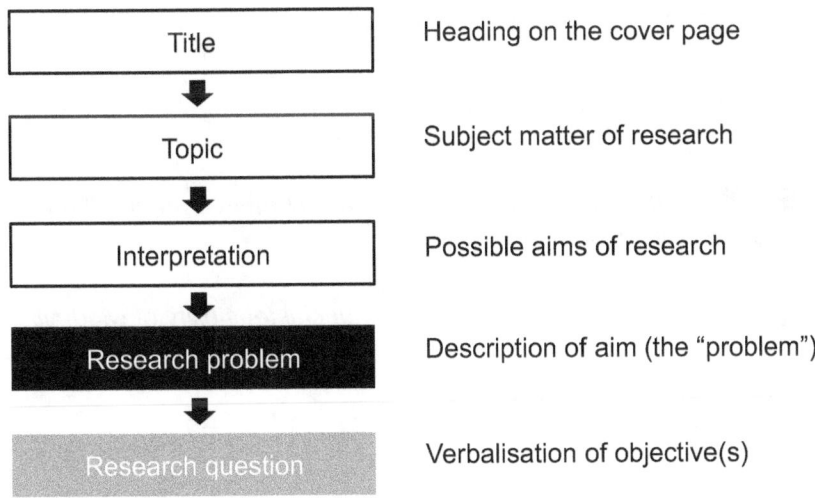

Figure 9.2: Refining a research question

An idealised process of refining a research question could be as follows:

- The starting point is the **title** of the research project. The title is the heading that appears on the cover page or at the top of the research paper.
- The **topic** is the subject matter of the research. In most cases, the topic and title of a research project are identical. Otherwise, the topic might have a more explanatory and comprehensive wording than the title.
- As explained in the previous chapter, each topic needs an **interpretation**. An interpretation is needed in order to identify possible aims of a research project.
- The **research problem** is a description of the aim of the research project. After one has identified the aims and decided for a specific one, it can be documented in the subchapter "Research problem", which finally leads to a research question.
- The **research question** is laid out in the last paragraph of the subchapter "Research problem". This paragraph verbalises the objectives of the research project.

Figure 9.3 exemplifies the idealised process of refining a research question.

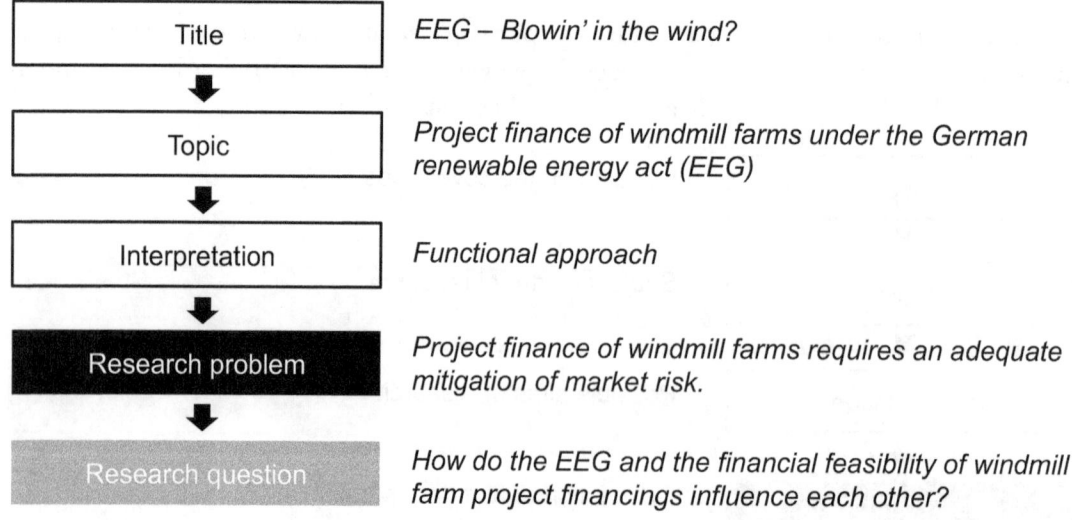

Figure 9.3: Refining a research question – example

As illustrated in Figure 9.3, the process of refining the research question can be as follows:

- The starting point is the **title** of the research project. The title of the fictitious research project is "EEG – Blowin' in the wind?"
- Obviously, this title is short and creative by metaphorically relating to a Bob Dylan song. Therefore, it needs a clarification with respect to the factual **topic**. The topic is "Project finance of windmill farms under the German renewable energy act (EEG)".
- The topic needs an **interpretation**. After having concluded a negative as well as a positive interpretation, one could decide to follow a functional approach.
- Now, one can start to define a provisional **research problem**. In short, the research problem could address that "Project finance of windmill farms requires an adequate mitigation of market risk."
- The culmination point of the research problem is its last paragraph, the **research question**. In this case, the research question could be stated as follows: "How do the German renewable energy act (EEG) and the financial feasibility of windmill farm project financings influence each other?"

9.2.2 Deduction of major components

There are various techniques of writing a research problem depending on scientific styles and personal preferences.

Deductive reasoning is a pragmatic way to write a research problem. As discussed in chapter 3, the principle of deductive logic is to advance from general components to more specific components.

Figure 9.4 shows an example of applying deductive reasoning.

9 Structuring technique

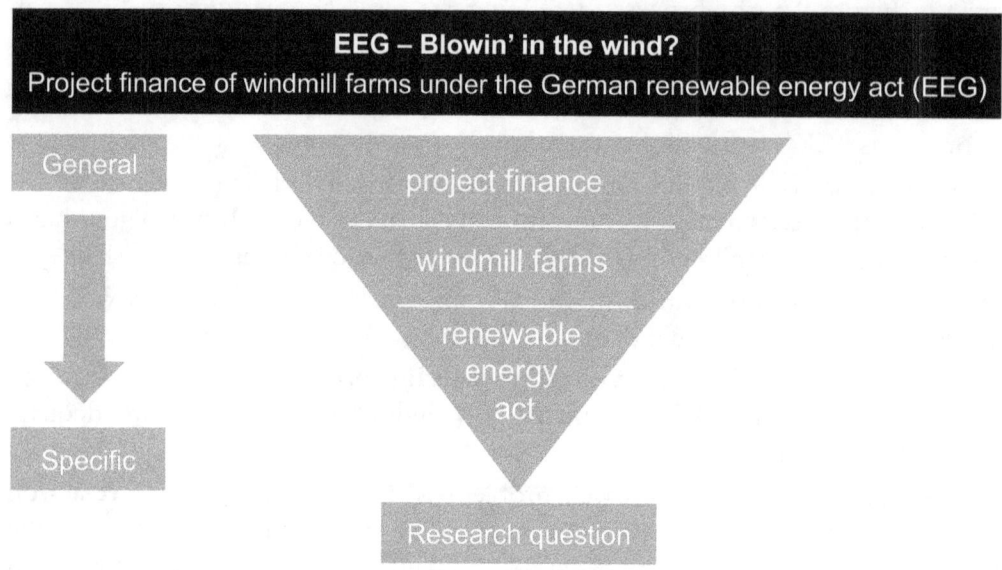

Figure 9.4: Deductive reasoning – example

As exemplified in Figure 9.4, the title of the research project is "EEG – Blowin' in the wind?" Since this title needs a clarification of the topic, the topic is defined as follows: "Project finance of windmill farms under the German renewable energy act (EEG)".

As deductive reasoning implies that researchers work from general information towards specific arguments and conclusions, the deductive logic can be symbolised by a reversed triangle.

From the topic of the research project, one can isolate three major components.

- The first major component could be "project finance" as a general component. The rationale is that project finance is a financing technique that is not only applied in renewable energy projects but also in various other sectors.
- The second major component could be "windmill farms" as a specific component. The rationale is that windmills represent only one type of a renewable energy investment. Thus, they can be considered a specific asset.
- The third major component could be "renewable energy act" as component with the highest degree of specificity. The rationale is that the renewable energy act is a specific law, which is only applicable in one specific country.

After one has identified the major components and their respective levels of specificity, the point has been reached where a research question can be formulated. This requires that an interpretation of the topic as explained in chapter 8 has taken place.

9.2.3 Structure of a research problem

The outcome of the deductive reasoning process can be linked to the text structure of the subchapter "Research problem" (Figure 9.5).

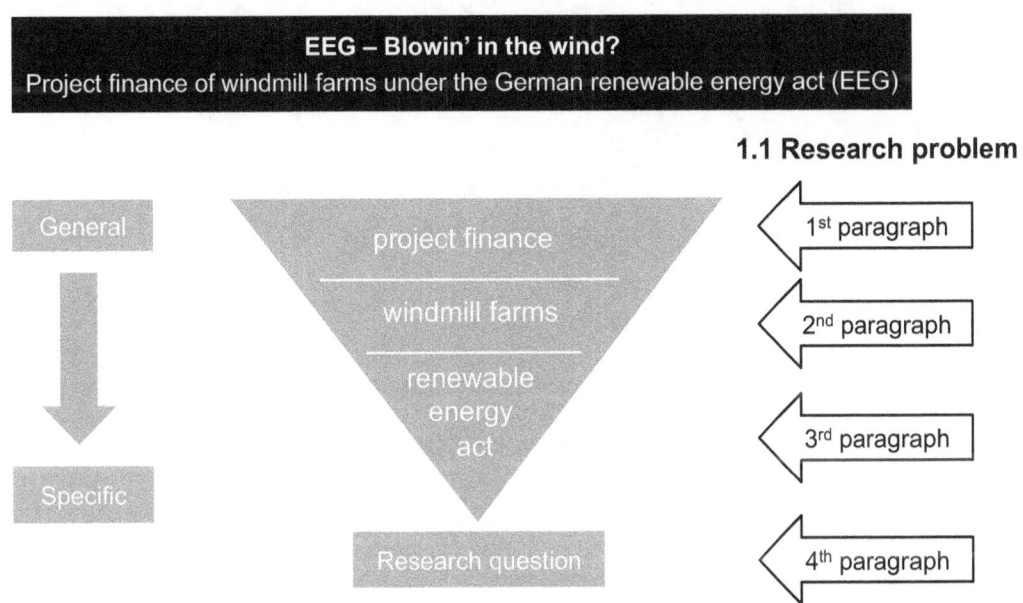

Figure 9.5: Deductive reasoning – structure of the subchapter "Research problem"

An individual paragraph is needed for each major component as well as for the research question:

- In the first paragraph, the general component of the topic is addressed.
- In the second paragraph, the specific component is introduced.
- The third paragraph is about the component with the highest specificity.
- Finally, there has to be a paragraph in which the research question is defined.

The structure of the research problem could look as exemplified in Figure 9.6.

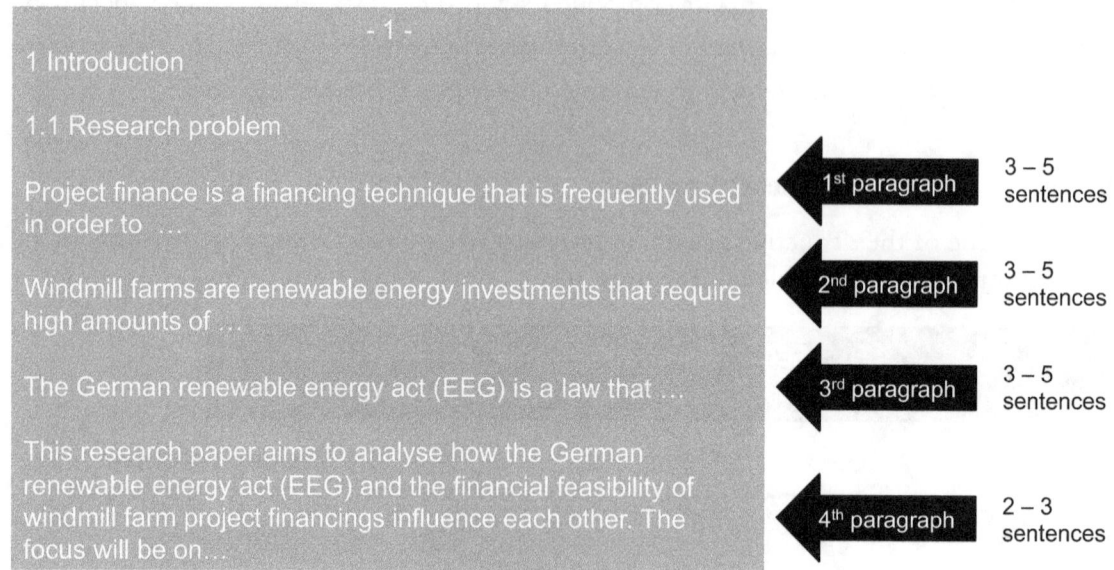

Figure 9.6: Structure of the research problem – sample text

The paragraphs of the subchapter are structured according to deductive logic:

- In the first paragraph the term "project finance" is covered.
- In the second paragraph, "windmill farms" are introduced as typical renewable energy investments.
- In the third paragraph, the EEG is briefly introduced.
- The fourth and final paragraph postulates the research question. The subchapter "Research problem" always ends with the research question.

In order to achieve a balanced structure, it is important to set a maximum number of sentences for each paragraph.

9.2.4 Rules

There are some rules of thumb while writing a research problem:

- Avoid a "journalistic" or colloquial writing style.
- Beware of superficial, general, political and/or personal statements.

- Focus on the topic and its components.
- Restrict the maximum length of the research problem to one or two pages.
- Keep in mind that the subchapter "Research problem" is typically shorter in term papers than in thesis projects.
- Consider stressing the relevance of the topic by providing numerical facts and statistical data.

9.3 Research problem, outline and course of investigation

9.3.1 Aligning research question and outline

Once the deductive reasoning process has been applied in order to structure a research problem and define a research question, the logic can be aligned with other structural elements of the research paper. First of all, the structure of the outline has to match the logic of the research question. Figure 9.7 exemplifies this rule of thumb.

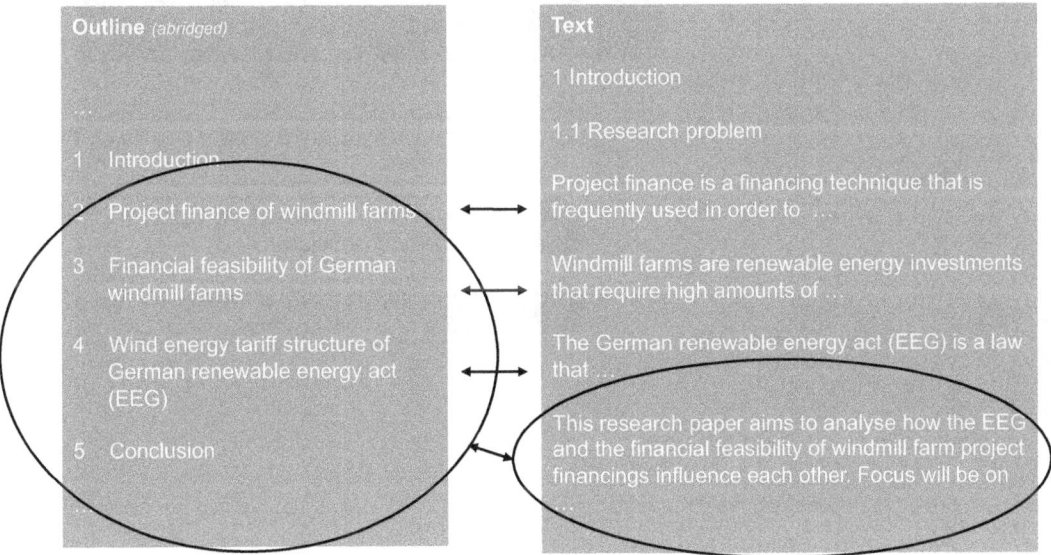

Figure 9.7: Aligning research question with structure of outline

The chapters of the outline have to be related to the subchapter "Research problem" and vice versa:

- The first paragraph of the research problem has to correspond with the heading of chapter two.
- The second paragraph of the research problem has to correspond with the heading of chapter three.
- The third paragraph of the research problem has to correspond with the heading of chapter four.
- The overall structure of the outline has to match the implicit aim stated in the last paragraph, the research question.

9.3.2 Structure of outline

The structure of the outline has to be aligned with the logic of the research question and, more specifically, with the aim that has been decided on.

The exemplification in Figure 9.8 is based upon the sample outline previously introduced.

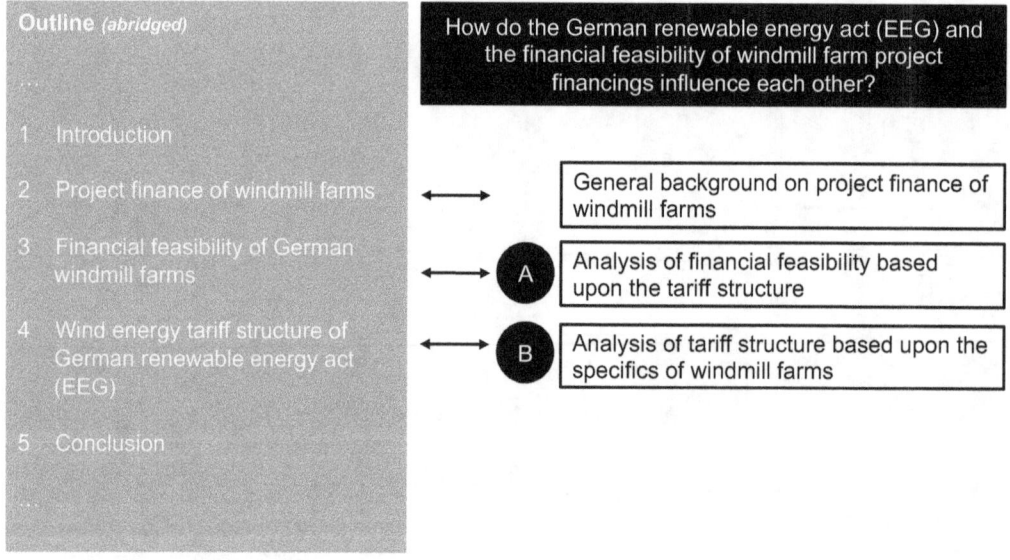

Figure 9.8: Structure of the outline – functional approach

Earlier, in the process of the interpretation of the topic, the decision on an aim lead to a functional approach implied in the research question "How do the EEG and the financial feasibility of windmill farm project financings influence each other?"

While structuring the outline, the use of the functional approach can have the following implications:

- The second chapter of the outline can be formulated in a way so that it will introduce the general background of project finance in the context of windmill farms.
- The third chapter could analyse the financial feasibility based upon the tariff structure (A). Thus, it analyses the impact of the tariff structure on the financial feasibility.
- Vice versa, the fourth chapter could analyse the tariff structure based upon the specifics of windmill farms (B). Thus, it analyses the impact of windmill farm specifics on the tariff structure to be set and to be occasionally adjusted by lawmakers.

Chapter structure and chapter headings within an outline vary according to the addressed aims. This will be addressed in detail in subchapter 9.5.

Tip

With regard to the proper structure of an outline, there are some rules of thumb for the beginner. Typically, the core of an outline has only five main chapters. In some cases, six main chapters may be needed. The introduction is always the first chapter and the conclusion is always the last chapter; some exceptions to these rules are introduced in subchapter 9.6 of this textbook.

9.3.3 Aligning course of investigation and outline

Similar to the logic discussed in the previous subchapter, there is a relation between the subchapter "Course of investigation" and the outline (Figure 9.9).

9 Structuring technique

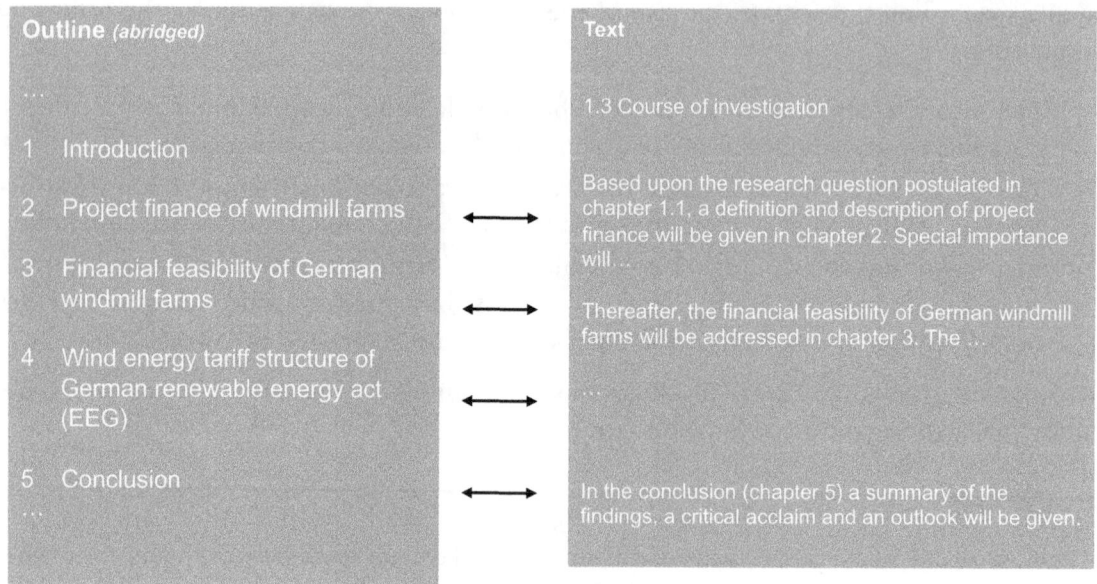

Figure 9.9: Aligning the outline with the course of investigation

The subchapter "Course of investigation" describes how one aims to derive an answer to the research question. It simply refers to the sequence of the chapters, not the method. Thus, it has to be reconciled with the outline:

- The first paragraph of the course of investigation refers to the research question and leads directly into a brief description of chapter 2.
- The second paragraph of the course of investigation briefly describes chapter 3.
- The third paragraph of the course of investigation addresses chapter 4.
- The last paragraph states that there will be a conclusion at the end of the research paper.

9.3.4 Aligning and the triangle of synchronisation

The relations explained in the previous subchapters can be visualised by means of a triangle (Figure 9.10).

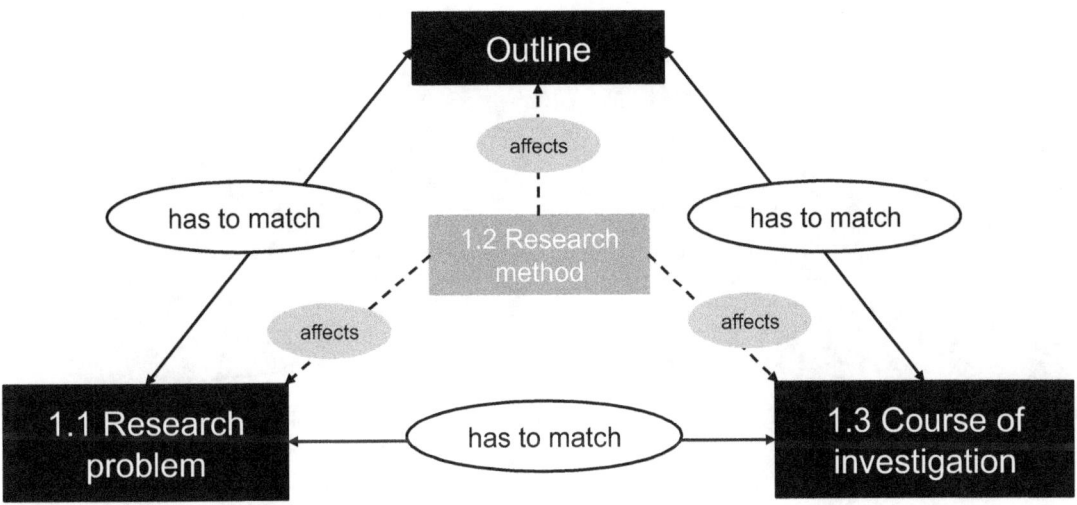

Figure 9.10: The triangle of synchronisation

The outline, the subchapter "Research problem", and the subchapter "Course of investigation" have to be logically matched. The aligning of the elements that form the triangle can be viewed as a process of synchronisation. The chosen research method can be explained in a separate subchapter "Research method".

9.3.5 Research method

The subchapter "Research method" is used in order to describe the applied methodology of the research project. The subchapter "Research method" is not identical with the subchapter "Course of investigation". In contrast to the subchapter "Course of investigation", in which the route of the research is described, the subchapter "Research method" is the place where the theoretical framework as well as the techniques and applied procedures are defined.

> Example
> "This paper (thesis) analyses the impact of the legal environment on the financing of windmill farms. Hence, a legal interpretation of the applicable law is required. For this purpose…"

As demonstrated in Figure 9.11, there are two options of placing the research method.

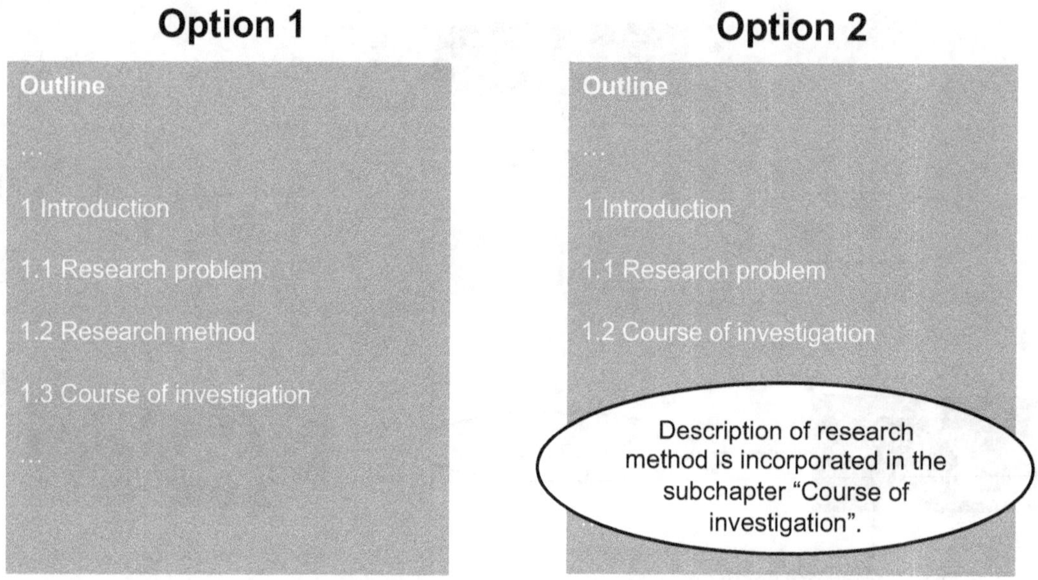

9 Structuring technique

Option 1

Outline

...

1 Introduction

1.1 Research problem

1.2 Research method

1.3 Course of investigation

...

Option 2

Outline

...

1 Introduction

1.1 Research problem

1.2 Course of investigation

(Description of research method is incorporated in the subchapter "Course of investigation".)

Figure 9.11: The two options of placing the description of the research method

The two options can be as follows:

1. A separate **subchapter 1.2** can be used for describing the research method.
2. One **paragraph** describing the research method can be incorporated at the beginning of the subchapter "Course of investigation".

Tip

In essay assignments, term papers and shorter thesis projects, a single paragraph consisting of four to five sentences can be used for describing the research method. In empirically focussed and/or extended research projects such as master's thesis projects, several subchapters and/or paragraphs with extended information on the applied methodology can be useful and might be expected.

9.4 Conclusion, summary, critical acclaim and outlook

9.4.1 Conclusion

A conclusion may consist of three elements:

1. Summary: a short résumé of the research project and the findings
2. Critical acclaim: a differentiated and critical reflection of the research findings
3. Outlook: a discussion of potential developments of the topic in the future

☙ Tip

The critical acclaim and the outlook are sometimes viewed as optional components. Therefore, it is advisable to check the applicable institutional requirements and expectations with respect to conclusions.

9.4.2 Summary

The first subchapter of a conclusion could be a summary (Figure 9.12).

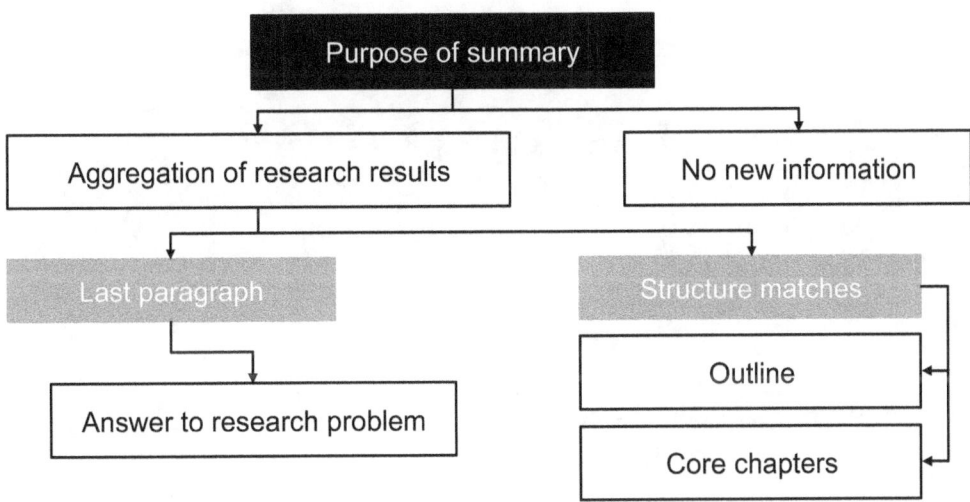

Figure 9.12: Summary – purpose and structure

The purpose of the summary is to aggregate the research result without providing new information:

- The last paragraph of the summary provides an answer to the research question that has been raised in subchapter "1.1 Research problem".
- The structure of the summary should match the structure of the outline and the structure of the core chapters of the research project.

9.4.3 Aligning summary and outline

Like the research problem and the course of investigation, the summary should be aligned with the structure of the outline (Figure 9.13).

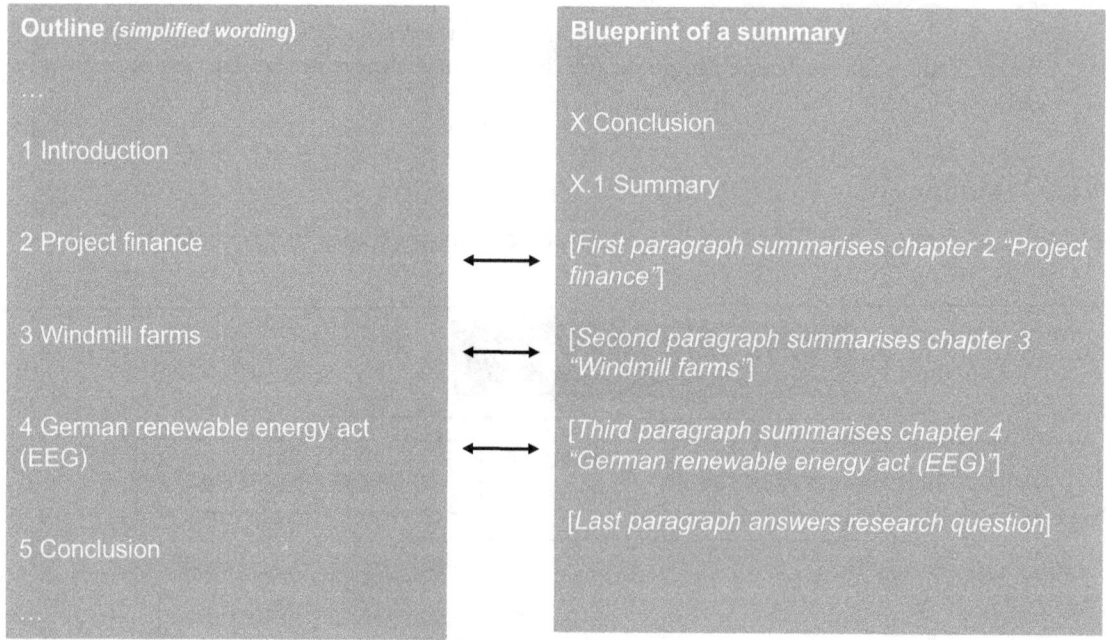

Figure 9.13: Aligning summary and outline – example

The alignment is as follows:

- The first paragraph of the summary has to summarise chapter 2.
- The second paragraph of the summary has to summarise chapter 3.
- The third paragraph of the summary has to summarise chapter 4.
- The last paragraph answers the research question.

9.4.4 Critical acclaim

The second subchapter of a conclusion could be a critical acclaim (Figure 9.14).

9.4 Conclusion, summary, critical acclaim and outlook

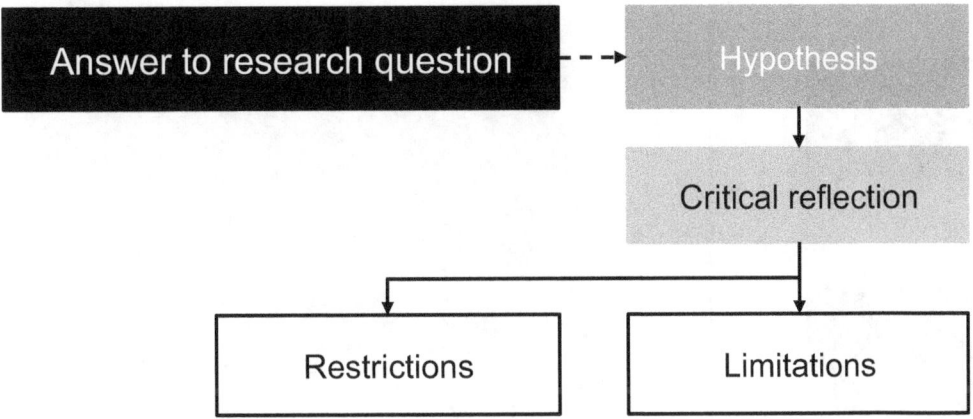

Figure 9.14: Critical acclaim

The answer to the research question is merely a newly developed hypothesis. Therefore, it is considered necessary and good academic style to critically reflect on one's own results. Academic restrictions and limitations of the research project have to be pointed out.

♛ Tip

The term "academic restrictions" is sometimes misunderstood. One has to avoid excusatory statements such as the following citations excerpted from previously submitted thesis projects:

- "There was not enough time for proper research."
- "It is difficult for a student to deal with such a topic."
- "There were not enough sources in our library."

Statements implying self-pity or sympathy with one's own incompetence degrade the quality of the research.

9.4.5 Outlook

The third subchapter of a conclusion could be an outlook (Figure 9.15). There, one can demonstrate an intellectual achievement that should reflect one's own research.

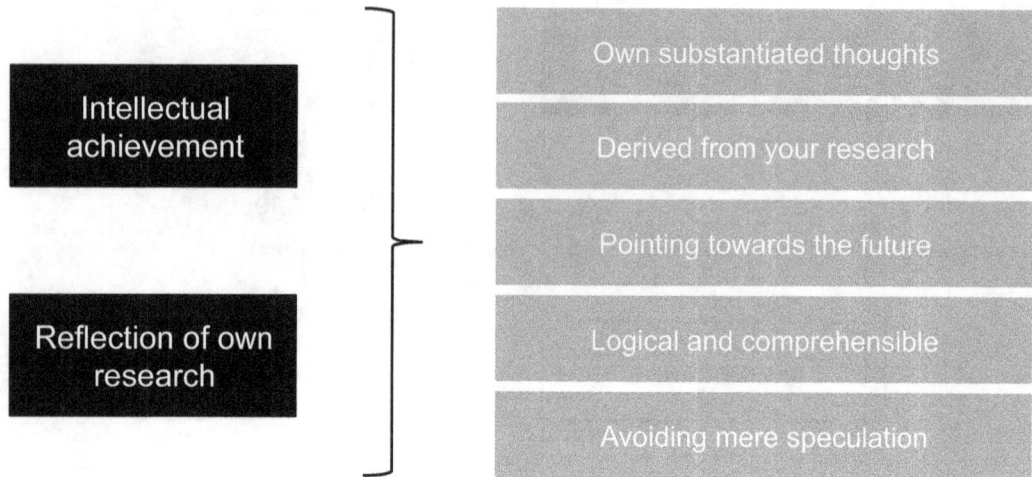

Figure 9.15: Outlook

An outlook provides a place for stating the substantiated thoughts a researcher has developed during the research project. These thoughts should point towards the future, should be logical and comprehensible and should not be of a speculative nature.

9.5 Interpretation-based structuring

9.5.1 Impact of interpretation on structuring

In chapter 8 "Interpretation of a topic", five potential aims were introduced.

In subchapter 9.3, it was exemplified how the structure of an outline has to be aligned with the aim that has been selected. Therefore, the **interpretation-based structuring** of a topic leads to different outlines according to the chosen aim. This can be demonstrated with an abstract example as shown in Figure 9.16.[1]

If the topic is "[A] and [B] in the context of [C]", five different outlines according to the five aims of description, causal connection, intention, function and comparison could be derived.

---

[1] A concrete sample topic will be discussed in subchapter 9.5.2.

9.5 Interpretation-based structuring

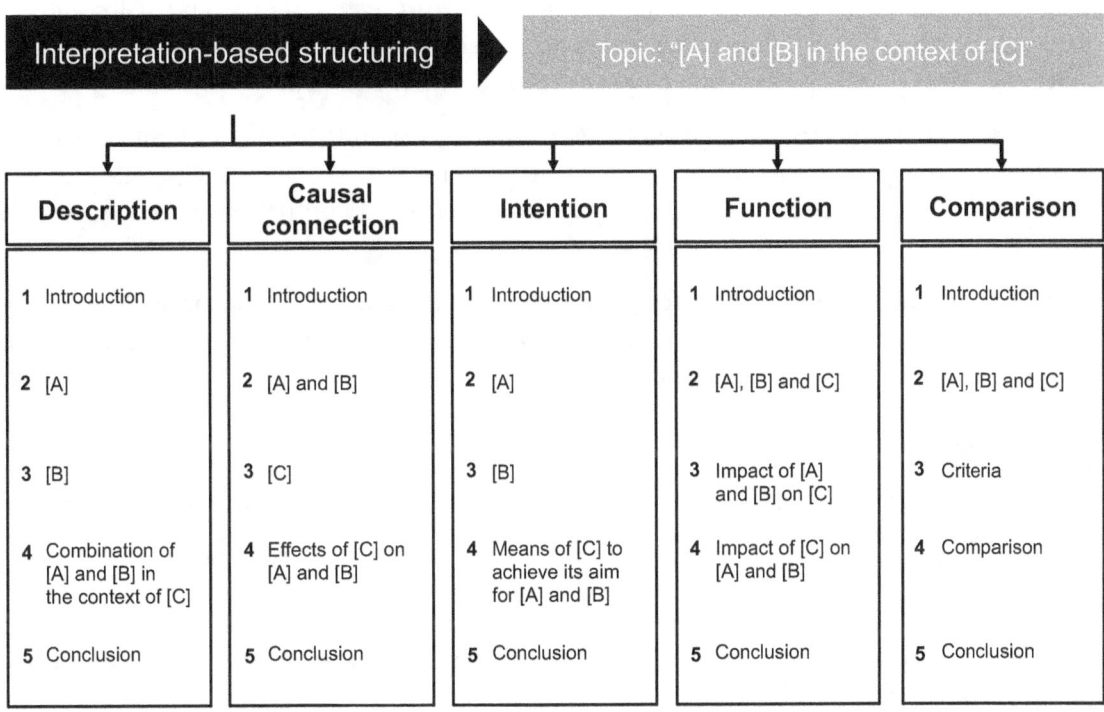

Figure 9.16: Interpretation-based structuring – overview

For demonstration purposes, all outlines are presented with a five-chapter structure. In some cases, a six-chapter structure could be used as well.

Using five chapters, the interpretation-based structuring can be as follows:

For all aims there could be a chapter 1 entitled "Introduction" and a chapter 5 entitled "Conclusion".

While choosing a **descriptive approach**, elements [A] and [B] could be described in chapters 2 and 3. A combined analysis of elements [A] and [B] in the context of element [C] could be undertaken in chapter 4.

While analysing a potential **causal connection**, elements [A] and [B] could be introduced in chapter 2. The specifics of element [C] could be analysed in chapter 3. The effects of element [C] on elements [A] and [B] could be dealt with in chapter 4.

If the aim would be to analyse an underlying **intention**, elements [A] and [B] could be introduced separately in chapters 2 and 3. Chapter 4 could elaborate on the means by which element [C] achieves its objectives for elements [A] and [B].

While applying a **functional approach**, elements [A], [B] and [C] could be introduced in chapter 2. In chapter 3, the impact of elements [A] and [B] on element [C] could be analysed. Vice versa, the impact of element [C] on elements [A] and [B] could be analysed in chapter 4.

If the aim is to make a **comparison**, elements [A], [B] and [C] could be introduced in chapter 2. In chapter 3, a set of criteria could be derived. Based on these criteria the comparison could be made in chapter 4.

> 🎓 **Tip**
>
> Please keep in mind that the presented chapter structures are merely suggestions. Indeed, each chapter structure depends on the structure of the topic and the individual approach applied in an academic research project.

In the following subchapter, the interpretation-based structuring technique will be applied to the sample topic "Project finance of windmill farms under the German renewable energy act (EEG)".

9.5.2 Examples

9.5.2.1 Description

Assuming the sample topic is "Project finance of windmill farms under the German renewable energy act (EEG)", a descriptive aim could be applied in order to analyse **the structure and the process** of windmill farm financing (Figure 9.21).

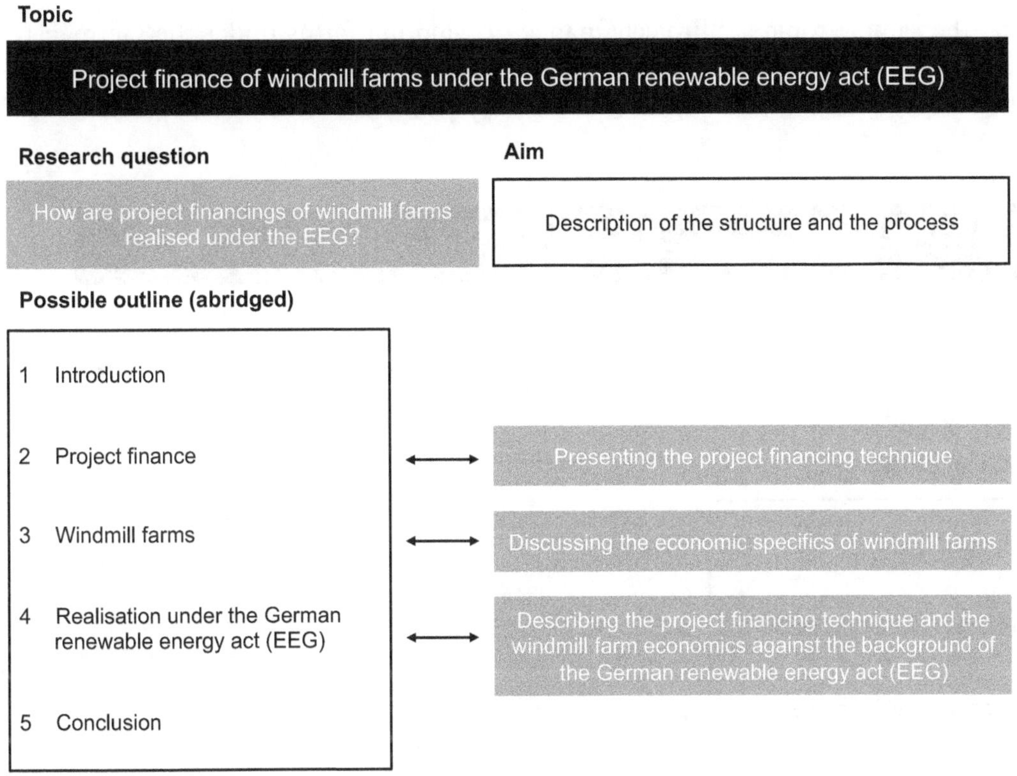

9.5 Interpretation-based structuring

Topic

Project finance of windmill farms under the German renewable energy act (EEG)

Research question

How are project financings of windmill farms realised under the EEG?

Aim

Description of the structure and the process

Possible outline (abridged)

1. Introduction

2. Project finance ⟷ Presenting the project financing technique

3. Windmill farms ⟷ Discussing the economic specifics of windmill farms

4. Realisation under the German renewable energy act (EEG) ⟷ Describing the project financing technique and the windmill farm economics against the background of the German renewable energy act (EEG)

5. Conclusion

Figure 9.17: Interpretation-based structuring – description

The research question could be formulated as follows: "How are project financings of windmill farms realised under the EEG?"

The research question would imply a description of the structure and the process.

In the second chapter entitled "Project finance", the project financing technique could be presented in a general way.

In the third chapter entitled "Windmill farms", the economic specifics of windmill farms could be discussed.

The fourth chapter entitled "Realisation under the German renewable energy act" could be used to describe the project financing technique at hand and windmill farm economics against the background of the German renewable energy act.

9.5.2.2 Causal connection

Assuming the sample topic is "Project finance of windmill farms under the German renewable energy act (EEG)", a causal approach could be applied for the analysis of the underlying causality in windmill farm financing (Figure 9.22).

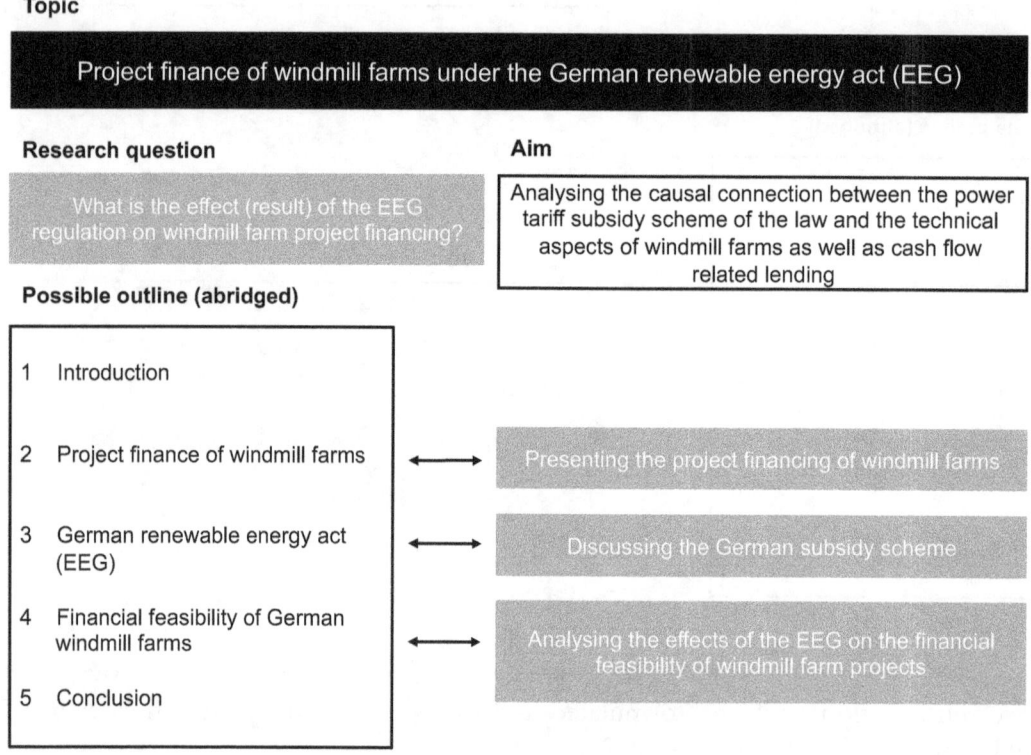

Figure 9.18: Interpretation-based structuring – causal connection

The research question could be formulated as follows: "What is the effect (result) of the EEG regulation on windmill farm project financing?"

This research question would imply a causal connection between the power tariff subsidy scheme of the law and the technical aspects of windmill farms as well as cash flow related lending.

In the second chapter entitled "Project financing of windmill farms", the project financing of windmill farms could be presented.

In the third chapter entitled "German renewable energy act (EEG)", the German subsidy scheme could be discussed.

In the fourth chapter entitled "Financial feasibility of German windmill farms", the effects of the EEG on the financial feasibility of windmill farm projects could be analysed.

9.5.2.3 Intention

Assuming the sample topic is "Project finance of windmill farms under the German renewable energy act (EEG)", an intentional aim could be applied in order to analyse the legal means by which the EEG seeks to influence windmill farm financing (Figure 9.23).

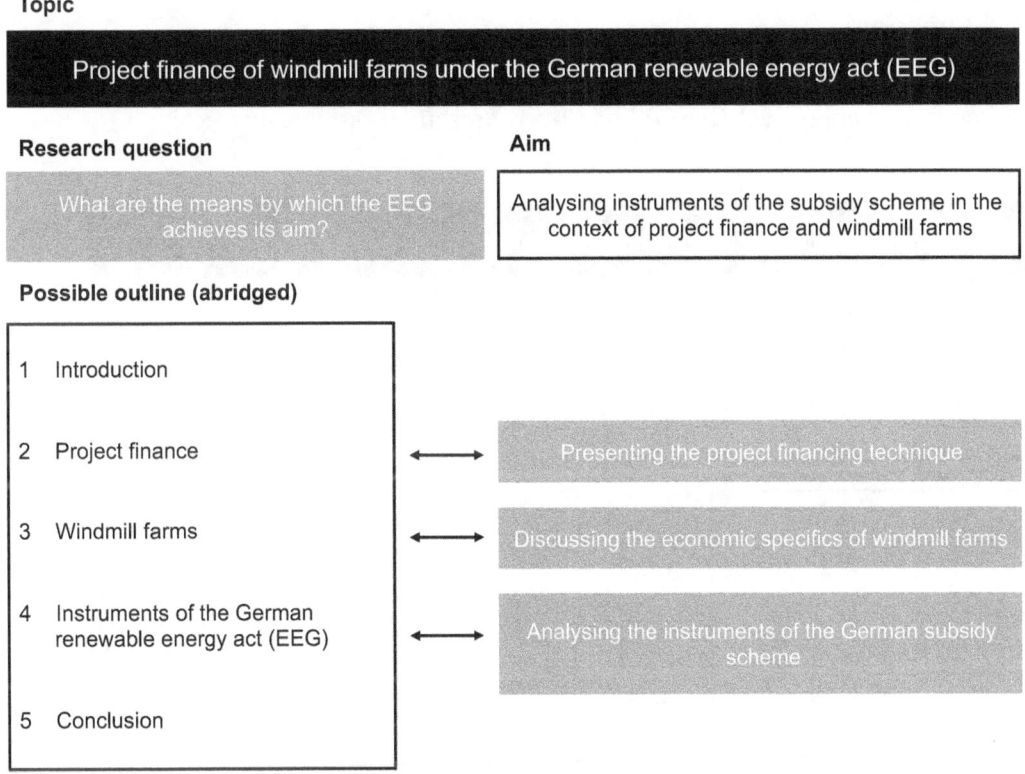

Figure 9.19: Interpretation-based structuring – intention

The research question could be formulated as follows: "What are the means by which the EEG achieves its aim?"

9 Structuring technique

This research question would address the instruments of the subsidy scheme in the context of project finance and windmill farms.

In the second chapter entitled "Project finance", the project financing technique could be presented in a general way.

In the third chapter entitled "Windmill farms", the economic specifics of windmill farms could be discussed.

The fourth chapter entitled "Instruments of the German renewable energy act (EEG)" could be used in order to analyse the instruments of the German subsidy scheme influencing the economics of project finance of windmill farms.

9.5.2.4 Function

A functional approach to the sample topic "Project finance of windmill farms under the German renewable energy act (EEG)" had been presented previously.

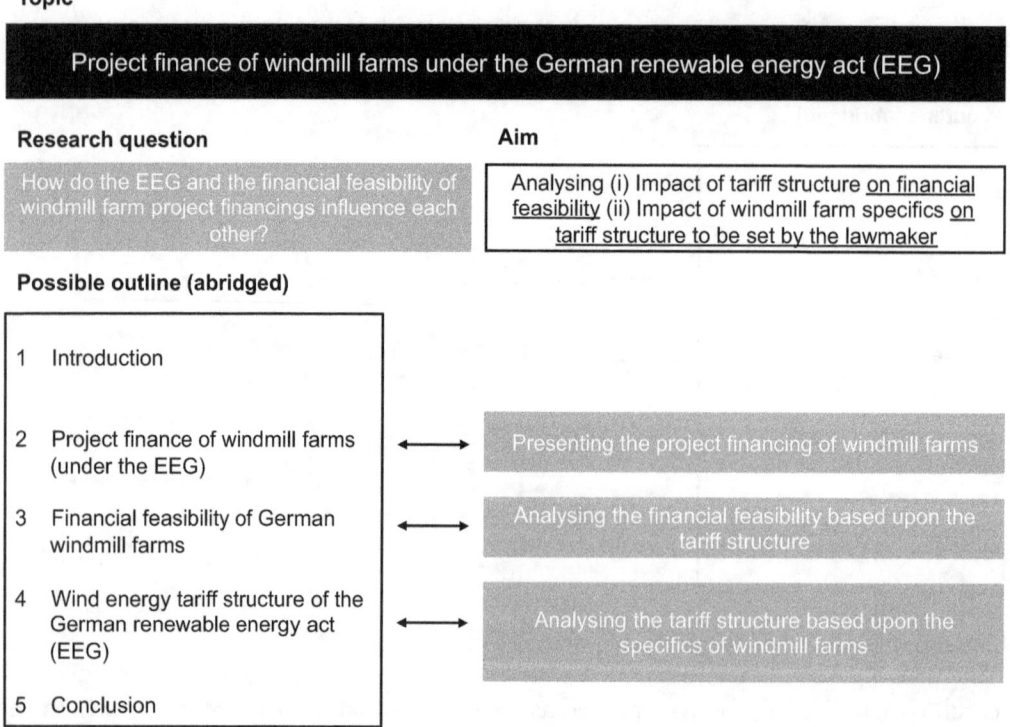

Figure 9.20: Interpretation-based structuring – function

206

As explained, a functional aim could be applied in order to analyse the relation between the financial feasibility of windmill farms and the tariff scheme of the German renewable energy act (Figure 9.24).

The research question could be formulated as follows: "How do the EEG and the financial feasibility of windmill farm project financings influence each other?"

This research question would address the impact of the tariff structure on financial feasibility as well as the impact of windmill farm specifics on the tariff structure to be set by the lawmaker.

In the second chapter entitled "Project finance of windmill farms", the project financing of windmill farms could be presented. The discussion would include the implications of the German renewable energy act.

In the third chapter entitled "Financial feasibility of German windmill farms", the financial feasibility based upon the tariff structure could be analysed.

In the fourth chapter entitled "Wind energy tariff structure of the German renewable energy act (EEG)", the tariff structure based upon the specifics of windmill farms could be analysed.

Tip

It has to be noted that while applying a functional approach to the topic, the interdependencies should be discussed in two separate main chapters.

9.5.2.5 Comparison

Assuming the sample topic is "Project finance of windmill farms under the German renewable energy act (EEG)", an assessment of the suitability of the subsidy scheme could be undertaken (Figure 9.25).

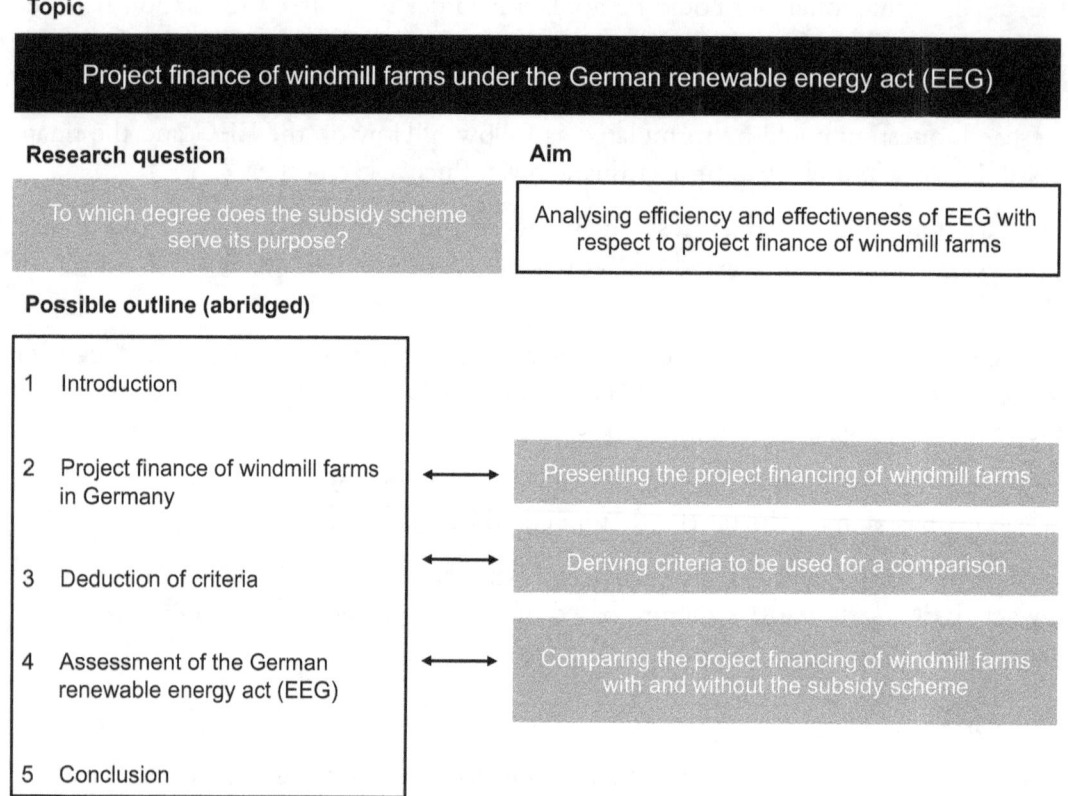

Figure 9.21: Interpretation-based structuring – comparison

The research question could be formulated as follows: "To which degree does the subsidy scheme serve its purpose?"

This research question would address the efficiency and effectiveness of the EEG with respect to project finance of windmill farms.

In the second chapter entitled "Project finance of windmill farms in Germany", the project financing of windmill farms could be presented.

In the third chapter, criteria for a comparison could be deduced from the research question.

In the fourth chapter entitled "Assessment of the German renewable energy act (EEG)", the project financing of windmill farms based on the German subsidy scheme could be compared with the project financing of windmill farms without a subsidy scheme.

9.6 Advanced structuring techniques

9.6.1 IMRaD

In some cases, research papers require an advanced structuring technique. In empirical research, the IMRaD structure is a commonly applied approach of structuring a research paper. IMRaD stands for:

- Introduction
- Methods
- Results
- and
- Discussion

A research paper structured according to the IMRaD approach has four main chapters. Depending on the institutional circumstances, these four main chapters might either be exactly named "Introduction", "Methods", "Results" and "Discussion" or carry individually formulated headings.

The structure has its origins in the field of life sciences. Consequently, the IMRaD approach describes and prescribes a certain logical flow of the research process, which is common in natural sciences. It has been adopted in social sciences such as psychology, sociology, and pedagogy. Furthermore, it is applied in certain fields of business sciences as for example marketing, organisational behaviour and human resource management.

As mentioned before, the IMRaD approach is primarily suitable for empirical research. This encompasses quantitative and qualitative research approaches as well as experimental research designs.

The IMRaD approach is recommended by academic associations (e.g. American Psychological Association). In many cases, the IMRaD approach is the mandatory standard for articles to be published in academic journals.

9.6.2 Variations

There are several variations derived from the IMRaD approach (Figure 9.22).

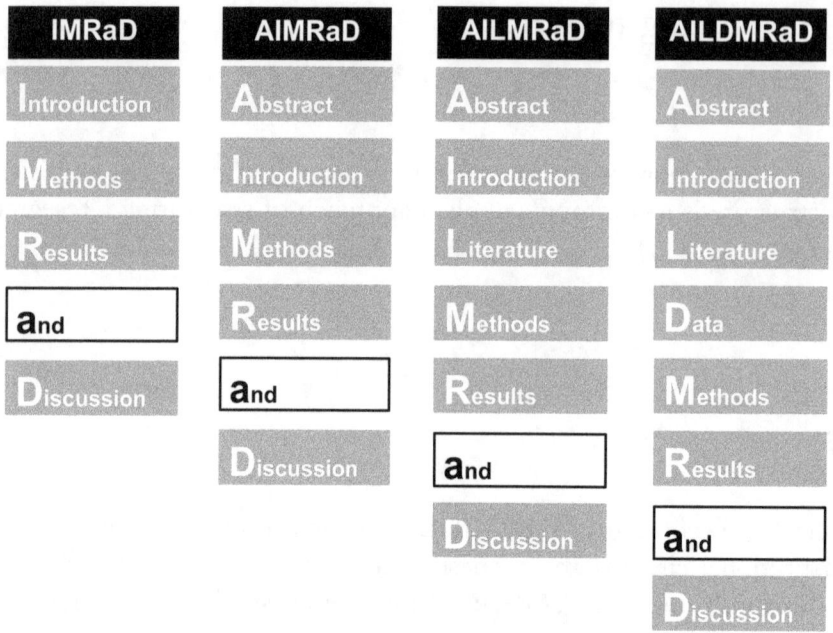

Figure 9.22: Variations of the IMRaD approach

As described, the basic IMRaD approach encompasses the chapters "Introduction", "Methods", "Results" and "Discussion". The most common variations are as follows:

- AIMRaD is a variation that emphasises the importance of an abstract, which might be a mandatory component depending on the institutional requirements.
- AILMRaD is a further variation explicitly establishing a chapter entitled "Literature" or "Literature review" related to the research problem.
- AILDMRaD is a variation that incorporates an additional chapter "Data".

It has to be noted that this is not a comprehensive list. There are more combinations derived from the basic IMRaD approach.

9.6.3 Sections

In short, the purposes of the individual sections according to the IMRaD approach and its derivatives are as follows:

- The abstract is a self-contained text that provides an abridged version of the research project.

- The chapter "Introduction" introduces the research problem, stating aim(s) and research question(s), as well as the course of investigation.
- The chapter "Literature" is a theoretical reflection of the academic status quo that leads to a deduction of one or more hypotheses.
- The chapter "Data" is a description of the data sets that have been generated or collected in primary research or used in secondary research.
- The chapter "Methods" is a description of the empirical methods that have been used in order to test the hypotheses.
- The chapter "Results" serves as an unbiased presentation of the findings without an interpretation.
- The chapter "Discussion" is a summary of the research project encompassing an interpretation of the results, a critical acclaim and an outlook.

9.6.4 Hourglass model

The IMRaD approach and its variations have been described by means of an hourglass model (Figure 9.23). The hourglass serves as a metaphor for the broadness or specificity of the different chapters. The hourglass model assumes that the introduction approaches the topic from a more generalised perspective. Thereafter, the chapters "methods" and "results" have to be very specific or "narrow". Then again, the chapter "discussion" can have a more general character.

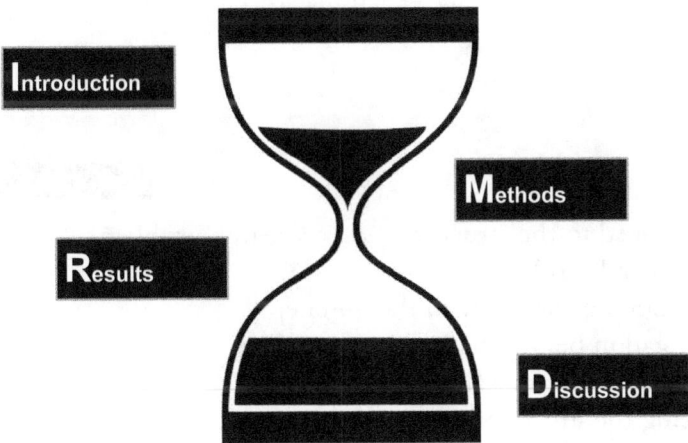

Figure 9.23: Hourglass model

It has to be noted that the shape of the hourglass does not correspond with the number of pages of the individual chapter. As pointed out, it solely indicates if a chapter is of a more general or more specific nature. Whether the hourglass model is a helpful guideline for writing a research paper according to the IMRaD approach, depends on the discipline and the character of a research project. Particularly in social sciences and business sciences, advanced variations of the IMRaD structure such as AILMRaD and AILDMRaD are used. In these cases, it should be analysed whether the hourglass model is appropriate.

9.7 Summary and exercises

9.7.1 Synopsis

In chapter 9, the following aspects of structuring were discussed:

- Advancement from general to more specific aspects while structuring and writing a research problem
- Synchronisation of the outline and the subchapters "Research problem", "Course of investigation" and "Summary"
- Providing a conclusion, which may consist of a summary, a critical acclaim and an outlook
- Applying interpretation-based structuring technique
- Considering the IMRaD approach or one of its variations for empirical and experimental research projects

9.7.2 Questions

Knowledge

1. How can deductive logic be applied to the structuring of a research problem?
2. What are rules for writing a research problem?
3. Why should the research question be aligned with the outline?
4. How can the course of investigation be matched with the outline?
5. What is the idea of the triangle of synchronisation?
6. What are the options of placing the information about the research method into the research paper?
7. What are the "rules of thumb" for structuring an outline?
8. What are the three elements of the chapter "Conclusion"?

9. What is the purpose of a summary?
10. How can the text of the summary be matched with the outline?
11. What is the rationale of a critical acclaim?
12. What is the idea of an outlook?
13. What is the purpose of interpretation-based structuring?
14. What does IMRaD stand for?
15. What are additional components of the AIMRaD, AILMRAD, and AILDMRaD structuring approach?

9.7.3 Problems

9.7.3.1 Aligning topic, aim and research question

Analysis **Synthesis**

Learning target

Being able to identify mismatches of topics, aims and research questions

Instructions

Please analyse the following five examples of topics, aims and research questions:

1. Identify and document shortcomings of the last paragraph of the research problem
2. Derive a suitable aim (description, causal connection, intention, function, comparison)
3. Develop suggestions for improvement by rephrasing the paragraph

Example 1

Topic: "The Internet and its impact on global business"

<u>Last paragraph of research problem:</u>

> "This research paper will analyse the impact that the Internet has on global business. The focus will be on the implementation of Internet services in the financial sector."

Example 2

Topic: "Due diligence in large-scale corporate buy-outs"

Last paragraph of research problem:

> "This paper aims to describe the process of due diligence in large-scale corporate buy-outs."

Example 3

Topic: "Crowd funding of biomedical start-ups"

Last paragraph of research problem:

> "This research paper aims to analyse the usage of crowd funding as a financing alternative for biomedical start-ups."

Example 4

Topic: "Crisis communication concepts for railroad companies"

Last and only paragraph of research problem:

> "A train accident does not happen very often, but when it does it can be devastating. The railroad industry is thus one of the most vulnerable businesses when it comes to a communication crisis. Like any other crisis, the communication crisis settles for different management strategies. In the railroad industry, these methods are individual since it is a peculiar type of business. Catastrophic events require a very delicate, sensitive and convincing way of communicating. Persuading the public to believe the theory stated and protected by the company is a science in itself."

Example 5

Topic: "Business models for providers of online education"

Last paragraph of research problem:

> "This paper aims to analyse how the Internet affects business models for online education providers. It examines how the existence of the Internet for education

has different impacts on business models for learning providers. By elaborating on positive and negative consequences, this paper takes various positions towards the impact of Internet on business models for two selected online education providers."

9.7.3.2 Aligning aim and structure of outline

Synthesis

Learning target

Being able to align the interpretation of a topic with the structure of the outline

Background

Please refer to the problem at the end of chapter eight, addressing a term paper project with the title/topic:

Intercultural communication in global supply chains

Instructions

Please develop a draft of possible outlines (structures) for a term paper that reflect the five different aims (description, causal connection, intention, function, comparison). Focus on the first indenture level (level of main chapters).

10 Referencing

Abstract

The academic principle of intersubjective comprehensibility requires the traceability of thoughts and conclusions. Thus, academic research and writing is characterised by meticulous referencing. Style guides or citation guidelines define the applicable rules of referencing. Generally, five different types of references are distinguished: citation, indication, cross references, information, and explanation. The two major types of referencing techniques are parenthetical referencing and footnote referencing. Parenthetical referencing can be performed by the use of the author-date method or the author-title method (author-page method). Parenthetical referencing requires an unstructured bibliography or an unstructured list of references. Footnote referencing with full information allows for a structured bibliography or a structured list of references.

Keywords

Citation, direct citation, indirect citation, in-text citation, quotation, paraphrase, indication, reference, cross reference, footnote, endnote, parenthetical referencing, footnote referencing, author-date method, author-title method, author-page method, Harvard style, style guides, APA style, MLA style

10.1 Context and relevance

10.1.1 Context of chapter 10

The context of this chapter is linked to the academic principle of intersubjective comprehensibility that demands the traceability of thoughts and conclusions, and therefore requires meticulous referencing.

Figure 10.1 shows how chapter 10 is embedded within the setting of a research project.

10 Referencing

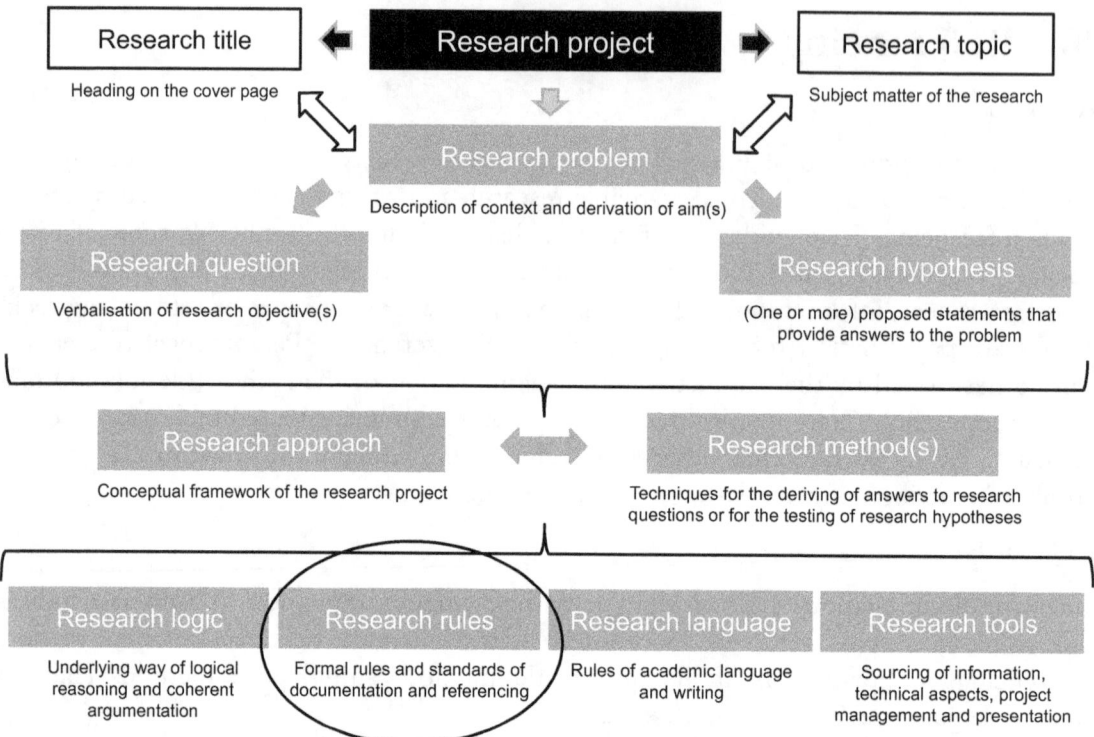

Figure 10.1: Context of chapter 10

In this chapter, formal rules and standards of referencing are addressed.

10.1.2 Relevance of chapter 10

If proper referencing is missing, the research work lacks credibility. Even worse, the violation of referencing rules may have drastic consequences. Furthermore, referencing helps to keep track of information sources that have been used during the research process.

10.1.3 Learning objectives of chapter 10

After having studied this chapter, the reader should be able to:

- understand the nature and importance of references
- distinguish different types of references and their application

- understand the logic and technique of parenthetical referencing
- understand the logic and technique of footnote referencing

10.2 Principles of referencing

10.2.1 Logic and importance of references

The term "reference" refers to the relation between one object or a group of objects and another object or a group of objects (Figure 10.2).

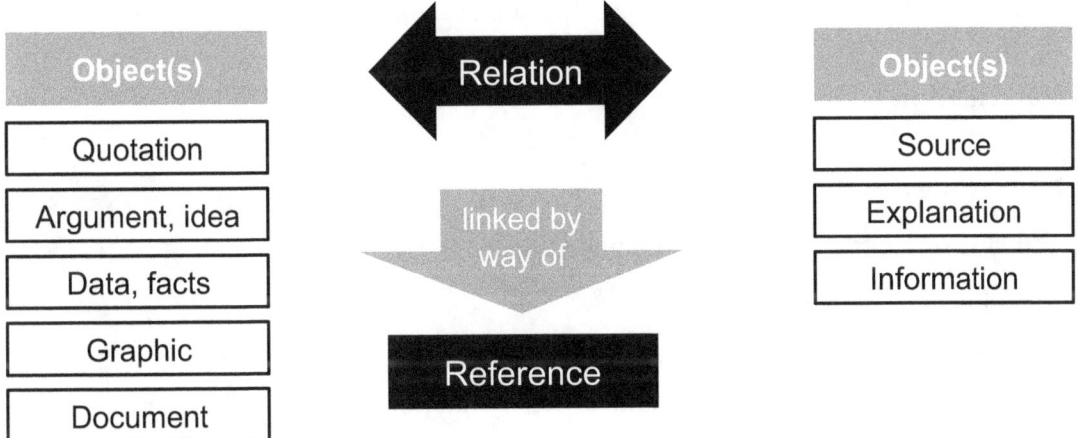

Figure 10.2: Logic of references

If the research paper contains a quotation, an argument, specific data, a graphic, or a document, it should be linked to the source it stems from. These objects might need additional explanation and information. The reference is the way by which these objects are related to one another.

According to the academic principles of accuracy and intersubjective comprehensibility, traceability is considered to be a key feature of academic research. Therefore, the following rules have to be obeyed:

- Every statement or fact has to be backed up by one or more references. However, excessive and/or repetitive citation of the same references in a paper or thesis has to be avoided.

- Numbers, data, tables, and graphics have to be referenced without exception.
- In case of doubt, every sentence has to be referenced to a source. Only one's own thoughts and conclusions are exempted from this general rule.

The following types of references can be distinguished:

- Citation
- Indication
- Cross references
- Information
- Explanation

The different types of references will be explained in the following subchapters.

10.2.2 Citation

10.2.2.1 Rules

Referencing by a citation can be differentiated into

- the direct citation or quotation
- the indirect citation or paraphrase

The direct citation or quotation is characterised by the following rules:

- Quoting means to repeat an original statement without any changes; the statement is cited verbatim.
- Unmarked modifications to the original text are not allowed.
- A quote has to be indicated by way of quotation marks.

The indirect citation or paraphrase is subject to the following rules:

- Paraphrasing means to reproduce an original statement in one's own words.
- Unmarked modifications to the original meaning are not allowed.
- A paraphrase is not indicated by way of quotation marks.

Direct and indirect citations have to be referenced, either by parenthetical or footnote referencing.

The following examples of citations are based on parenthetical referencing. The same rules apply in footnote referencing. The details of parenthetical and footnote referencing will be discussed further below.

10.2.2.2 Direct citations (quotations)

Direct citations have to be denoted with quotation marks.

> Example
> "A financing of a particular economic unit in which a lender is satisfied to look initially to the cash flows and earnings of that economic unit as the source of funds from which a loan will be repaid and to the assets of the economic unit as collateral for the loan" (Nevitt and Fabozzi, 1995, p. 1).

Omitted parts of a direct citation have to be denoted by ellipsis points.

> Example
> "A financing of a particular economic unit in which a lender is satisfied to look initially to the cash flows . . . of that economic unit as the source of funds from which a loan will be repaid and to the assets of the economic unit as collateral for the loan" (Nevitt and Fabozzi, 1995, p. 1).

If one or more words are omitted, they are replaced by three spaced points.

If text is omitted between two sentences, the omission is indicated by four spaced points.

Amended parts within a direct citation have to be denoted with square brackets.

> Example
> "A financing of a particular economic unit [the project] in which a lender is satisfied to look initially to the cash flows and earnings of that economic unit as the source of funds from which a loan will be repaid and to the assets of the economic unit as collateral for the loan" (Nevitt and Fabozzi, 1995, p. 1).

If a direct citation is included within a direct citation, it has to be denoted with single quotation marks.

> Example
> "Kookmin Bank, South Korea's largest, plans to use covered bonds as a long-term funding tool in place of government-guaranteed debt. 'Covered bonds allow us to fund on an independent basis and to a longer tenor than under the government guarantee program,' Kang Chung-won said on a conference call with reporters today" (Smith, 2009, p. 1).

If it is necessary to place a citation of considerable length, a block quotation is applied. The paragraph stating the long citation is indented. Whether the quotation marks are omitted, depends on the applicable requirements. The same holds true for the formatting.

> Example
> Nevitt and Fabozzi (1995, p. 1) developed the following definition:
>
>> A financing of a particular economic unit in which a lender is satisfied to look initially to the cash flows and earnings of that economic unit as the source of funds from which a loan will be repaid and to the assets of the economic unit as collateral for the loan.
>
> This definition emphasises ...

Adhering to local academic standards while writing a research paper in English may be challenging. Different research traditions have led to different referencing and citation styles (Figure 10.3).

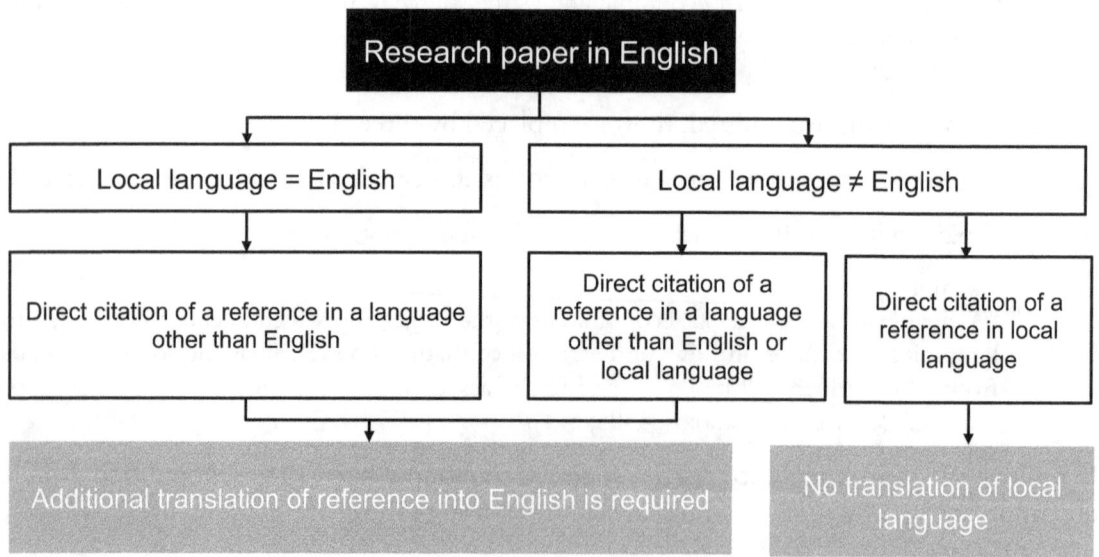

Figure 10.3: Translation of citations

The following rules are applicable:

- Assuming the language of the academic environment is English and the direct citation is in a different language, an additional translation into English is required.

- If the local language is not English and the citation is in a third language, which is neither English nor the local language, an additional translation into English is required.
- If the local language is not English and the citation is in the local language, no additional translation is required.

10.2.2.3 Indirect citations (paraphrases)

Indirect citations or paraphrases have to be referenced as well.

> Example
> The three major features that can be used in order to define project finance are (i) the existence of an independent economic unit (the project), (ii) the application of the principles of cash flow related lending, and (iii) the availability of assets that serve as collateral (Nevitt and Fabozzi, 1995, p. 1).

There are two important rules for indirect citation:

1. An indirect citation is not denoted with quotation marks.
2. There must be no change of the original meaning while paraphrasing an original statement.

Generally, paraphrases are preferable to quotations in order to support the flow and cohesion of one's own argumentation.

10.2.3 Indication

With regard to the referencing of indications, there are two forms. An indication can address an opinion considered supporting or informative, or it can state an opinion, which is diverting.

- Supporting or informative opinions can be derived from sources that either (potentially) support the researcher's argumentation or might be of general interest to the reader.
- Diverting opinions can be derived from sources (or authors) that do not support the researcher's argumentation or thoughts of cited sources.

Both supporting/informative opinions as well as diverting opinions should be referenced in order to demonstrate comprehensive, critical and diligent literature research. Indications are referenced by means of an indicative wording (e.g. see, also, different, deviant etc.).

Examples
When referencing a supporting or informative opinion, the wording could be:
See Smith, 2008, p. 24
Also Meyer, 2009, p. 310

When referencing a diverting opinion, the wording could be:
Different Smith, 2008, p. 24
Deviant Baker, 2005, p. 11

10.2.4 Cross reference

Cross-referencing is referencing within the research paper. A cross reference refers to information that has either been given in a previous chapter or will be presented in one of the following chapters.

A cross reference can be placed in a separate footnote. Alternatively, parenthetical cross-referencing is possible.

Examples
Project finance is referred to as structured finance (see subchapter 2.3).
Project finance is referred to as structured finance (see subchapter 2.3, p. 20).

Modern work processing software allows for dynamic cross-referencing that automatically updates cross references if the numbering of chapters and pages changes.

10.2.5 Information

Any information that is linked to one's argumentation has to be incorporated in the respective paragraph of the research paper. However, in some cases it may be necessary to provide the reader with additional information that is not linked to the author's argumentation. This information is given as a reference that is placed in a separate footnote.

 Tip

Additional information has to be provided cautiously. It must not be misunderstood as a divergence that is not linked to the research question.

10.2.6 Explanation

In a research paper, it may be necessary to provide different forms of explanations addressing formulas, logical conclusions, additional aspects, or specific terminology. The reference type explanation is placed in a separate footnote. However, there are certain restrictions:

- A formula is only explained if an additional explanation of the formula is needed.
- A logical conclusion is only explained if the complexity of one's logical reasoning requires a further explanation.
- Additional aspects are only explained if further aspects seem to be noteworthy and would disturb the text flow.
- Terminology is only explained if it needs explanation and the research paper does not include a glossary as a structural element.

10.3 Parenthetical referencing

10.3.1 Major styles

With regard to parenthetical referencing, two major styles are distinguished:

- author-date method
- author-title or author-page method

The author-date method refers to the style systems named "Harvard style", "Harvard referencing", "Harvard system", "APA style" and others.

The author-title/author-page method refers to the style system named "MLA style".

> **Tip**
>
> Since there are many variations of the major referencing techniques and almost every academic institution or department follows its own guidelines, it is absolutely necessary to refer to the applicable citation guidelines of the institution or department or the applicable style guides (e.g. APA, ACS, CMS, MLA, etc.).

The examples in the following subchapters are for demonstration purposes and may differ from the specific citation standards of the institution where the research paper is written.

10.3.2 Academic styles

A selection of styles is listed in Table 10.1.

Abbreviation/term	Source	Publisher
ACS Style	ACS Style Guide	American Chemical Society
AMA Style	AMA Manual of Style	American Medical Association
APA Style	Publication Manual of the American Psychological Association	American Psychological Association
ASA Style	ASA Style Guide	American Sociological Association
CMOS (or CMS)	Chicago Manual of Style	University of Chicago Press
ISO 690	ISO 690:2010	International Organization for Standardization
MHRA Style	MHRA Style Guide	Modern Humanities Research Association
MLA Style	MLA Style Manual	Modern Language Association of America
Turabian Style	A Manual for Writers of Research Papers, Theses, and Dissertations	University of Chicago Press

Table 10.1: Major styles

It has to be noted that the term "Harvard style" may be used as a

- collective term for parenthetical referencing
- synonym for the author–date–method

10.3.3 Author-date method

The following examples demonstrate how the author-date method of parenthetical referencing is used. The examples are based on the APA style.

The in-text citation is placed in parentheses at the end of the sentence that is to be supported.

> Example
> There are three major features that can be used in order to characterise project finance (Smith, 2008, p. 10).

The in-text citation can also be placed at the end of a part of the sentence that is to be supported.

> Example
> Whereas Smith (2008, p. 10) refers to three major features, other authors refer to five features (Meyer, 1993, p. 2) that can be used in order to characterise project finance.

If the reference contains the names of two authors, both authors are named and connected by "and" or "&".

> Example
> … (Decker and Paesler, 2004, p. 8)
> … (Decker & Paesler, 2004, p. 8)

If there are more than two authors, all authors are mentioned the first time the reference occurs.

> Example
> … (Yin, Lee, and Smith, 2005, p. 9)

Thereafter, only the first author is mentioned and amended by "et al." (et alii/et aliae; "and others").

> Example
> … (Yin et al., 2005, p. 9)

If an author has published more than one publication within the same year, the date of the year is amended with a lowercase letter.

> Example
> … (Smith 2008a, p. 20)
> … (Smith 2008b, p. 10)

Square brackets or a virgule (slash) are used in order to show the original publication date when citing a reprint.

> Example
> … (Popper [1934] 2005, p. 10)
> … (Popper 1934/2005, p. 10)

If it is not referred to a specific page but to the entire publication, there is no page number reference.

> Example
> ... (Popper 1934)

If a publication does not carry a date of publication, there is "n. d." for "no date of publication".

> Example
> ... (Brown and Smith, n. d., p. 20)

If a publication is not paginated, there are two options:

> (i) Stating "n. pag." for "not paginated"
>
> Example
> ... (Mueller, 1962, n. pag.)
>
> (ii) Counting the number of the cited paragraph
>
> Example
> ... (Mueller, 1962, para. 2)

10.3.4 Author-title method/author-page method

In comparison to the author-date method, the author-title method or author-page method recommended by the MLA style guide is used in a slightly different way.

The parentheses of the reference include the author's name, a short version of title (if more than one source by the same author is cited), and the page number.

> Example
> There are three steps in performing a DCF analysis (Titman and Martin, *Valuation*, 21).

In the bibliography or list of references, the source is listed as in the following example:

> Titman, Sheridan, and John D. Martin. *Valuation: The Art and Science of Corporate Investment Decisions*. 2nd ed. Boston: Pearson, 2011. Print.

10.3.5 Unstructured bibliography or unstructured list of references

Parenthetical referencing requires that used or cited sources be alphabetically listed in an unstructured bibliography or an unstructured list of references – as shown in the following example (APA style):

List of references

Hempel, C. G., & Oppenheim, P. (1948). Studies in the Logic of Explanation. *Philosophy of Science, 15*(2), 135–175. doi:10-1086/286983

Hogue, A., & Hogue, J. (2003). The Essentials of English: A Writer's Handbook (with APA Style). Harlow, England: Longman.

Kumar, R. (2014): *Research Methodology: A step-by-step guide for beginners* [Kindle edition] (4th ed.). London: Sage.

Lapakko, D. (2014). *Argumentation: Critical Thinking in Action* (3rd ed.). New York City: iUniverse.

Macgilchrist, F. (2014). *Academic Writing.* Stuttgart: UTB

10.3.6 Advantages and disadvantages

Parenthetical referencing has its advantages and disadvantages.

The advantages are:

- The abridged information of the reference is immediately available at the end of the sentence.
- It saves space compared to a footnote, which requires a whole line.
- It gives the work an Anglo-Saxon, modern image.
- It is suitable for researchers who are familiar with the cited literature.
- It saves time since the referencing is done during the writing process.

The disadvantages are:

- It provides limited information: The reader has to refer to the bibliography or list of references in order to obtain the full information on the reference.
- It may distract the reader or impede the readability of the text.
- It requires an unstructured bibliography or an unstructured list of references.
- It implies additional effort if more literature of the same author will be added at a later point in time.

10.4 Footnote referencing

10.4.1 Major styles and rules

In contrast to parenthetical referencing within the text, the footnote reference is placed – as its name implies – at the bottom of the text page. The footnote referencing system includes two options, which are not supposed to be mixed within a research paper:

1. The footnote provides **full information**.
2. The footnote contains **abridged information**.

> ⬥ **Tip**
>
> It should be noted that there is a difference between footnotes and endnotes. Footnotes appear at the bottom of a page, whereas endnotes appear at the end of the text. Endnotes are common in humanities.

The footnote providing full bibliographic information is written as in the following example:

> There are three major features that can be used in order to characterise project finance.[1]
>
> ―――
> [1] Cf. Nevitt, Peter K., Fabozzi, Frank J.: Project Financing, London 1995, p. 1.

In footnotes with abridged information, the wording of the footnote is similar to parenthetical referencing ("author – date method" or "author – title method") – as shown in the following example:

> There are three major features that can be used in order to characterise project finance.[1]
>
> ―――
> [1] Nevitt and Fabozzi, 2008, p. 1.

Referring to the same source cited in the previous reference is indicated by the abbreviation "Ibid.". In the following example, footnote 2 indicates that the citation refers to the same source but a different page. Footnote 3 indicates that the citation refers to the same source and the same page:

> There are three major features that can be used in order to characterise project finance.[1] .... [2] .... [3]
>
> ―――
> [1] Cf. Nevitt, Peter K., Fabozzi, Frank J.: Project Financing, London 1995, p. 1.
> [2] Ibid., p. 12.
> [3] Ibid.

10.4.2 Structured bibliography or structured list of references

The following (abridged) example shows a structured bibliography or a structured list of references usually required by the footnote system:

Monographs
Nevitt, Peter K., Fabozzi, Frank J.: Project Financing, London: Euromoney 1995.

Articles in journals
Decker, Christian; Julius, Hinrich: Project Financing under the German Export Credit Guarantee Programme, in: European Financial Services Law, Vol. 6 (1999), No. 5 (May), pp. 192 – 196.

Working papers
Decker, Christian; Paesler, Stephan: Financing of Pay-on-Production-Models, in: Berichte aus dem Weltwirtschaftlichen Colloquium der Universität Bremen, Nr. 92, Bremen 2004.

Examples of structural elements are:

- Monographs
- Articles in journals
- Concise dictionaries
- Working papers
- Conference proceedings

Tip

While applying footnote referencing, the applicable rules of structured bibliographies and/or a structured list of references should be consulted.

10.4.3 Advantages and disadvantages

Footnote referencing has its advantages and disadvantages.

The advantages are:

- It does not distract the flow of reading.
- Full information footnotes provide complete information about the source, immediately accessible at the bottom of the page.
- It is informative for readers who are not familiar with cited sources.

- It allows for a structured bibliography/list of references.

The disadvantages are:

- It is rather time-consuming during the writing process.
- It takes up more space than parenthetical referencing due to page formatting; therefore it might shorten the core text. This is a potential problem in the case of a restricted length of main body.

10.5 Academic abbreviations

Table 10.2 lists academic abbreviations commonly used in parenthetical referencing, footnote referencing, bibliographies and lists of references.

Abbreviation/term	Latin and/or English
ca.	circa, approximately
cf.	confer (bring together, compare, consult)
e.g.	exempli gratia (for example)
etc.	et cetera
et al.	et alii/aliae (and other people)
ff.	follis (from pages)
i.a.	inter alia (among other things)
ibid.	ibidem (in the same place)
i.e.	id est (that means)
l.c.	loco citato (in the place cited)
n. d.	no date

10.5 Academic abbreviations

Abbreviation/term	Latin and/or English
n. p.	no place of publication and/or no publisher
n. pag.	not paginated
ca.	circa, approximately
cf.	confer (bring together, compare, consult)
e.g.	exempli gratia (for example)
etc.	et cetera
et al.	et alii/aliae (and other people)
ff.	follis (from pages)
i.a.	inter alia (among other things)
ibid.	ibidem (in the same place)
i.e.	id est (that means)
l.c.	loco citato (in the place cited)
n. d.	no date
n. p.	no place of publication and/or no publisher
n. pag.	not paginated

Table 10.2: Academic abbreviations

It has to be noted that some style guides might deviate from the abbreviations listed in Table 10.2.

10.6 Summary and exercises

10.6.1 Synopsis

The referencing techniques introduced in chapter 10 imply the following aspects:

- Refer to the applicable style guides or citation guidelines
- Distinguish the five different types of referencing
    - Citation
    - Indication
    - Cross references
    - Information
    - Explanation
- Distinguish the methods of parenthetical referencing and footnote referencing
- Decide on either parenthetical referencing or footnote referencing
    - Parenthetical referencing requires an unstructured bibliography or an unstructured list of references.
    - Footnote referencing with full information allows for a structured bibliography or a structured list of references.

10.6.2 Questions

Knowledge

1. What is a direct citation?
2. What is an indirect citation?
3. What is the difference between a quotation and a paraphrase?
4. What is an indication?
5. What is a cross reference?
6. What is the difference between information and explanation?
7. What are the two major referencing styles?
8. What are advantages of parenthetical referencing?
9. What are disadvantages of parenthetical referencing?
10. What is footnote referencing with abridged information?
11. What is the difference between footnotes and endnotes?
12. What is a structured bibliography or a structured list of references?
13. What are advantages of footnote referencing?
14. What are disadvantages of footnote referencing?

10.6.3 Problem

Analysis

Learning target

Being able to differentiate standards of referencing

Instructions

Please research the citation and referencing standards of the faculties and/or departments of your university.

10.6.4 Additional reading

Chernin, E. (1988). The "Harvard" system: A mystery dispelled. *British Medical Journal, 297*, 1062–1063. Retrieved from http://www.ncbi.nlm.nih.gov/pmc/articles/PMC2056883/

11 Academic language and writing style

Abstract

Chapter 11 provides a brief introduction to academic language and academic writing style. Academic writing can be differentiated from other forms of writing, for example literary writing. Furthermore, different academic disciplines favour different styles of writing, which have to be studied on an individual basis. Independent of specific academic styles, the principles of accuracy and clarity provide a general framework that prescribes to be specific, to omit the needless, to beware of adjectives, to avoid subjectivity, to apply factual tonality and to focus on clear phrasing. The elements of coherence, structure and cohesion, further support the logic of argumentation. Logical links between and within sentences as well as linking repetition are techniques to enhance the intersubjective comprehensibility. The academic writer has inter alia to differentiate between British and American English and should use punctuation, special characters, symbols and figures in a way that supports the documentation of research projects.

Keywords

Academic language, research language, academic writing, phrasing, cohesion, coherence, syntax, spelling, punctuation

11.1 Context and relevance

11.1.1 Context of chapter 11

The academic principles have an immediate impact on the language. Conducting proper research work implicitly requires applying an academic language and an appropriate writing style.

Figure 11.1 shows how chapter 11 is embedded within the setting of a research project.

11 Academic language and writing style

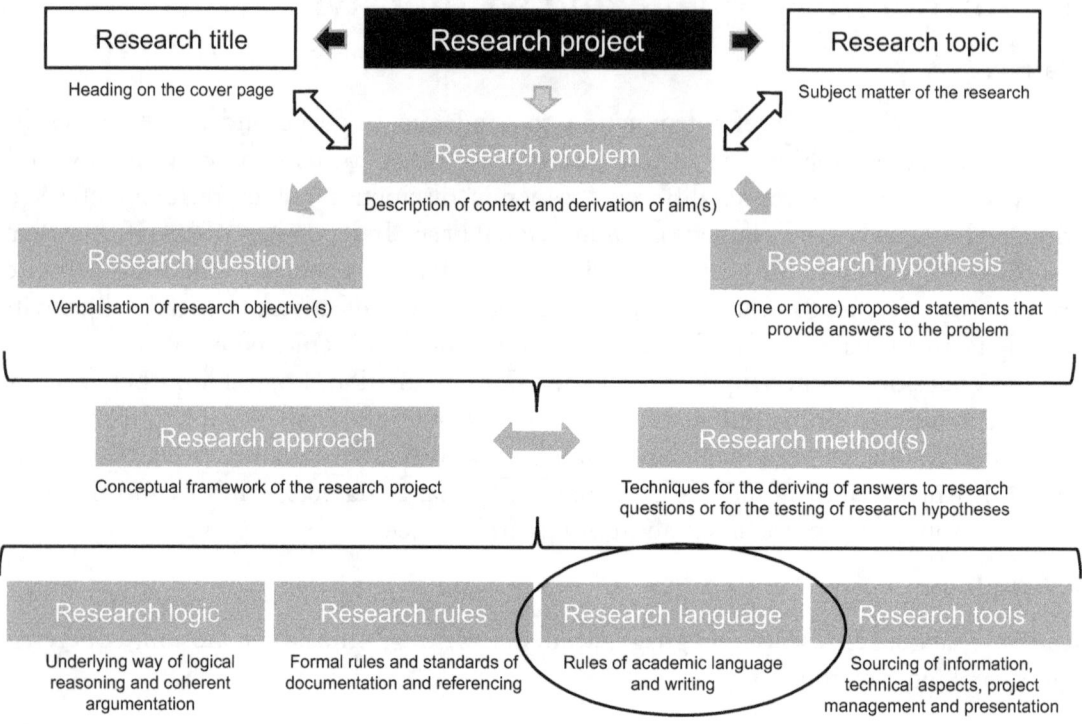

Figure 11.1: Context of chapter 11

In this chapter, rules of academic language and writing are addressed.

11.1.2 Relevance of chapter 11

If researchers want their work to be taken seriously and acknowledged, they have to lay it out according to the common rules of academic language and writing style. Of course, academic writing, with its proper argumentation, phrasing and spelling, will make one's thinking comprehensible.

11.1.3 Learning objectives of chapter 11

After having studied this chapter, the reader should be able to:

- differentiate between academic writing and literary writing
- apply the principles of academic writing

- write in a coherent and cohesive way
- master substantial rules of grammar, spelling and punctuation

11.2 Principles of academic writing

11.2.1 The language of science

There are several means to state information within a research paper: language, symbols, formulas, figures, and sometimes pictures (Figure 11.2).

The language used to present a research project is academic language. Academic language has to follow comprehensive and generally defined rules of formality and structure. It differs widely from non-academic language, which is characterised by undefined or inconsistently defined levels of formality.

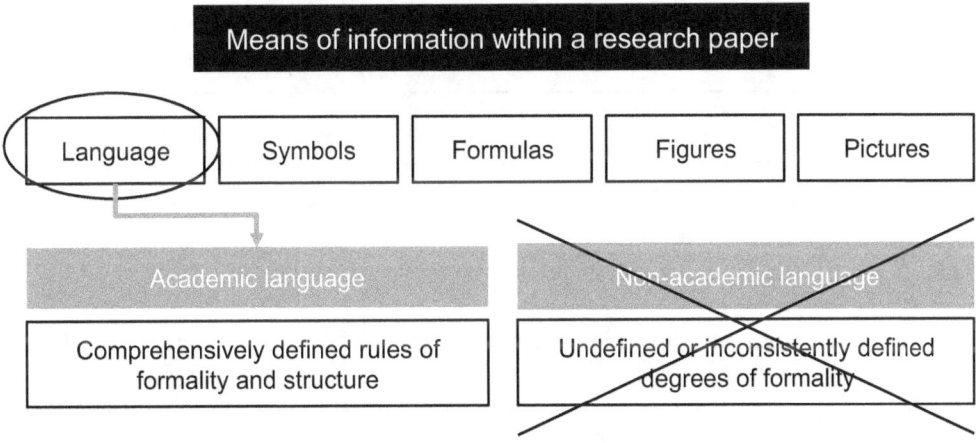

Figure 11.2: The language of science

Non-academic language has to be avoided in academic writing.

11.2.2 Examples of non-academic language

Non-academic language with its different levels of formality occurs in many different areas: common speech, jargon as a special language used by a special group, printed or e-correspondence, journalism in its various forms, advertising, bureaucracy, the non-fictional literature that is not academic, and, of course, fictional literature. A phenotype of a young language is the so-called space limited language that has developed along with the use of electronic media. It is characterised by reduced, condensed and coded elements.

Obviously, it is the non-academic language that is predominant in spoken and printed communication. That is why special emphasis has to be put on identifying and mastering academic language.

11.2.3 Academic and literary writing

A possible way to define academic writing is to differentiate it from its counterpart literary writing by analysing the characteristics of the different writing styles (Table 11.1).

	Academic writing	**Literary writing**
Content	Comprehensible, clear, complete, stringent	Unexpected, interpretable, redundant, sometimes open-ended
Perspective	Objective, factual	Subjective, imaginative
Subject matter	Real	Real and/or fictional
Sources	Systematically documented, traceable	Unknown
Rules	Strict rules for style, structure, grammar	"Artistic" freedom of style, structure, even grammar
Language	Pure, unadorned, formal	Optionally metaphorical, colloquial, particular, unconventional

Table 11.1: Characteristics of writing styles

A criterion for recognizing and applying academic writing is to follow the academic principles of accuracy, completeness, clarity, comparability, and materiality. Accordingly, the content of a research project should be comprehensible, clear, complete, and stringent. In distinct contrast, literary written content may provide surprising, unexpected information, may allow individual interpretations, may be redundant due to stylistic reasons, and may even end without a final result or conclusion. Whereas an academic perspective has to be objective and factual, dealing with real life phenomena, the author of a literary piece writes from a subjective and imaginative perspective about subject matters that are either real, fictional or a mix of both. A research project has to be based on traceable sources, whereas literary writing does not state its source of information and inspiration, or at least not in a systematic way. Likewise, literary writing is characterised by a total freedom in writing style, text structure and sometimes grammar, whereas, on the contrary, academic writing should strictly observe the rules and norms of scientific structuring and language. Consequently, the academic piece is characterised by a pure, unadorned and formal language, whereas literary writing can use every kind of language: metaphorical descriptions and expressions, colloquial speech etc.

One should note that there are research-based publications that address a broad public beyond the research community. These are typically presented in a mix of academic and literary writing. This approach is called popular science and considered inappropriate in scientific work.

11.2.4 Academic writing styles

As explained, the criteria of academic writing can be sharply distinguished from those of literary writing. However, within the area of academic writing, the writing style or mode of expression that is common and expected may differ across different academic disciplines.

Academic writing styles may expand from a more concise, factual tone to a more expansive, lively character. Which tone is appropriate, may sometimes depend on the approach – be it quantitative or qualitative. The tonality may also depend on the conventions of the broad academic disciplines reaching from Natural Sciences, Engineering Sciences to Humanities. Generally, the area of business and social sciences can be placed somewhere in between.

A possible way to familiarise oneself with the appropriate writing style in a specific field of study, is reading high quality journal publications. While doing so, it is advisable to pay attention not only to the thematic focus of the articles but also to the structure and length of sentences, the choice of words and the article's general tonality.

11.2.5 Principles of accuracy and clarity

11.2.5.1 Be specific

Above all, it is the principles of accuracy and clarity that should guide the researcher's writing. Apart from simple writing mistakes that might be rarely made by students and researchers, there are rules that seem less obvious, but lead to inaccuracy and lack of clarity when disregarded.

Some of these rules can be bundled under the imperative "Be specific" (Table 11.2).

Rule	Remarks
Beware of generalisations	Inaccuracy is often implicit in wordings such as "all", "most people", "It is generally believed that…" etc.
Beware of false completeness	The heading "2.4 The applications of project finance" implies that all applications are mentioned which rarely proves to be true. Better: "2.4 Applications of project finance".
Choose the correct word	Do not confuse "effective" with "efficient", "continuous" with "continual", "discrete" with "discreet" etc.
Choose the specific word within a context	Avoid for example the non-scientific word "get" in favour of one of its numerous possible meanings such as "receive, obtain, become, acquire, grow, develop, comprehend, arrive" etc.

Table 11.2: Principles of accuracy and clarity – be specific

A typical source of inaccuracy is making generalisations. Because of the implicit inaccuracy, one should be careful with generalising words and statements.

A frequently made mistake is creating false completeness by using the definite article in headings.

Similar sounding words often have a different meaning. One has to make sure to choose the correct word.

Accurate, clear writing also means using the full range of vocabulary and choosing the specific, most suitable word within a context.

11.2.5.2 Omit the needless

Another rule in favour of accurate and comprehensible writing is to omit the needless (Table 11.3).

Rule	Remarks
Avoid double negatives	"It is not clear if there is no change."
Avoid unnecessary foreign words and unexplained jargon	Not "aficionado", but "keen supporter"; not "Spreads have tightened.", but "Spreads have decreased."
Avoid redundancies in structure, argumentation and wording	Exceptionally, repetition of wording is appropriate to generate cohesion within the text (keywords) and if synonyms are impossible or misleading (names of persons, organisations, locations etc.).
Beware of hidden redundancy (pleonasm)	"Plan forward", "first introduction", "repeat again", "integrated element", "positive success", "the possibility to be able to do" etc.
Recognise and avoid needless words	Omit superfluous adverbs (filler words) such as "now", "somehow", "no doubt", "actually" etc.

Table 11.3: Principles of accuracy and clarity – omit the needless

Double negatives may turn arguments into unnecessarily complicated sentences. It is advisable to avoid negative sentences wherever possible, since positive sentences are generally more comprehensible.

The use of unnecessary foreign words as well as unexplained jargon is considered inappropriate in academic writing.

While writing or proofreading text, one should check carefully whether there are any redundancies in structure, argumentation and wording. One should avoid unnecessary repetition in any form. However, repetition of words is sometimes appropriate or even necessary. For example, the repetition of keywords is used to generate cohesion within the text. Furthermore, certain words have to be repeated if the use of synonyms does not make sense or would even be misleading. More information on repetition is given below.

A means to enhance the quality of an academic text is the avoidance of hidden redundancies such as pleonastic wording. A pleonasm can be defined as an expression in which the additional word is implicit.

Writing is not about piling up numerous words. On the contrary: Needless words reduce the quality of the writing. By examining a text thoroughly, one will find surprisingly many words that are simply superfluous. A good start to purify a text is to omit useless adverbs.

11.2.5.3 Beware of adjectives

An additional prerequisite for accurate and clear writing is the careful handling of adjectives (Table 11.4).

Rule	Remarks
Avoid needless adjectives	Many adjectives are simply dispensable (and require special scrutiny during proof-reading).
Beware of measuring adjectives	The implicit judgement of measuring adjectives (e.g. "weak", "strong", "good", "poor", "big", "small" etc.) and their degrees (e.g. "weaker", "weakest", "stronger", "strongest", "better", "best" etc.) has to be proved by a reference (e.g. data, statistics).
	Exaggerating adjectives ("huge", "incredible") are both inaccurate and bad style.
Recognise incomparable adjectives	Do not grade and do not compare the incomparable: e.g. very unique, totally perfect, completely false, too ineffective, straighter, more vertical, most independent, less general.

Table 11.4: Principles of accuracy and clarity – beware of adjectives

Adjectives are superfluous, whenever they do not provide additional information. Therefore, adjectives deserve special attention during writing or proofreading.

A typical source of inaccuracy is the use of adjectives of a measuring nature. They imply a judgement that has to be proved by adding a reference. Exaggerating adjectives such as huge, incredible etc. are not only vague, but also considered poor style in academic writing.

A further rule regarding the proper handling of adjectives is recognising whether they are incomparable. A non-gradable or incomparable adjective describes an attribute that cannot be graded or compared. This is obvious in adjectives such as pregnant, dead, empty, full etc. Other incomparable adjectives are not as easily identified. Here is a range of examples. Do not write "very unique", "totally perfect", "completely false", "too ineffective", "straighter", "more vertical", "most independent", "less general". All these adjectives are of an absolute nature and must not be combined with a grading adverb. Accordingly, whenever applying a grading adverb such as very, rather, too, totally, more, less and so on, one should examine carefully, if the following adjective can be meaningfully graded or compared.

11.2.5.4 Avoid subjectivity

Academic writing should not contain statements of a subjective nature (Table 11.5).

Rule	Remarks
Avoid personalised writing	Personal style contains words related to the first person such as "I", "we", "myself", "me", "us", "my", "mine", "I, personally", "our", "ours" etc.
	Avoid directly addressing your reader and words related to the second person such as "you", "your", "yours", "yourself" including "you" as a generic pronoun.
Avoid biased language and stereotypes	"Germans are …"
Avoid humour and cynicism	Humour, especially if derogative, and cynicism are considered inappropriate in academic writing.

Table 11.5: Principles of accuracy and clarity – avoid subjectivity

Typically, in academic writing, one should avoid personalised writing and the use of words related to the first person.

> **🎓 Tip**
>
> From time to time, one will find academics that favour the use of personalised writing. However, one should keep in mind that a pure and traditional academic writing style avoids personalised writing. Thus, it is advisable to clarify the position of the academic advisor.

One should avoid biased language and stereotypes by stating unqualified opinions.

Additionally, it is advisable to avoid humour and cynicism in academic writing.

11.2.5.5 Apply factual tonality

In accordance with avoiding a subjective perspective, a scientific author should apply a factual tonality (Table 11.6).

Rule	Remarks
Avoid colloquial language	Avoid contractions ("it isn't", "he doesn't").
	Avoid incomplete sentences; each sentence must include a verb – exception: titles, captions, figure descriptions.
Be careful with metaphoric language	Avoid metaphors, especially, if the metaphoric expression tends toward being a cliché such as "This hits the nail on the head" or the like.
	Exceptionally, metaphors, expressions in the figurative sense, or plays of words may be applied in titles (e.g. "EEG – Blowin' in the wind?").
Do not formulate chapter headings or sentences within the main body as questions	Not "2.1 What is the definition of project finance?", but "2.1 Definition of project finance"

Table 11.6: Principles of accuracy and clarity – apply factual tonality

With regard to an academic context, it is expected to avoid colloquial language in all its manifestations.

Figurative language, for example metaphors and analogies, is a sophisticated way of writing, however, not always considered appropriate in academic writing. Therefore, one should be careful with adopting or creating metaphors and analogies in a text. Figurative language is definitely inappropriate when consisting of clichés. An exception to this guideline is that metaphors, expressions in the figurative sense, and plays of words may be applied in titles (e.g. "EEG – Blowin' in the wind?").

In favour of a factual tone, one should not address the reader directly. Accordingly, one should not formulate chapter headings or sentences within the main body as questions. It should be remarked that, in some cases, one might find headings, which are posed as questions. This is especially true for academic textbooks and working papers. Nevertheless, one should keep in mind that a substantial part of the recipients will consider this inappropriate.

11.2.5.6 Focus on clear phrasing

A focus on clear phrasing supports the comprehensibility of the author's thoughts (Table 11.7).

Rule	Remarks
Avoid long and complicated sentences	Long and complicated sentences disturb the intersubjective comprehensibility.
Balance your text	Mix short main clauses including subject and verb and somewhat longer sentences with additionally one or two subordinate clauses at the most.
Avoid unnecessary passive constructions	Write active sentences instead of passive constructions when possible ("Popper explained that …" instead of "It was explained by Popper that …").
	In contrast, use passive in order to avoid first person statements ("The findings are summarised in the last chapter." instead of "I summarise the findings in the last chapter.")

Table 11.7: Principles of accuracy and clarity – focus on clear phrasing

Above all, one should avoid long and complicated sentences that disturb the intersubjective comprehensibility and might even require repeated reading. On the other hand, the exclusive use of short sentences may prevent an adequate argumentation.

Therefore, one should try to balance the text. A paragraph should consist of a mix of short main clauses including subject and verb and somewhat longer sentences with additionally one or two subordinate clauses at the most.

Whenever possible, one should avoid sentences in a passive voice. Typically, active sentences are shorter and less complicated than passive sentences. However, using a passive construction is useful if the acting person (or issue) is unknown or irrelevant. In this sense, the use of the passive voice is a reliable way of avoiding personal style and formulations in the first person.

11.3 Logic of argumentation, phrasing and syntax

11.3.1 Logical writing

According to the academic principles, the text of a research project has to be accurate and clear. This also refers to the logic of argumentation. Once researchers have made a decision about tackling their research objectives, they do not want to lose track, change their direction or become lost in a random selection of ideas. Blurred or even contradictory argumentation threatens the research project to fail.

A research project has to apply an underlying logic of reasoning, for example deductive reasoning. Progressing on this argumentative path, it has to follow its logical thread without contradictions and deviations. Researchers should derive one argument from the other, and avoid jumping back and forth.

As illustrated in Figure 11.3, there are three prerequisites to increase the intersubjective comprehensibility and ensure the proper composition of academic writing:

- Structure
- Cohesion
- Coherence

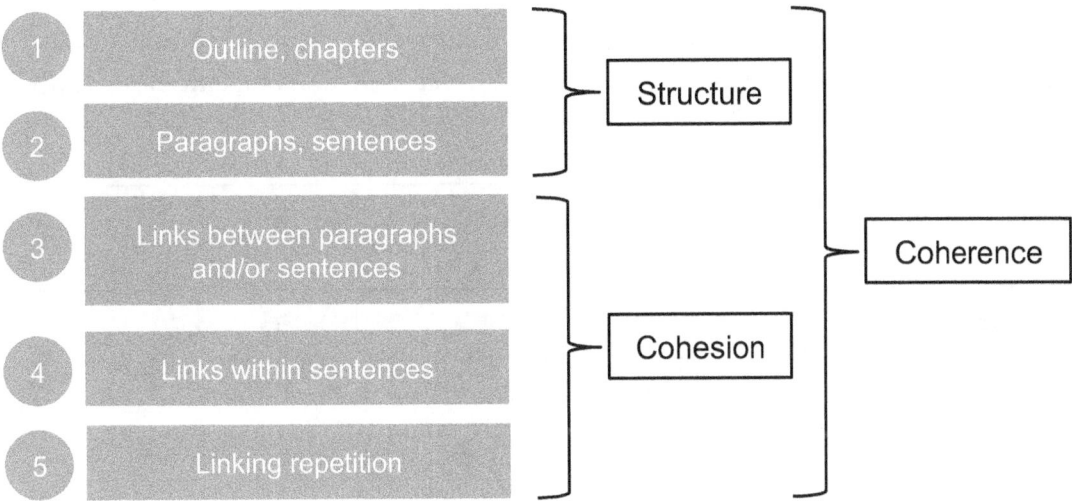

Figure 11.3: Structure, cohesion, coherence

Accordingly, the components of a research paper consisting of outline, chapters, paragraphs and sentences are organised in a logical structure.

Developing an argumentation by using links between sentences, links within sentences and linking repetitions increases the cohesion of the text.

To sum it up: An argumentation that is organised in a logical structure and phrased in cohesive sentences will indicate that a researcher has mastered one of the main challenges of academic writing: logical coherence.

11.3.2 Cohesion

11.3.2.1 Links between sentences

In order to achieve cohesion **between** paragraphs or sentences, one should link the arguments according to their meaning by using adverbs with a transitional function. These adverbs are called conjunctive adverbs. Conjunctive adverbs serve as guiding connectors that signal the purpose of one's information. Accordingly, one should apply the conjunctive adverb that indicates the purpose of the intended reasoning.

Table 11.8 provides a list of examples.

Conjunctive adverb (examples)	Purpose
However, in contrast, on the other hand, nevertheless, conversely, in another sense, but, yet, on the contrary, though (adv.), still (adv.)	Contrast, difference, change
Additionally, in addition, furthermore, moreover, besides, finally	Addition
First, second, next, then, last, finally	Order
Thereafter, then, since then, at last, at length, afterwards, before, previously, meanwhile, now, presently, ultimately, simultaneously, subsequently	Time sequence
Indeed, in fact, above all	Emphasis
Therefore, consequently, thus, hence	Effect, result, conclusion
Similarly, likewise	Equal value
For example, for instance, specifically	Apposition
Of course, accepting this, certainly	Concession
Accordingly, consistently	Accordance

Table 11.8: Conjunctive adverbs

Of course, this is not to be considered as a complete list of conjunctive adverbs. There are more options of transitional words and expressions.

11.3.2.2 Links within sentences

Cohesion is also achieved by links **within** sentences. Therefore, it is important to structure logical links within sentences according to the function of the information.

One should state the main argument in a main clause, which is always an independent clause. A simple independent clause consists of at least a subject and a verb.

> Example
> "A market failure can occur."

Typically, an independent clause consists of three elements: subject, verb and object.

> Example
> "The student hands in a paper."

One should put additional arguments of equal importance in coordinate clauses.

> Example of two joined independent clauses
> "The student writes the paper, and the professor reviews it."

Coordinating words such as "and", "or", "but", "for", "nor" connect independent clauses. Therefore, these words are called coordinating conjunctions.

> Examples of connected independent clauses
> "The plan has been finalised, and its realisation will start next week."
> "There are two options: The cost will be cut, or the sales will be increased."
> "The prices do not rise, nor is the market share affected."

Related information is given in relative clauses. A relative clause is always a dependent clause that cannot exist without an independent clause. It literally depends on the main clause.

An independent clause and a relative clause are connected by a relative pronoun such as "who", "whose", "whom", "which", "that".

> Examples
> "The graphic shows a list of investment projects, which can be distinguished according to the risk involved."
> "Papers that are handed in earlier will be reviewed earlier."
> "The author, who is known for his different point of view, raises several objections."

While the main information is given in an independent clause, dependent additional information should be stated in a dependent clause.

Dependent and independent clauses are connected by the use of subordinating conjunctions. Subordinating conjunctions are for example "if", "although", "while", "because", "in order to".

> Examples
> "Although he had been working under time pressure (dependent clause), the author handed in an excellent paper (independent clause)."

> "The author has to draft a revised version (independent clause) because his paper was rejected by the publisher (dependent clause)."

In Table 11.9, the most common subordinating conjunctions, the subordinating connectors, are related to their function.

Subordinating connectors	Function
Because, since, as	Cause
If, even if, unless	Condition
Whereas, while, although	Contrast
Before, after, as long as, since, when	Time sequence
While, as, just as	Simultaneity
(So) that, in order to (+ infinitive clause)	Purpose, aim
That	Statement, reason, result
As	Accordance

Table 11.9: Subordinating connectors and their function

One should note that some subordinating conjunctions have more than one meaning.

> Examples
> "While" can indicate a contrast or simultaneity.
> "Since" can indicate a cause or a time period.
> "As" can indicate a cause or simultaneity or accordance.

11.3.2.3 Linking repetition

Another characteristic of cohesive academic texts is linking repetition. That is, cohesion within an academic text can also be achieved by the repetition of certain words or phrases. This does not mean that the writing should be repetitive and boring. Cohesion by words refers to the repeating and restating of keywords and phrases. The repetition of words and phrases that are of central meaning to the text is not an option, but a must.

Keywords may be names, main subjects and central terms or phrases of the text.

> Examples
> United States (name)
> Project finance (main subject)
> Hedging (central term)
> A new financial product named container freight derivatives enables companies to lock in future transportation costs. The main characteristics of container freight derivatives are … (text with linking repetition)

If a word or phrase is of central meaning, there is no need to search for synonyms. Firstly, unnecessary synonyms would reduce cohesion because the repetition of central terms provides a kind of structure guiding the reader's eyes and supporting the reader's comprehension of the information. Additionally, the synonym of an accurately defined central word may lack precision.

> Example
> If the subject of the research is "vendor finance", it must not be replaced by the term "sales finance" as a synonym, because the latter term implies a broader perspective.

The repetition of central words includes the whole word family.

> Example
> If the main subject of the text is "organisation", the additional use of related words such as the verb "organise" and the adjective "organisational" may serve the purpose of cohesive repetition.

11.4 Rules of spelling and punctuation

11.4.1 British or American English

If applying the above-explained insights on proper academic style and coherent logical argumentation, writers will communicate the content and aim of their research. However, it is possible to spoil a structured and coherent text by neglecting some fundamental rules of proper English. Being on safe ground regarding grammar, spelling and punctuation in an English written research paper starts with the decision whether to use British English or American English. After the language is chosen according to the requirements of the research context, it has to be used consequently and thoroughly.

British English and American English differ in certain spelling rules and grammar rules and sometimes in vocabulary. Accordingly, one should adjust the spellchecker and grammar checker to the language decided on.

Independent of the language chosen, one should not entirely rely on the error-spotting programs, since their corrections or non-corrections might not match the context.

11.4.2 British versus American English – Spelling

The main differences between British and American spelling consist in the different use of certain endings, doubled consonants and umlauts.

(i) The different notation of endings is as follows:

The ending "re" in British English is spelled "er" in American English.

> Examples
> BE: centre, theatre, litre, fibre
> AE: center, theater, liter, fiber

The ending "ise" in British English is spelled "ize" in American English.

> Examples
> BE: organise, recognise, realise
> AE: organize, recognize, realize

British verbs ending in "yse" always end in "yze" in American English.

> Examples
> BE: analyse, paralyse
> AE: analyze, paralyze

Accordingly, nouns derived from a verb with these endings are spelled either with "s" in British or with "z" in American.

> Examples
> BE: globalisation, securitisation
> AE: globalization, securitization

Regarding the above-mentioned endings, the American spelling – containing the "z" – is sometimes accepted in British English. In academic writing, however, it is preferable to use the spelling as shown in the list.

The verb "practise" ends in "ise" in British English, whereas it is ends in "ice" in American.

Nouns ending in "our" in British English lose the " u" in American English.

>Examples
>BE: labour, colour, behaviour, neighbour
>AE: labor, color, behavior, neighbor

The British ending "ce" is spelled "se" in American English.

>Examples
>BE: licence, defence, offence
>AE: license, defense, offense

The British ending "gue" is spelled "g" in American, while the British "gue" is also accepted.

>Examples
>BE: catalogue, analogue
>AE: catalog or catalogue, analog or analogue

(ii) In British and American spelling, some distinctions are made in doubled consonants.

If the consonant "l" is followed by a vowel, it doubles in British English.

>Examples
>BE: modelling, traveller, counsellor
>AE: modeling, traveler, counselor

However, the infinitive form of the verb fulfil is "fulfil" in British and "fulfill" with double l in American spelling.

British nouns ending in "mme" end in "m" in American spelling.

>Examples
>BE: programme, kilogramme
>AE: program, kilogram

(iii) Umlauts are sometimes spelled in a simplified way in American English.

>Examples
>BE: encyclopaedia, paediatric, aesthetic, manoeuvre, homoeopathic
>AE: encyclopedia, pediatric, esthetic, maneuver, homeopathic

In British English, the past simple and past participle of some verbs are spelled in the irregular form ending in "t". In American spelling the regular form and the irregular form are possible.

> Examples
> BE: learnt, spoilt, burnt
> AE: learned or learnt, spoiled or spoilt, burned or burnt

In British English, headings are written in upper and lower case, whereas, in American English, essential words within the heading are often capitalised.

> Examples
> BE heading: Differences in spelling and punctuation
> AE heading: Differences in Spelling and Punctuation

11.4.3 British versus American English – Vocabulary

In addition to different spelling, there are some differences in British and American vocabulary. Different terms can have the same meaning.

> Examples
> BE: solicitor, AE: attorney
> BE: shop, AE: store
> BE: black economy, AE: underground economy
> BE: financial year, AE: fiscal year
> BE: share option, AE: stock option
> BE: trade union, AE: labor union

11.4.4 Punctuation

11.4.4.1 Comma

Punctuation is not just a matter of rules. Skilfully applied punctuation serves as a guide for the reader and defines the precise meaning of the text. This is particularly the case when using or not using commas.

There is no comma before dependent clauses beginning with "that", "what" or "whether".

> Examples
> "The author states that she has supervised the experiment."
> "The professor explains whether the graphic is important or not."
> "It is the result that counts."

There is no comma before and after defining (restrictive) relative clauses. A defining or restrictive clause is a clause that cannot be omitted without changing the meaning of the sentence.

> Example
> "Students who succeed in writing receive better grades."
> If the defining relative clause "who succeed in writing" is omitted, the sentence "Students receive better grades." has lost its meaning.

The same rule applies to defining or restrictive participles. There is no comma before and after defining or restrictive participles.

> Example
> "Authors writing a research paper should use academic language."
> If the defining participle "writing a research paper" is omitted, the remaining sentence "Authors should use academic language." has lost its meaning.

Do not use a comma before an adverbial clause.

> Example
> "The research is inadequate (no comma) if it is not laid out in proper writing."

Accordingly, one does not use a comma before an infinitive phrase.

> Example
> "He submitted the paper (no comma) to finish the course."

However: If an adverbial clause or infinitive phrase serve as an introductory element of the sentence, the adverbial clause or infinitive phrase are followed by a comma. Accordingly, use a comma after an adverbial clause.

> Example
> "If students practise academic writing, (comma) their results improve."

Likewise, one uses a comma after an infinitive phrase.

> Example
> "To obtain the certificate, (comma) the student had to finish the paper."

Generally, the introductory element of a sentence is followed by a comma.

- Introductory elements are for example adverbs.

> Examples
> "However, (comma) the findings do not confirm that…"
> "Thus, (comma) it can be concluded…and so on".

- Furthermore, introductory elements can be prepositional phrases. Accordingly, prepositional phrases, if placed at the beginning of the sentence, are set off by a comma.

  Examples
  "From a banks perspective, (comma) the financing will have to be structured …"
  "After the successful completion of the research, (comma) the article will be published."

If a specific element of a sentence is supposed to be emphasised, it can be put it in front of the sentence and has to be separated by a comma.

> Example
> "To him, (comma) the approaches are not as different as the colleague researchers consider them."

Commas are used to delineate parenthetical elements. Parenthetical elements are parts of sentences that are not essential to the main information and can be omitted without changing the central meaning of the sentence. A typical parenthetical element is the apposition or appositive. A non-restrictive apposition gives information about the preceding subject, but can be omitted without changing the meaning of the sentence.

> Example
> "An academic research project, a typical challenge for every student, requires special efforts."

Commas are used for demarcating non-defining (which means non-restrictive) relative clauses.

> Example
> "Miller, who has published three books on the topic, takes a different approach."
> (The non-restrictive relative clause gives additional information about the subject, but – if omitted – does not alter the meaning of the sentence. The sentence "Miller takes a different approach." is still valid.)

A similar parenthetical element is the non-defining (or non-restrictive) participle phrase.

> Example
> "Miller, known for his expertise on finance, has published his third book."

11.4.4.2 Exclamation mark, question mark, hyphen, dash

In academic writing, special attention should be put on exclamation marks, question marks, hyphens and dashes.

Exclamation marks and question marks should be avoided. The same applies to interjections, exclamations and questions.

> Example
> Do not state exclamations such as "What a precise definition this is!" Prefer a regular sentence such as: "This is a precise definition."
> Do not write: "Why round this number? The reason is…", but: "The number has to be rounded because …"

Some written pieces lack accuracy, because the author had not thoroughly distinguished between hyphen and dash.

Hyphens (-) are used to create hyphenated compound words.

> Examples
> "a twenty-year-old"
> "the so-called Pay-on-Production-model"

Dashes (–) are used to demarcate a parenthetical part of a sentence.

> Example
> "Funding – (dash) if private or public – (dash) has to be structured thoroughly."

11.4.5 Special characters, symbols, figures

In academic writing, it is advisable to avoid the careless use of special characters, symbols and figures.

Avoid the unnecessary use of special characters in headings and texts. In the following examples of headings, the use of slash, backslash, @ etc. makes no sense:

> 2.2 Finance/Project finance
> 2.2 Project finance\Cash flow*.*
> 3.4 Controlling@Work

It goes without saying that the use of special characters is necessary in case of computer codes, technical terms and names.

> Examples
> @{url | file_name[.ext] } [arg...]
> john.doe@master-mail.com
> Chicago@work

One must not use the ampersand as a substitute for a regular "and".

> Example
> Not: bonds & (ampersand) loans
> But: bonds and loans

In contrast, the ampersand has to be used as a substitute for "and", if it is part of technical terms and names.

> Examples
> Mergers & Acquisitions
> Miller & Sons Limited

One must not use mathematical symbols as substitutes for words.

> Example
> Not: bonds + loans
> But: bonds and loans

One must not use figures as artificial substitutes for words.

> Example
> Not: strategy 4 marketing
> But: strategy for marketing

One must not decorate the text by using graphic symbols, icons etc.

11.5 Summary and exercises

11.5.1 Synopsis

Chapter 11 provided a brief introduction to academic language and writing style:

Academic and literary writing have to be differentiated.

Within the world of sciences, different styles of different academic disciplines can be distinguished.

The principles of accuracy and clarity require the observation of major imperatives:

- Be specific
- Omit the needless
- Beware of adjectives
- Avoid subjectivity
- Apply factual tonality

- Focus on clear phrasing

Structure and cohesion are the elements of coherence.

Cohesion can be achieved by logical links between sentences, logical links within sentences and by linking repetition.

Differences between British English and American English have to be obeyed.

Rules of punctuation help the recipients to comprehend the argumentation.

Special characters and symbols have to be carefully used.

11.5.2 Questions

Knowledge

1. What are the means of information within a research paper?
2. What is the difference between academic and non-academic language?
3. What are examples of non-academic language?
4. What are characteristics of the academic writing style?
5. What are characteristics of the non-academic writing style?
6. What are the two different modes of expression, which are used by academic disciplines?
7. What are rules to be applied in order to "be specific" in academic writing?
8. What are rules to be applied in order to "omit the needless" in academic writing?
9. What are rules to be applied in order to "beware of adjectives" in academic writing?
10. What are rules to be applied in order to "avoid subjectivity" in academic writing?
11. What are rules to be applied in order to "apply factual tonality" in academic writing?
12. What are rules to be applied in order to "focus on clear phrasing" in academic writing?
13. What is the meaning of structure, cohesion and coherence?
14. How can "links between paragraphs/sentences" be established?
15. How can "links within paragraphs/sentences" be established?
16. What does "linking repetition" mean?
17. Why is a decision for British or for American English important in academic writing?
18. What are examples of spelling differences in British and American English?
19. What are examples of the different vocabulary usage for words of the same meaning in British and American English?
20. What are the major comma rules discussed in this chapter?

21. What are rules for the application of exclamation marks (exclamation points) and question marks in academic writing?
22. What is the difference between a hyphen and a dash?
23. What are rules for the use of special characters in academic writing?
24. What are rules for the use of symbols and figures in academic writing?

11.5.3 Additional reading

Coleman, R. (2003, December 1). Pardon My Proper English. *The Scientist*. Retrieved from http://www.the-scientist.com

Jaffe, S. (2003, March 10). No Pardon For Poor English in Science. *The Scientist*. Retrieved from http://www.the-scientist.com

12 Argumentation

Abstract

Rigour and flow of argumentation have a major impact on the quality of academic research. An essential component of argumentation is providing definitions. Definitions can be derived with the help of standard, advanced or professional approaches. Furthermore, the deduction of individual arguments is documented in paragraphs and chapters, which serve as the units of an academic paper. The logic of arguments has to be mirrored in the paragraph structure, which consists of three logical text elements: topic sentence, supporting sentences and concluding sentence. Transitioning between sentences as well as between paragraphs supports the flow of argumentation and provides cohesion within the text. During the development of an argumentation, the structuring of paragraphs and chapters shows an iterative character. Referencing that supports the argumentation can enhance the academic quality of the research output. Thus, arguments of other sources should be carefully combined instead of randomly compiled.

Keywords

Argumentation, reasoning, definitions, paragraph structure, topic sentence, supporting sentences, concluding sentence, cohesion, indenting, referencing

12.1 Context and relevance

12.1.1 Context of chapter 12

The quality of academic research is, among other aspects, determined by the rigour and logical flow of argumentation.

Figure 12.1 shows how chapter 12 is embedded within the setting of a research project.

12 Argumentation

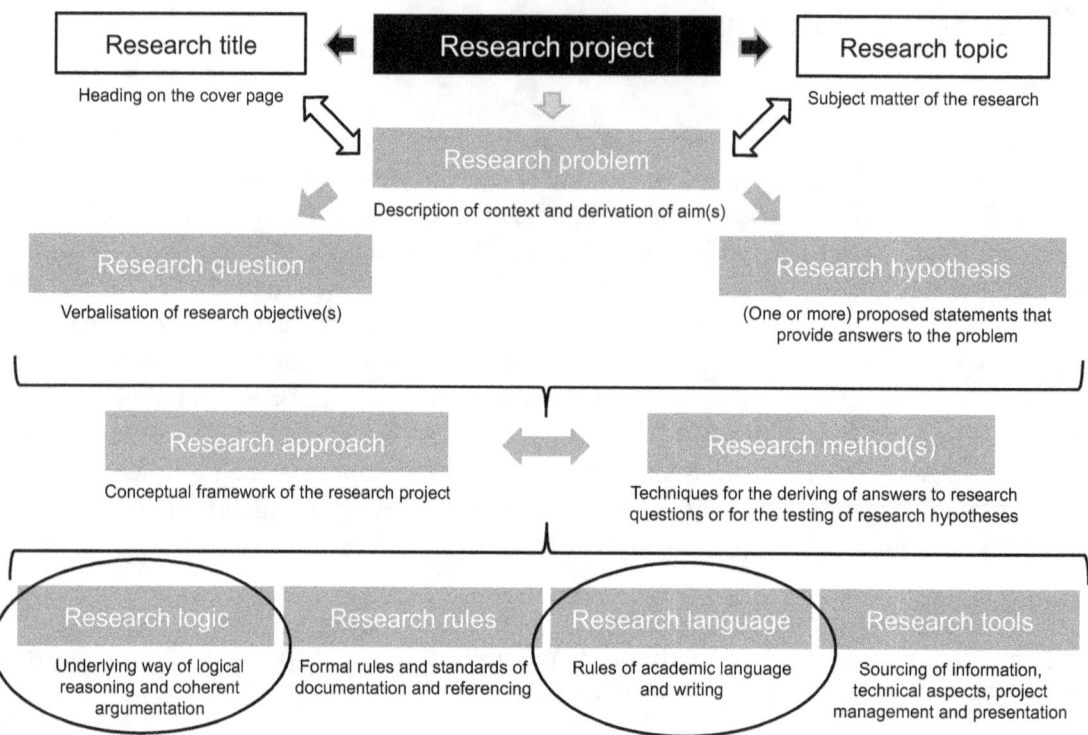

Figure 12.1: Context of chapter 12

In this chapter, selected aspects of research logic and research language are addressed.

12.1.2 Relevance of chapter 12

A deduction of arguments serves as a means of self-control in the research process. Furthermore, a rigorous line of reasoning helps potential recipients to understand the conclusions. Thus, a stringent argumentation signals a certain level of intellectual quality.

12.1.3 Learning objectives of chapter 12

After having studied this chapter, the reader should be able to:

- understand different ways of deriving definitions
- understand the characteristics of a paragraph and explain the structure of a paragraph

- point out the flow of paragraphs within a chapter and its implications for chapter structuring
- understand the logical nexus between reasoning and referencing

12.2 Definitions

12.2.1 Purpose

Metaphorically speaking, definitions are like buoys, which help to guide a writer on the "research journey" (Figure 12.2).

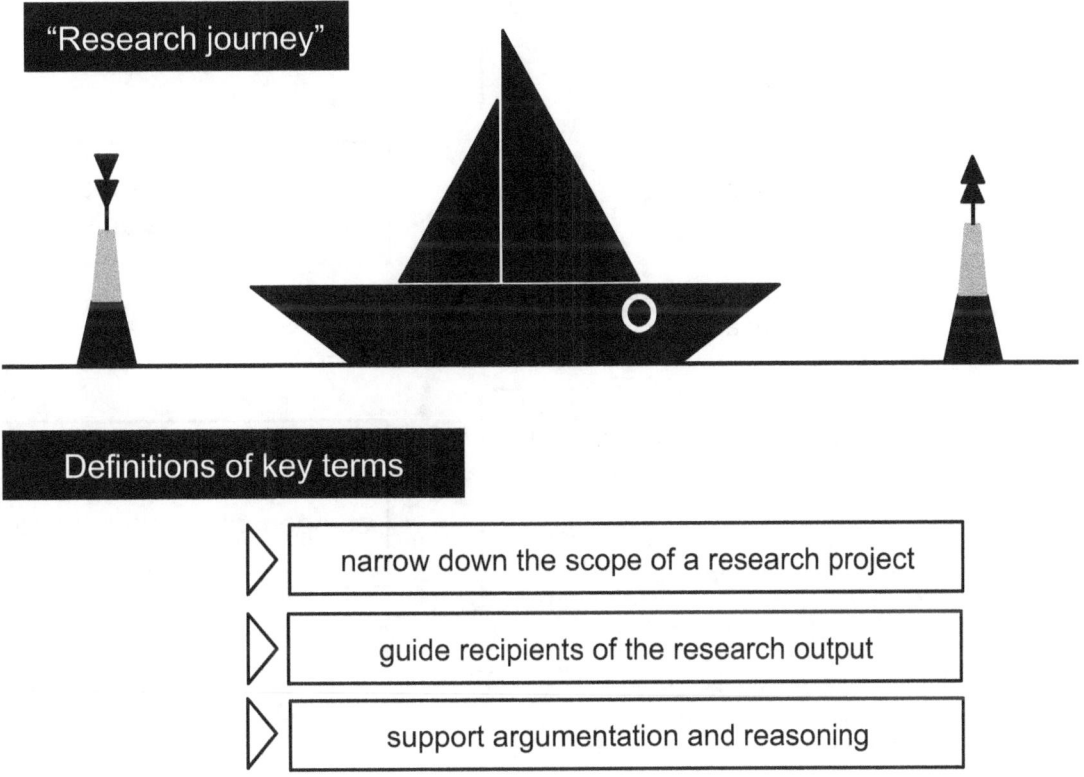

Figure 12.2: Purpose of definitions

Definitions of key terms are essential in order to narrow down the scope of a research project. Furthermore, definitions provide guidance for the recipients of the research output. Last but not least, definitions support the argumentation and reasoning within a research paper.

12.2.2 Coverage

Definitions are the building blocks of every research paper (Figure 12.3).

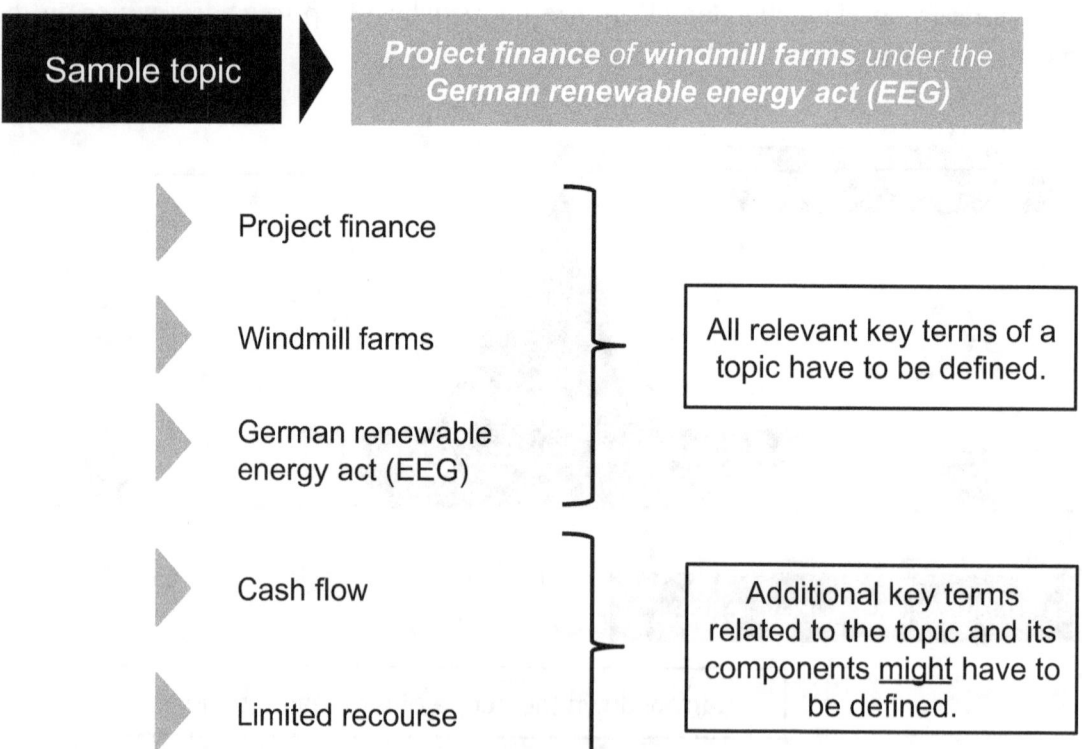

Figure 12.3: Definitions – coverage

Definitions covered within a research paper are:

- All relevant key terms of a topic that have to be defined
- Additional key terms related to the topic and its components that might have to be defined

12.2.3 Technique

Figure 12.4 shows how proper definitions can be derived.

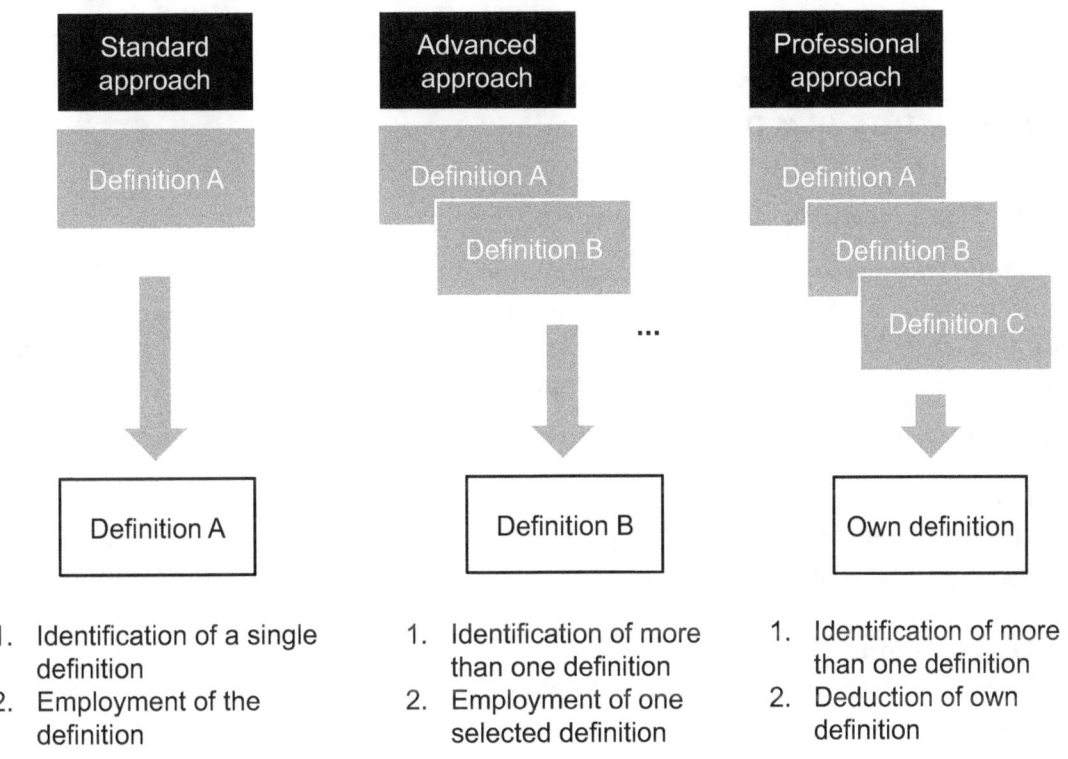

Figure 12.4: Definitions – technique

Roughly, there are three scenarios that can be distinguished:

- The standard approach would be, first, the identification of a single definition of a given key term and, second, the employment of the definition in the research process.
- A slightly more advanced approach would be, first, the identification of more than one definition of a given key term and, second, the employment of one selected definition in the research process. It is expected to explain the reason for having selected a specific definition.

- A professional approach would be, first, the identification of more than one definition of a given key term and, second, the deduction of one's own definition in the research process. Typically, this would take place by combining elements from different definitions, adding personalised amendments and explaining the resulting creation.

12.3 Structure of a paragraph

12.3.1 Characteristics of a paragraph

Paragraphs, the units of a text, play a central role for the quality of the written documentation of a research project. Particularly in academic texts, as they are subject to academic principles such as clarity, paragraphs must not appear as a random collection of text blocks. In fact, they serve as an important means to organise one's writing.

Accordingly, good paragraphing shows the following characteristics:

- **Entity**
  Each paragraph forms a logical unit presenting one main idea. If a new main argument emerges, it has to be discussed in a new paragraph.

- **Organisation**
  The sentences within a paragraph should be organised in a reasonable structure that helps to unfold the writer's arguments in a linear and logical way.

- **Cohesion**
  Connective and transitional wording should support the logical flow within a paragraph.

- **Transition**
  If possible, a transition to the next paragraph of a chapter should be provided.

As pointed out, it is advisable that each paragraph is organised in a logical structure. Hence, the sentences within a paragraph are not ordered randomly, but according to their logical purpose (Figure 12.5).

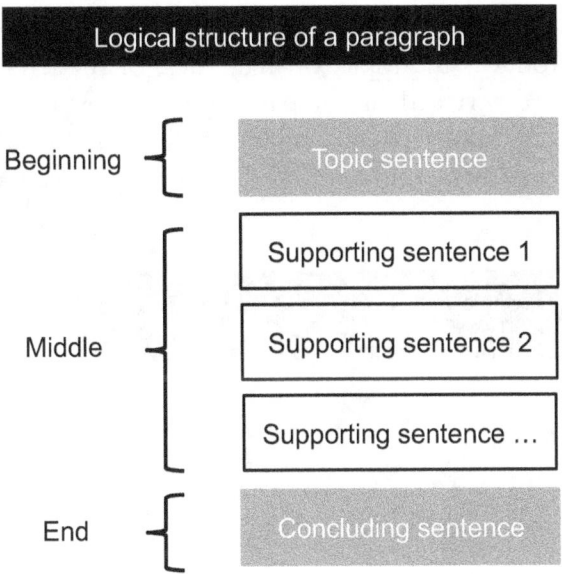

Figure 12.5: Logical structure of a paragraph

To achieve a logical order, it is useful to construct each paragraph as a unit consisting of three parts: beginning, middle and end. Furthermore, each of the three parts should consist of a certain category of sentences.

The three categories of sentences within a paragraph are:

- Beginning: topic sentence
- Middle: supporting sentences
- End: concluding sentence

With few exceptions, a paragraph typically consists of at least three or more sentences.

It should be noted that the three-part structure is a helpful means for logical argumentation in a text. However, there are categories of text units where the three-part structure does not necessarily apply. These text units refer to the research problem, the course of investigation, the summary, the critical acclaim, and the outlook.

Additionally, if a paragraph consists of a simple list of facts, data etc., the three-part structure is not applied.

12.3.2 Topic sentence

As its name implies, the topic sentence introduces the topic, or main idea, of the paragraph. Accordingly, the topic sentence is stated very early in the paragraph; in most cases it is the first sentence. The topic sentence has to be formulated carefully. The way of formulating a topic sentence determines the following sentences of the paragraph (Figure 12.6).

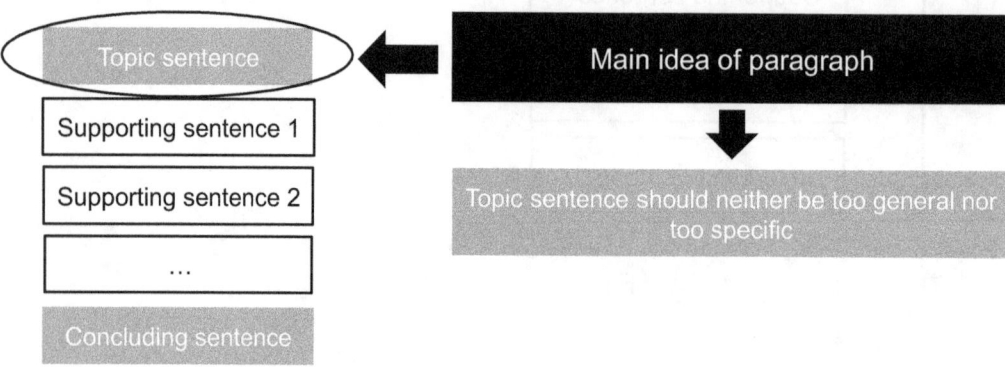

Figure 12.6: Topic sentence – from too general to too specific

Because of its impact on the following sentences, the topic sentence should neither be too general nor too specific:

If the topic sentence contains a statement that is too general, it will take too many supporting sentences to elaborate on the overly general point. In this case, the paragraph will be too long.

> Example of a topic sentence that might be too general:
> "The EEG has a positive impact on energy projects."

If the topic statement is too specific, there might not be enough left to elaborate on. In this case, the topic sentence does not state a topic, but an already elaborated argument.

> Example of a topic sentence that might be too specific:
> "The EEG is regarded as an instrument that removes the market risk in a renewable energy project by enabling a realisation that otherwise would not be feasible due to uncertain market conditions, i.e. insufficient sales volumes as well as insufficient sales prices."

Figure 12.7 provides an example of the beginning of a three-part paragraph.

12.3 Structure of a paragraph

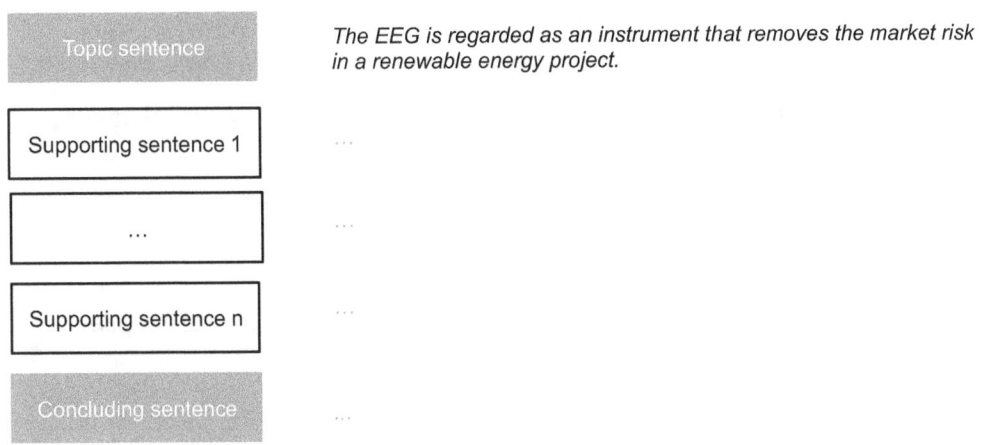

Figure 12.7: Topic sentence – example

The introductive topic sentence could be as follows:

> "The EEG is regarded as an instrument that removes the market risk in a renewable energy project."

12.3.3 Supporting sentences

At least one or, typically, several supporting sentences follow the topic sentence (Figure 12.8).

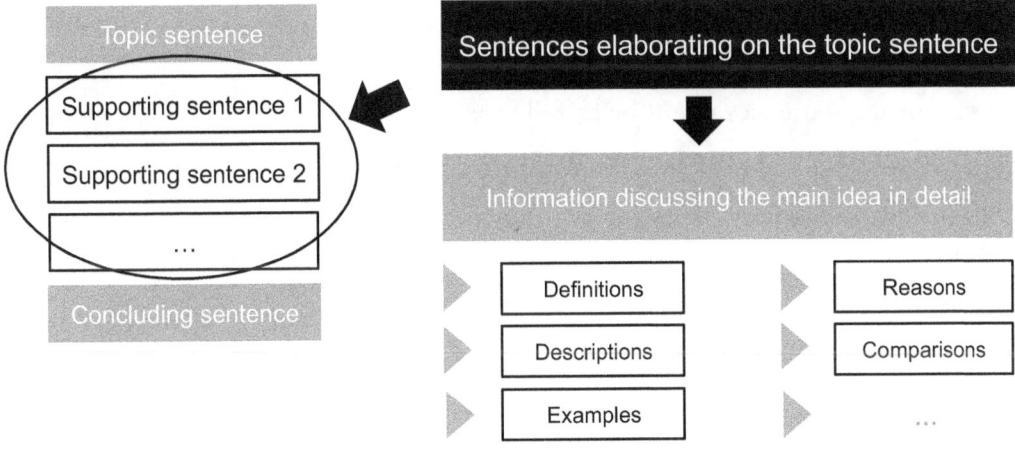

Figure 12.8: Supporting sentences

12 Argumentation

The supporting sentences contain information discussing the main idea in detail. This information can consist of definitions, descriptions, examples, reasons, comparisons etc.

In the following, the previous example paragraph is continued by sentences that support and elaborate the topic sentence (Figure 12.9).

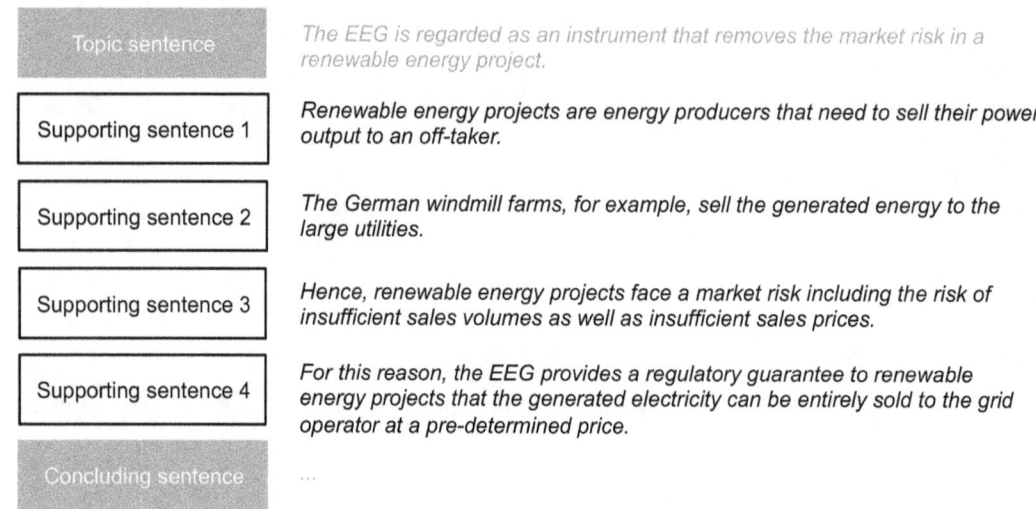

Figure 12.9: Supporting sentences – example

As shown above, the topic sentence of the example is

> "The EEG is regarded as an instrument that removes the market risk in a renewable energy project."

Now, the supporting sentences might be as follows:

Supporting sentence 1 could provide a **description** such as

> "Renewable energy projects are energy producers that need to sell their power output to an off-taker."

Supporting sentence 2 could provide an **example**:

> "The German windmill farms, for example, sell the generated energy to the large utilities."

Supporting sentence 3 could provide a further **specification**:

"Hence, renewable energy projects face a market risk including the risk of insufficient sales volumes as well as insufficient sales prices."

Supporting sentence 4 could state a **reason**:

"For this reason, the EEG provides a regulatory guarantee to renewable energy projects that the generated electricity can be entirely sold to the grid operator at a pre-determined price."

It should be noted that the elaboration on a main idea might follow a deductive flow, a progress from the general to the specific. A more general argument is introduced in the topic sentence, which, in the supporting middle part, is followed by descriptions and explanations leading from the general to the more specific. However, not every supporting part necessarily follows a deductive logic. It may as well support the topic by just stating examples, addressing a comparison or listing a number of events and so on.

12.3.4 Concluding sentence

A well-structured paragraph typically ends with a concluding sentence. A concluding sentence can be either of a summarising or transitional nature; it can even provide both a summarising and transitional function (Figure 12.10).

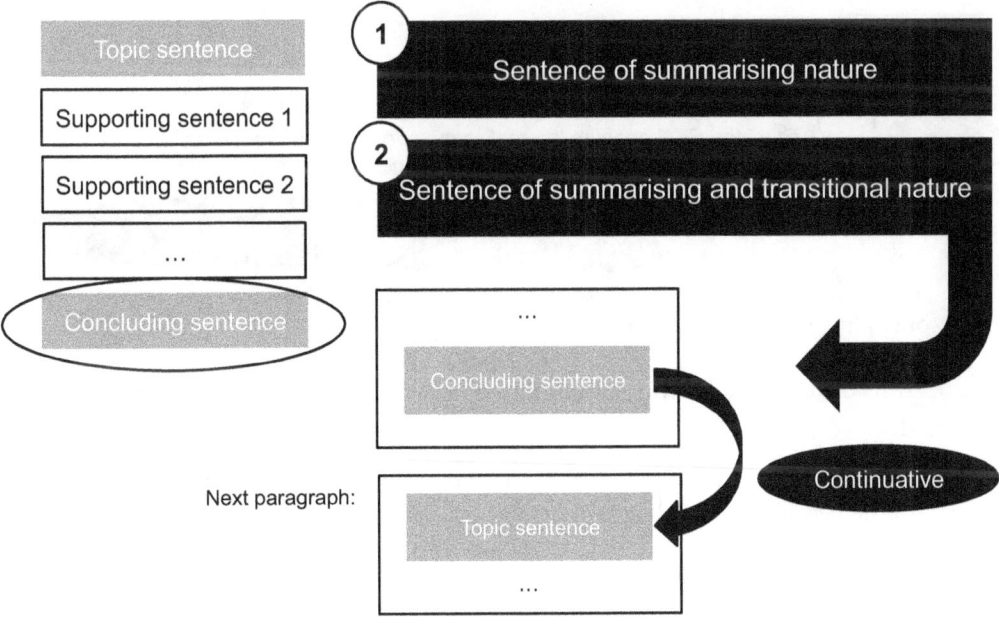

Figure 12.10: Concluding sentence

12 Argumentation

Ideally, the final sentence of a paragraph is continuative. It presents a step forward referring to the main idea stated in the topic sentence and leads on to the next main argument that will be dealt with in the next paragraph.

In the following, the example paragraph is continued by sentences that support and elaborate the topic sentence.

The first example of a concluding sentence has a summarising function (Figure 12.11):

> "Thus, the EEG enables the realisation of renewable energy projects that otherwise would not be feasible due to uncertain market conditions."

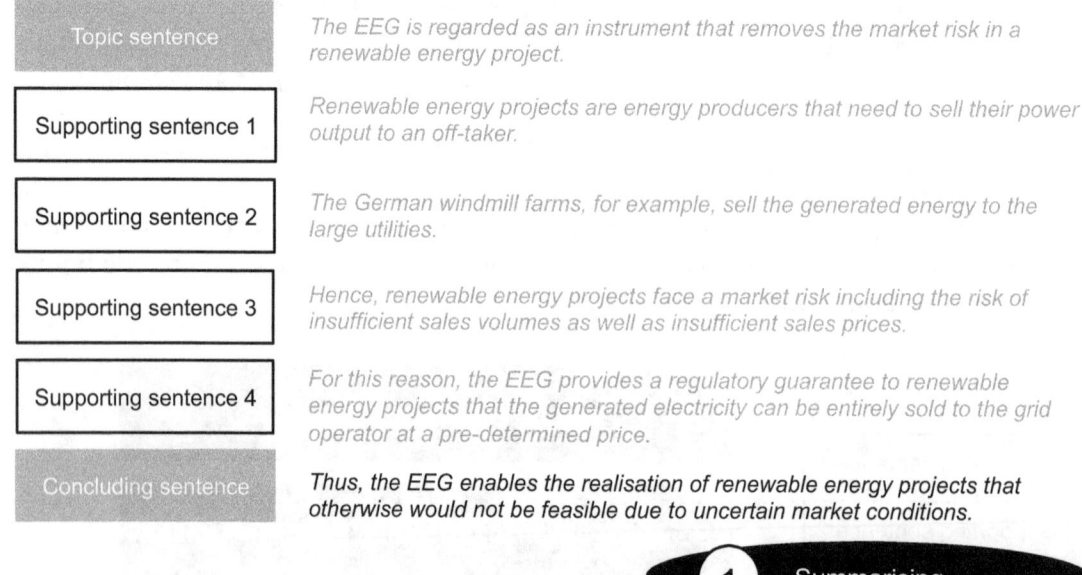

Figure 12.11: Concluding sentence – summarising

The second example of a concluding sentence has a summarising and transitional function (Figure 12.12):

> "Currently, the EEG enables the realisation of renewable energy projects that otherwise would not be feasible due to uncertain market conditions."

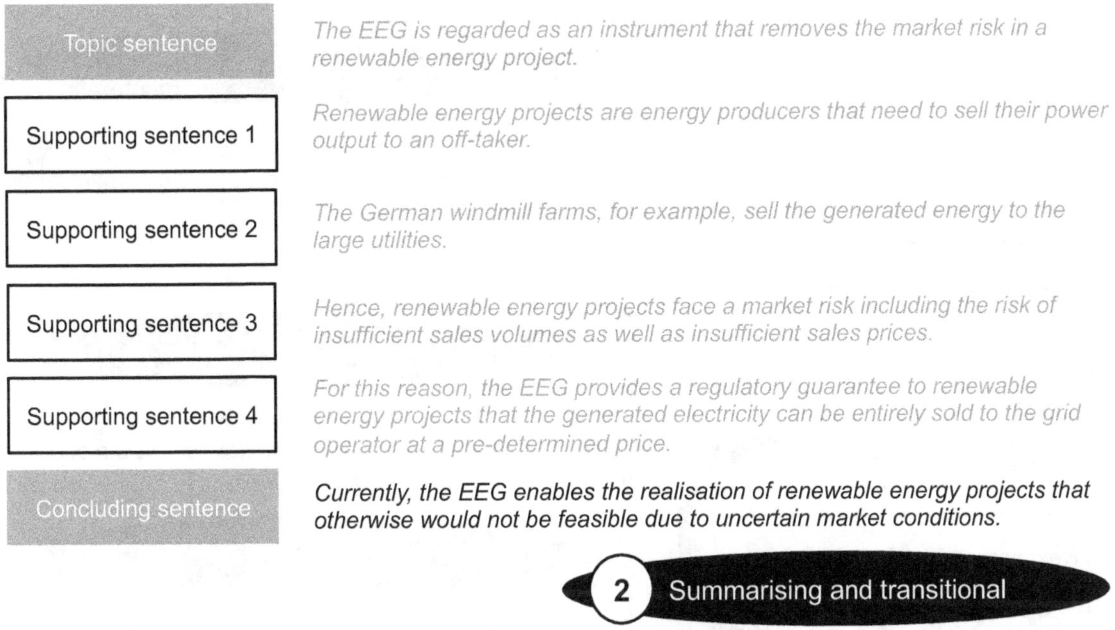

12.3 Structure of a paragraph

Topic sentence	*The EEG is regarded as an instrument that removes the market risk in a renewable energy project.*
Supporting sentence 1	*Renewable energy projects are energy producers that need to sell their power output to an off-taker.*
Supporting sentence 2	*The German windmill farms, for example, sell the generated energy to the large utilities.*
Supporting sentence 3	*Hence, renewable energy projects face a market risk including the risk of insufficient sales volumes as well as insufficient sales prices.*
Supporting sentence 4	*For this reason, the EEG provides a regulatory guarantee to renewable energy projects that the generated electricity can be entirely sold to the grid operator at a pre-determined price.*
Concluding sentence	*Currently, the EEG enables the realisation of renewable energy projects that otherwise would not be feasible due to uncertain market conditions.*

(2) Summarising and transitional

Figure 12.12: Concluding sentence – summarising and transitional

A closer look at the two options of concluding sentences is provided in Figure 12.13.

- As explained, the first example of a concluding sentence has a summarising function. This is indicated by the adverb "thus" in the beginning of the sentence.
- The second example of a concluding sentence additionally has a transitional function. The adverb "currently" provides a transitional indication of the next argument, laid out in the next paragraph.

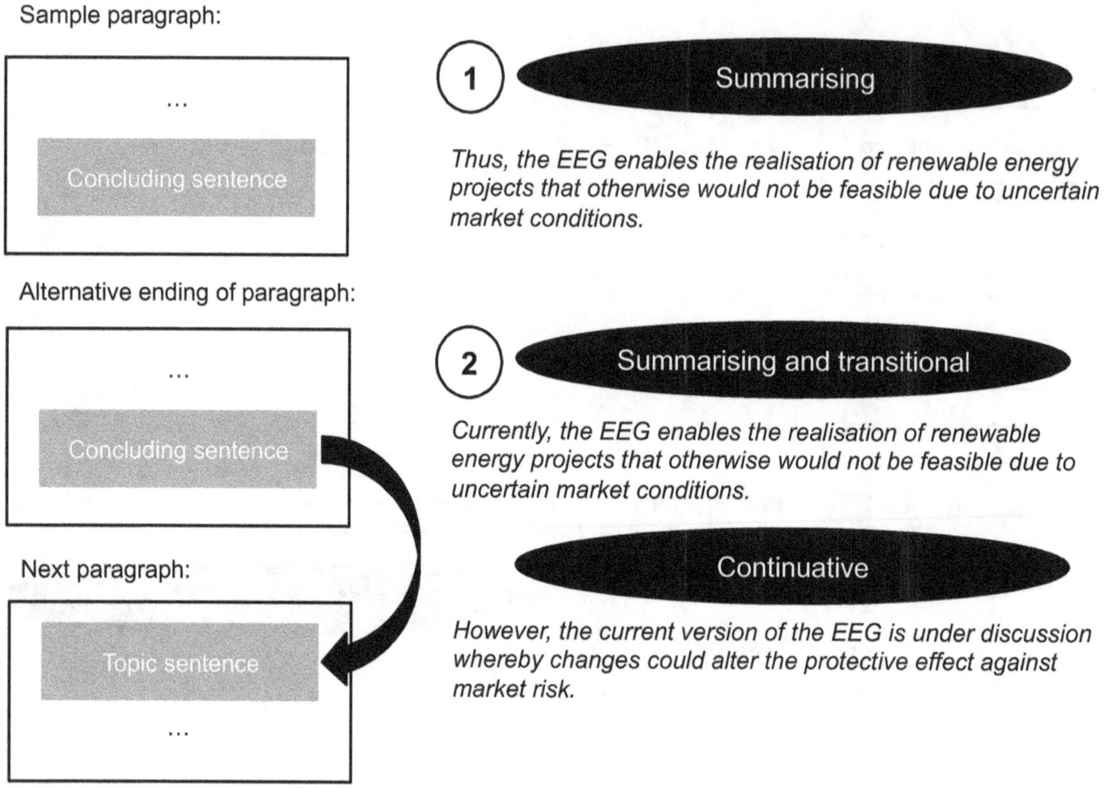

12 Argumentation

Sample paragraph:

1 Summarising

Thus, the EEG enables the realisation of renewable energy projects that otherwise would not be feasible due to uncertain market conditions.

Alternative ending of paragraph:

2 Summarising and transitional

Currently, the EEG enables the realisation of renewable energy projects that otherwise would not be feasible due to uncertain market conditions.

Continuative

However, the current version of the EEG is under discussion whereby changes could alter the protective effect against market risk.

Figure 12.13: Concluding sentence – continuative

Referring to the transitional character of the concluding sentence, the next paragraph could start with the following topic sentence continuing the discussion:

> "However, the current version of the EEG is under discussion whereby changes could alter the protective effect against market risk."

12.3.5 Cohesion

As discussed in subchapter 11.3.2, arguments have to be provided with cohesion. Accordingly, connective and transitional wording should support the logical flow within a paragraph. This is shown in the following example:

> The EEG is regarded as an instrument that removes the market risk in a renewable energy project. Renewable energy projects are energy producers that need to sell their power output to an off-taker. The German windmill farms, **for example**, sell the gener-

ated energy to the large utilities. **Hence**, renewable energy projects face a market risk including the risk of insufficient sales volumes as well as insufficient sales prices. **For this reason**, the EEG provides a regulatory guarantee to renewable energy projects that the generated electricity can be entirely sold to the grid operator at a pre-determined price. **Currently**, the EEG enables the realisation of renewable energy projects that otherwise would not be feasible due to uncertain market conditions.

In the example, the connective words are highlighted.

12.3.6 Indentation

There are two options of paragraph layout in British English:

- If the paragraph is the first paragraph after a heading, the first line should not be indented.

    The EEG is regarded as an instrument that removes the market risk in a renewable energy project. Renewable energy projects are energy producers that need to sell their power output to an off-taker. The German windmill farms, for example, sell the generated energy to the large utilities. Hence, ...

- If the paragraph is not the first paragraph after a heading, the first line should be indented.

    The EEG is regarded as an instrument that removes the market risk in a renewable energy project. Renewable energy projects are energy producers that need to sell their power output to an off-taker. The German windmill farms, for example, sell the generated energy to the large utilities. Hence, ...

It should be noted that in American English the beginning of a paragraph is always indented whether under a heading or not.

ᵂ Tip

With regard to the applicable indentation, it is advisable to refer to the required style guide standards or the individual institutional rules.

12.4 Flow of paragraphs

12.4.1 From paragraph to paragraph

As pointed out, a paragraph is a collection of sentences structured into a beginning, middle and end. Nevertheless, paragraphs are not isolated text elements, but merely the smaller units of a larger piece of argumentation: the chapter. Accordingly, it is preferable that paragraphs support the flow of argumentation within the chapter. Just as the sentences within a paragraph should follow a logical flow – ideally driven forward by connective elements such as adverbs and conjunctions – the whole ensemble of paragraphs should show a logical structure and cohesion as well.

A helpful technique to ensure the logical flow of paragraphs is transitioning (Figure 12.14).

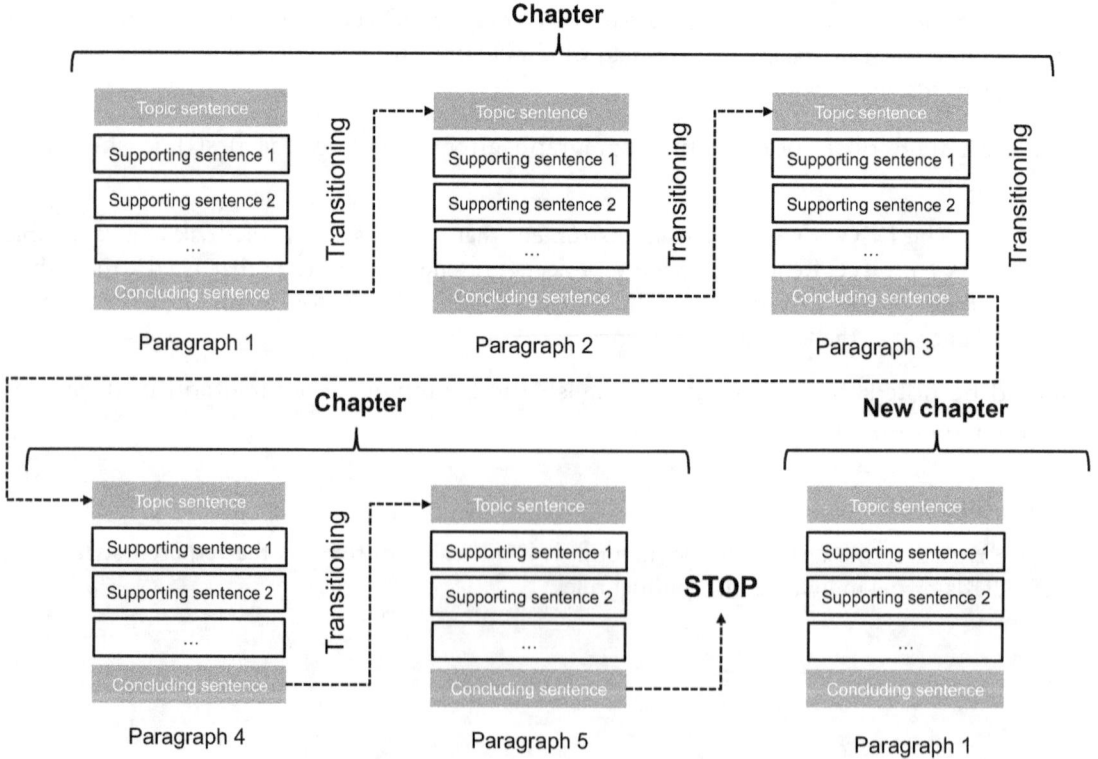

Figure 12.14: From paragraph to paragraph

At some point, it is not possible to generate a transition from one paragraph to the other, because the main idea of the new paragraph cannot be connected to the previously said. Then, the new paragraph might be logically disconnected and should be placed elsewhere, maybe even in another chapter. Therefore, the method of connecting and transitioning helps to test the logic of one's argumentation and guides the reader through the writer's thinking.

As explained before, transitioning between paragraphs can provide cohesion within a chapter. Figure 12.15 shows examples of transitional elements.

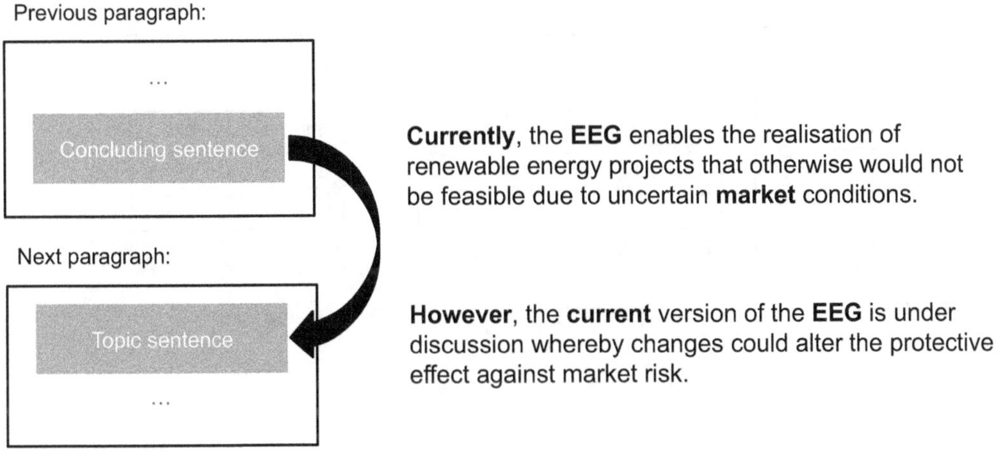

Previous paragraph:

Currently, the **EEG** enables the realisation of renewable energy projects that otherwise would not be feasible due to uncertain **market** conditions.

Next paragraph:

However, the **current** version of the **EEG** is under discussion whereby changes could alter the protective effect against market risk.

Figure 12.15: Sample transitioning

The paragraph ends with the concluding sentence:

> "Currently, the EEG enables the realisation of renewable energy projects that otherwise would not be feasible due to uncertain market conditions."

Referring to this, the next paragraph could start with the following topic sentence.

> "However, the current version of the EEG is under discussion whereby changes could alter the protective effect against market risk."

The linguistic means to indicate the connection between the arguments of the previous and the next paragraph and to provide cohesion within the text are

- using the adverb currently and restating the word current
- starting the next paragraph with the transitional adverb "However"

- restating key terms such as " EEG" and "market (conditions/risk)"

12.4.2 From paragraph to chapter

As discussed above, the flow of paragraphs within a chapter should be developed by logically structuring one's arguments. However, at some point, the flow of paragraphs within a chapter will come to an end. This indicates that the logical structure requires a new chapter (Figure 12.16).

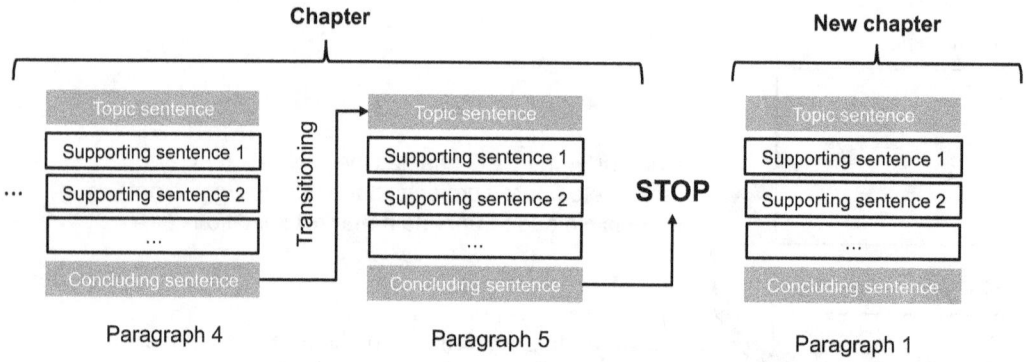

Figure 12.16: From paragraph to chapter

The following indicates that it is not necessary to start a new paragraph, but rather a new chapter:

- The next argument deviates from the topic of the chapter and cannot be subsumed under the chapter heading. In other words, within a given chapter there is no main idea left that could be stated in a new topic sentence.
- There are new key terms and elements that have not been introduced. In other words, new key terms and facts have to be tackled within a new chapter.

12.4.3 Iterative character of chapter structuring

Writing a research paper is an on-going process. As one dives deeper into the research question to be addressed, new ideas and insights to the topic will develop. An adjustment of the previously drafted outline might be necessary. For example, one might come to the conclusion that there is no need for a previously planned chapter. Moreover, one might realise that a chapter corresponds with another chapter already under construction. Here, it becomes necessary to merge two chapters as illustrated in Figure 12.17.

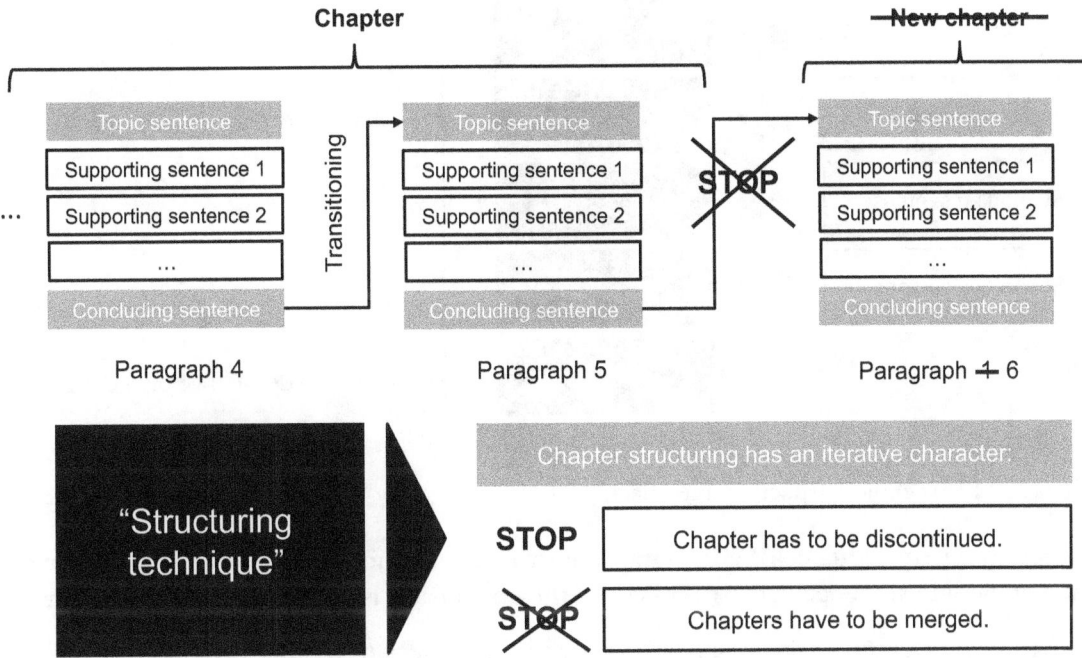

Figure 12.17: Iterative chapter structuring

While the rules of structuring technique are applied, it may be necessary to adjust the details of an outline. Therefore, chapter structuring has an iterative character:

- In some cases, chapters have to be discontinued in order to start a new chapter.
- In other cases, chapters have to be merged.

12.5 Reasoning

12.5.1 Technical aspects

The principle of accuracy requires meticulous and complete referencing (Figure 12.18).

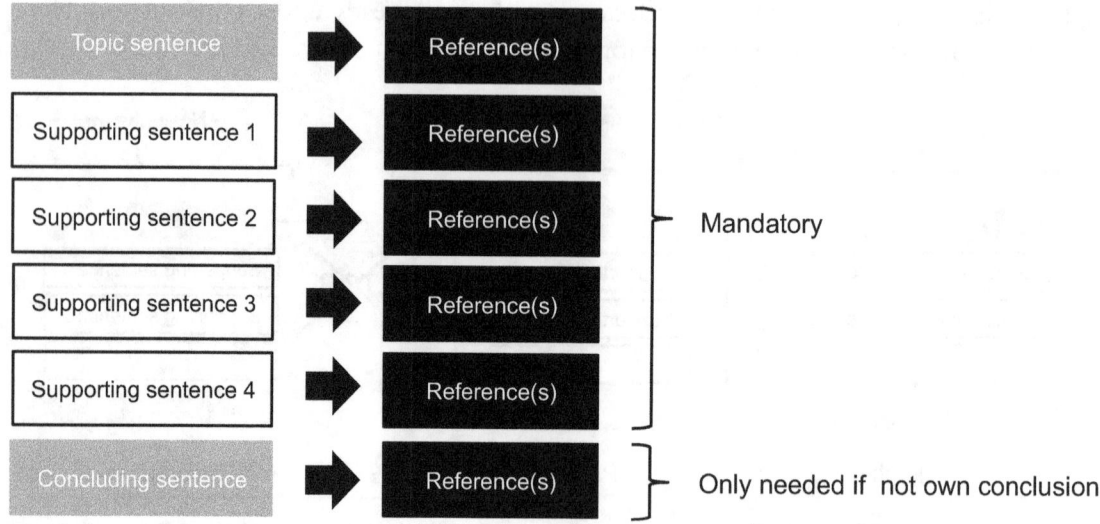

Figure 12.18: Technical aspects – references

Generally, every sentence of a paragraph has to be referenced to a source. A reference to the concluding sentence is not necessary if the conclusion is based upon own thoughts.

The following example shows a paragraph with references (references are highlighted):

> The EEG is regarded as an instrument that removes the market risk in a renewable energy project **(Meyer, 2007, p. 15)**. Renewable energy projects are energy producers that need to sell their power output to an off-taker **(Schmidt, 2010, p. 235)**. The German windmill farms, for example, sell the generated energy to the large utilities **(Braun, 2012, p. 130)**. Hence, renewable energy projects face a market risk including the risk of insufficient sales volumes as well as insufficient sales prices **(Black, 2014, p. 445)**. For this reason, the EEG provides a regulatory guarantee to renewable energy projects that the generated electricity can be entirely sold to the grid operator at a pre-determined price **(Peterson, 2011, p. 3)**. Currently, the EEG enables the realisation of renewable energy projects that otherwise would not be feasible due to uncertain market conditions **(Baker, 2014, p. 47)**.

As illustrated, all sentences have been referenced to a source.

12.5.2 Qualitative aspects

There are some aspects of signalling quality that have to be considered while referencing arguments:

- One should avoid excessive and/or repetitive citation of the same sources.
- If available and reasonable, more than one source should be stated for a sentence.
- One should indicate supportive references that fortify the argumentation.
- One should indicate contradictory references that do not support the argumentation.

The following (negative) example shows a paragraph with excessive referencing of the same source (references are highlighted):

> The EEG is regarded as an instrument that removes the market risk in a renewable energy project **(Meyer, 2007, p. 15)**. Renewable energy projects are energy producers that need to sell their power output to an off-taker **(Schmidt, 2010, p. 235)**. The German windmill farms, for example, sell the generated energy to the large utilities **(Meyer, 2007, p. 15)**. Hence, renewable energy projects face a market risk including the risk of insufficient sales volumes as well as insufficient sales prices **(ibid)**. For this reason, the EEG provides a regulatory guarantee to renewable energy projects that the generated electricity can be entirely sold to the grid operator at a pre-determined price **(ibid, p. 16)**. Currently, the EEG enables the realisation of renewable energy projects that otherwise would not be feasible due to uncertain market conditions **(ibid)**.

As demonstrated in the example, Schmidt has been cited once and Meyer has been cited five times. These references signal that proper literature research probably did not take place.

The following example shows a paragraph with references stating more than one source for a sentence (references are highlighted):

> The EEG is regarded as an instrument that removes the market risk in a renewable energy project **(Meyer, 2007, p. 15, McDougal, 2012, p. 5)**. Renewable energy projects are energy producers that need to sell their power output to an off-taker **(Schmidt, 2010, p. 235, Black, 2014, p. 445)**. The German windmill farms, for example, sell the generated energy to the large utilities **(Braun, 2012, p. 130, Jackson, 2005, p. 7, Moore, 20013, p. 56)**. Hence, renewable energy projects face a market risk including the risk of insufficient sales volumes as well as insufficient sales prices **(Black, 2014, p. 445, Miller, 2006, p. 24)**. For this reason, the EEG provides a regulatory guarantee to renewable energy projects that the generated electricity can be entirely sold to the grid operator at a pre-determined price **(Peterson, 2011, p. 3, Johnson, 2010, p. 67)**. Currently, the EEG enables the realisation of renewable energy projects that otherwise would not be feasible due to uncertain market conditions **(Baker, 2014, p. 47, Stone, 2012, p. 22)**.

These references signal proper literature research and a deep knowledge of the available academic literature.

The following example shows a paragraph with references of a supporting or a contradictory nature (references are highlighted):

> The EEG is regarded as an instrument that removes the market risk in a renewable energy project (Meyer, 2007, p. 15, **also Braun 2012, p. 129**). Renewable energy projects are energy producers that need to sell their power output to an off-taker (Schmidt, 2010, p. 235). The German windmill farms, for example, sell the generated energy to the large utilities (Braun, 2012, p. 130). Hence, renewable energy projects face a market risk including the risk of insufficient sales volumes as well as insufficient sales prices (Black, 2014, p. 445). For this reason, the EEG provides a regulatory guarantee to renewable energy projects that the generated electricity can be entirely sold to the grid operator at a predetermined price (Peterson, 2011, p. 3). Currently, the EEG enables the realisation of renewable energy projects that otherwise would not be feasible due to uncertain market conditions (Baker, 2014, p. 47, **deviant Jackson, 2005, p. 9**).

Whereas the first sentence is complemented with a supportive source, indicated by the word "also", the last sentence is amended with a contradictory source that states a contradictory opinion, indicated by the word "deviant". Again, these references signal proper literature research and a deep knowledge of the available academic literature.

12.5.3 Personal contribution

After having discussed some technical and qualitative aspects of reasoning and referencing, finally, the aspect of one's personal contribution needs to be addressed.

Often students that have to work on a research project ask the question:

> "If every sentence can be traced back to a source, what is my personal contribution?

This question addresses the issue of compilation versus combination (Figure 12.19):

- In case of a meaningless compilation, a sequence of sentences and corresponding references does not support the argumentation.
- In case of meaningful combination, the sequence of sentences and corresponding references supports the argumentation.

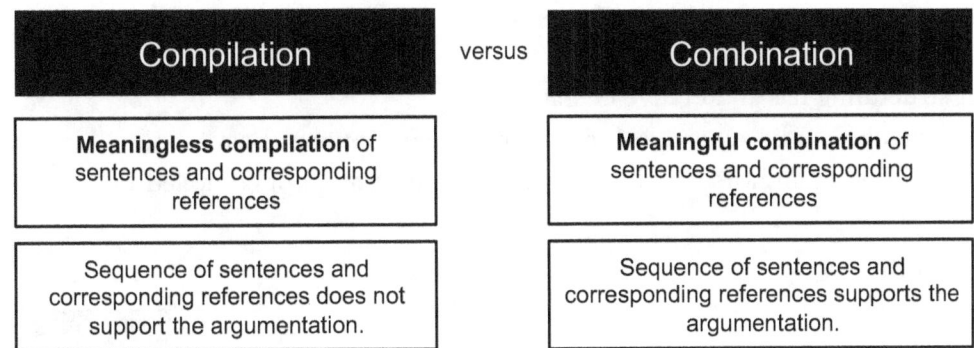

Figure 12.19: Personal contribution

In other words, the personal contribution lies in designing a paragraph that is logically driving one's reasoning while being referenced to relevant academic sources.

Advancing from a compilation to a combination style can be a challenge. The best way to rise to this challenge is to practise the art of meaningfully combining sentences and their corresponding references.

12.6 Summary and exercises

12.6.1 Synopsis

Chapter 12 provided a brief introduction to the principles of argumentation:

- Defining key terms is essential for every research project.
- Definitions can be derived with the help of the standard, advanced or professional approach.
- Paragraphs are units of academic papers.
- Topic sentence, supporting sentences and concluding sentence represent the logical structure of a paragraph.
- Connective and transitional wording supports the logical flow within a paragraph and provides cohesion.
- Indenting in British English differs slightly from indenting in American English.
- Transitioning from paragraph to paragraph supports the flow of argumentation within the chapter.

- Transitioning from paragraph to chapter supports the flow of argumentation between chapters.
- Chapter structuring has an iterative character.
- Academic quality can be achieved by referencing that supports the reasoning.
- Arguments of other authors should rather be combined and not compiled.

12.6.2 Questions

Knowledge

1. What is the purpose of providing definitions?
2. Which terms have to be defined in a research paper?
3. What are the three approaches of deriving definitions for a research paper?
4. What are the four characteristics of a paragraph?
5. What is the basic logical structure of a paragraph?
6. Which chapters of a research paper are exempted from the basic logical structure of a paragraph?
7. What is a topic sentence?
8. What are general rules of formulating a topic sentence?
9. What are supporting sentences?
10. What may be discussed in supporting sentences?
11. What is a concluding sentence?
12. What are two characteristics of a concluding sentence?
13. How can cohesion within a paragraph be achieved?
14. What are the rules for indenting?
15. What is transitioning within a chapter?
16. What are indications to start a new chapter?
17. Why is chapter structuring an iterative process?
18. Which sentences of a paragraph require mandatory referencing?
19. In which case is it not necessary to reference a concluding sentence of a paragraph?
20. What signals quality while referencing arguments?

12.6.3 Final problem

Synthesis

Learning target

Being able to transform a journalistic article into a research paper based on the principles of academic research and writing

Instructions

Please read the following article:

Anonymous (2015, March 28). Universities: The world is going to university, *The Economist*. Retrieved from http://www.economist.com

1. Derive a topic, an aim and a corresponding research question from the information provided in the article
2. Develop an outline that matches your research question
3. Search and retrieve additional literature
4. Develop advanced definitions for selected key terms
5. (Re-)Formulate the text based on a logical paragraph structure

12.6.4 Additional reading

Lapakko, D. (2014). *Argumentation: Critical Thinking in Action* (3rd ed.). New York City: iUniverse.

List of figures

Figure 1.1: Similarities of sample cases 4
Figure 1.2: Academia – overview 5
Figure 1.3: Dimensions of the term theory 8
Figure 1.4: Method, set of methods, methodology 9
Figure 1.5: Reality, truth, ontology 10
Figure 1.6: Theories of truth 11
Figure 1.7: Ontological positions 12
Figure 1.8: Epistemic objectives 14
Figure 1.9: Reductive models and constructive models 16
Figure 1.10: Topic structure of academic research and writing 17
Figure 2.1: Context of chapter 2 26
Figure 2.2: Intersubjective comprehensibility 28
Figure 2.3: Status quo of discipline 35
Figure 2.4: Expectancy of deviations 36
Figure 2.5: Reduction of inherent complexity 37
Figure 2.6: Decision usefulness 38
Figure 3.1: Context of chapter 3 44
Figure 3.2: Types of reasoning 45
Figure 3.3: Inductive reasoning 46
Figure 3.4: Deductive reasoning 47
Figure 3.5: Syllogism 48
Figure 3.6: Quantity and quality of conclusions 49
Figure 3.7: Types of propositions 50

List of figures

Figure 3.8: Deductive-nomological model – explanation 51
Figure 3.9: Deductive-nomological model – forecast 52
Figure 3.10: Inductive-statistical model 53
Figure 3.11: Problems of inductive-statistical reasoning 55
Figure 3.12: Modus ponens 56
Figure 3.13: Modus tollens 57
Figure 3.14: Falsification, verification 58
Figure 3.15: Falsification of a hypothesis with modus tollens 60
Figure 3.16: Generation of indicator hypotheses 61
Figure 3.17: Indicator hypotheses – examples 61
Figure 3.18: Causal hypothesis – example 62
Figure 3.19: Induction, deduction and theory 64
Figure 4.1: Context of chapter 4 70
Figure 4.2: Differentiation of questions 72
Figure 4.3: Interrogative words 73
Figure 4.4: Types of hypothesis – overview 74
Figure 4.5: Research approaches – overview 78
Figure 4.6: Philosophical research 79
Figure 4.7: Developmental research 79
Figure 4.8: Empirical research 80
Figure 4.9: Mixed research approach – example 81
Figure 4.10: Three types of scientific style 82
Figure 4.11: Theoretical solution-driven style – technique 83
Figure 4.12: Empirical solution-driven style – technique 84
Figure 4.13: Hypothesis-driven style 85

List of figures

Figure 5.1: Context of chapter 5 ... 90

Figure 5.2: Combinations of topic and title ... 96

Figure 5.3: Clarity while verbalising a topic ... 97

Figure 5.4: Refining a topic – example 1 ... 98

Figure 5.5: Refining a topic – example 2 ... 99

Figure 6.1: Context of chapter 6 ... 104

Figure 6.2: Relevance of academic literature ... 105

Figure 6.3: Relevance of empirical data ... 106

Figure 6.4: Double-blind peer review ... 114

Figure 6.5: Journal Impact Factor (JIF) – sample calculation ... 116

Figure 6.6: Information access and retrieval ... 118

Figure 6.7: OPAC search logic – example ... 120

Figure 6.8: Thesaurus – example ... 122

Figure 6.9: Boolean operations ... 125

Figure 6.10: Phrase searching – example ... 126

Figure 7.1: Context of chapter 7 ... 132

Figure 7.2: The four sections of a research paper ... 133

Figure 7.3: Page numbering ... 134

Figure 7.4: Structural elements always used in a research paper ... 136

Figure 7.5: Structural elements optionally used in a research paper ... 137

Figure 7.6: Structural elements selectively used in a research paper ... 138

Figure 7.7: Keywords of an abstract – example ... 142

Figure 7.8: Decadal numbering system – example ... 143

Figure 7.9: Alphanumerical numbering – example ... 144

Figure 7.10: List of figures and list of tables – options ... 145

List of figures

Figure 7.11: Abbreviation – example 146

Figure 7.12: Incomplete numbering, illogical structure – example 148

Figure 7.13: Complete numbering, illogical structure – example 149

Figure 7.14: Complete numbering, logical structure – example 150

Figure 7.15: Incomplete structuring – example 150

Figure 7.16: Intermediate text – example 151

Figure 7.17: Parenthetical referencing vs. footnote referencing 153

Figure 7.18: Structured bibliography or list of references – sample 154

Figure 8.1: Context of chapter 8 160

Figure 8.2: Interpretation of a topic – process steps 161

Figure 8.3: Negative interpretation – definition of terminology 162

Figure 8.4: Interpretation – possible aims 163

Figure 8.5: Deciding on an aim by identifying the nature of the task 164

Figure 8.6: Sample case "Windy decision" – context, nature of the task, functional aim 165

Figure 8.7: Abstract analysis of potential aims 166

Figure 8.8: Abstract analysis – description 167

Figure 8.9: Description – examples of research questions 168

Figure 8.10: Abstract analysis – causal connection 168

Figure 8.11: Causal connection – examples of research questions 169

Figure 8.12: Abstract analysis – intention 170

Figure 8.13: Intention – examples of research questions 171

Figure 8.14: Abstract analysis – functional approach 171

Figure 8.15: Functional approach – examples of research questions 172

Figure 8.16: Abstract analysis – comparison 173

Figure 8.17: Comparison – examples of topics and research questions 173

List of figures

Figure 8.18: Sample case, nature of the task, research question – examples 179

Figure 9.1: Context of chapter 9 184

Figure 9.2: Refining a research question 185

Figure 9.3: Refining a research question – example 186

Figure 9.4: Deductive reasoning – example 188

Figure 9.5: Deductive reasoning – structure of the subchapter "Research problem" 189

Figure 9.6: Structure of the research problem – sample text 190

Figure 9.7: Aligning research question with structure of outline 191

Figure 9.8: Structure of the outline – functional approach 192

Figure 9.9: Aligning the outline with the course of investigation 194

Figure 9.10: The triangle of synchronisation 195

Figure 9.11: The two options of placing the description of the research method 196

Figure 9.12: Summary – purpose and structure 197

Figure 9.13: Aligning summary and outline – example 198

Figure 9.14: Critical acclaim 199

Figure 9.15: Outlook 200

Figure 9.16: Interpretation-based structuring – overview 201

Figure 9.17: Interpretation-based structuring – description 203

Figure 9.18: Interpretation-based structuring – causal connection 204

Figure 9.19: Interpretation-based structuring – intention 205

Figure 9.20: Interpretation-based structuring – function 206

Figure 9.21: Interpretation-based structuring – comparison 208

Figure 9.22: Variations of the IMRaD approach 210

Figure 9.23: Hourglass model 211

Figure 10.1: Context of chapter 10 218

List of figures

Figure 10.2: Logic of references 219

Figure 10.3: Translation of citations 222

Figure 11.1: Context of chapter 11 238

Figure 11.2: The language of science 239

Figure 11.3: Structure, cohesion, coherence 249

Figure 12.1: Context of chapter 12 264

Figure 12.2: Purpose of definitions 265

Figure 12.3: Definitions – coverage 266

Figure 12.4: Definitions – technique 267

Figure 12.5: Logical structure of a paragraph 269

Figure 12.6: Topic sentence – from too general to too specific 270

Figure 12.7: Topic sentence – example 271

Figure 12.8: Supporting sentences 271

Figure 12.9: Supporting sentences – example 272

Figure 12.10: Concluding sentence 273

Figure 12.11: Concluding sentence – summarising 274

Figure 12.12: Concluding sentence – summarising and transitional 275

Figure 12.13: Concluding sentence – continuative 276

Figure 12.14: From paragraph to paragraph 278

Figure 12.15: Sample transitioning 279

Figure 12.16: From paragraph to chapter 280

Figure 12.17: Iterative chapter structuring 281

Figure 12.18: Technical aspects – references 282

Figure 12.19: Personal contribution 285

List of tables

Table 3.1: Advantages and disadvantages of models 54
Table 3.2: Comparison of induction and deduction 63
Table 5.1: Characteristics of abstract and problem-based aims – overview 93
Table 5.2: Idealised process of identifying and refining a topic 94
Table 6.1: Sample titles of textbooks, advanced textbooks, and monographs 107
Table 6.2: Examples of citation indices 115
Table 6.3: Sample literature search 121
Table 6.4: Truncation – examples 123
Table 7.1: Structural elements and their application 139
Table 7.2: Non-physical elements, electronic submission 155
Table 10.1: Major styles 226
Table 10.2: Academic abbreviations 233
Table 11.1: Characteristics of writing styles 240
Table 11.2: Principles of accuracy and clarity – be specific 242
Table 11.3: Principles of accuracy and clarity – omit the needless 243
Table 11.4: Principles of accuracy and clarity – beware of adjectives 244
Table 11.5: Principles of accuracy and clarity – avoid subjectivity 245
Table 11.6: Principles of accuracy and clarity – apply factual tonality 246
Table 11.7: Principles of accuracy and clarity – focus on clear phrasing 247
Table 11.8: Conjunctive adverbs 250
Table 11.9: Subordinating connectors and their function 252

List of abbreviations

ACS	American Chemical Society, Washington, D.C./USA
AE	American English
AMA	American Medical Association, Chicago, Illinois/USA
APA	American Psychological Association, Washington, D.C./USA
ASA	American Sociological Association, Washington, D.C./USA
BE	British English
cf.	confer (bring together, compare, consult)
CMOS	Chicago Manual of Style
CoCo	contingent convertible (bank bonds)
DN	deductive-nomological
doi	digital object identifier
EBSCO	EBSCO Information Services, Birmingham, Alabama/USA
Ed.	editors
ed.	edition
EEG	German renewable energy act
et al.	et alii/aliae (and other people)
HO	Hempel-Oppenheim
ibid.	ibidem (in the same place)
IS	inductive-statistical
ISBN	International Standard Book Number
ISSN	International Standard Serial Number
ISO	International Organization for Standardization, Vernier, Switzerland
JEL	Journal of Economic Literature
JIF	Journal Impact Factor

List of abbreviations

JSTORE	Journal STORage
l.c.	loco citato (in the place cited)
MHRA	Modern Humanities Research Association, Cambridge, England/UK
MLA	Modern Language Association, New York, NY/USA
n. d.	no date
n. p.	no place of publication and/or no publisher
n. pag.	not paginated
OPAC	Open Public Access Catalogue
Ph.D.	Doctor of Philosophy
SCCI	Social Science Citation Index
SSRN	Social Sciences Research Network

Bibliography

American Psychological Association (2013). *Publication Manual oft the American Psychological Association* [Kindle edition] (6th ed.), Washington, DC: Author.

Anonymous (2010, August 19). Boxing clever: Are container derivatives poised for bumper growth? *The Economist*. Retrieved from http://www.economist.com

Anonymous (2009, July 16). Financial Economics: Efficiency and beyond. *The Economist*. Retrieved from http://www.economist.com

Anonymous (2008, April 3). German lessons: An ambitious cross-subsidy scheme has given rise to a new industry. *The Economist*. Retrieved from http://www.economist.com

Anonymous (2005, September 15). Limited appeal. One giant step across Europe may find few imitators. *The Economist*. Retrieved from http://www.economist.com

Anonymous (2009, January 23). Lip service: What lipstick sales tell you about the economy. *The Economist*. Retrieved from http://www.economist.com

Anonymous (2013, February 9). Merkel Loses Minister: Schavan Steps Down amid Plagiarism Scandal. *Spiegel Online International*. Retrieved from http://www.spiegel.de

Anonymous (2012, July 14). QE, or not QE? An assessment oft the most controversial weapon in the central banker's armoury. *The Economist*. Retrieved from http://www.economist.com

Barnes, J. (2000). *Aristotle. A Very Short Introduction* [Kindle edition]. New York, NY: Oxford University Press.

Bell, J., & Waters, S. (2014). *Doing Your Research Project: A Guide for First-time Researchers* (6th ed.). Maidenhead, England: Open University Press/McGraw-Hill-Education.

Bhattacharjee, Y. (2013, April 26). The Mind of a Con Man. *New York Times*. Retrieved from http://www.nytimes.com

Biggam, J. (2015). *Succeeding with Your Master's Dissertation. A step-by-step handbook* [Kindle edition] (3rd ed.). Maidenhead, England: Open University Press/McGraw-Hill-Education.

Booth, W. C., Colomb, G. G., & Williams, J. M. (2008). *The Craft of research* (3rd ed.). Chicago, Il: The University of Chicago Press.

Briggle, A, & Mitcham, C. (2012). *Ethics and Science: An Introduction*. Cambridge, England: Cambridge University Press.

Briotta Paroloa, P. D., Pan, R. K., Ghoshb, R., Hubermanc, B. A., Kaskia, K., & Fortunato, S. (2015, March 9). *Attention decay in science*. Preprint. Retrieved from http://arxiv.org

Bibliography

Bryman, A., & Bell, E. (2011). *Business Research Methods*. [Kindle edition] (3rd ed.). Oxford, England: Oxford University Press.

Chalmers, A. (2013). *What is this thing called science?* (4th ed.)., Maidenhead, England: Open University press/McGraw-Hill-Education.

Chernin, E. (1988). The "Harvard" system: A mystery dispelled. *British Medical Journal, 297*, 1062–1063. Retrieved from http://www.ncbi.nlm.nih.gov/pmc/articles/PMC2056883/

Coleman, R. (2003, December 1). Pardon My Proper English. *The Scientist*. Retrieved from http://www.the-scientist.com

Coyne, K. P., & Coyne, S. T. (2011, March). Seven steps to better brainstorming. *McKinsey Quarterly*. Retrieved from http://www.mckinsey.com

Creswell, J. W. (2014). *Educational Research: Planning, Conducting and Evaluating Quantitative and Qualitative Research* [Kindle edition] (4th ed.). Harlow, England: Pearson Education.

D'Angelo, J. (2012). *Ethics in Science: Ethical Misconduct in Scientific Research*. Boca Raton/Florida, USA: CRC Press, Taylor & Francis Group.

Dollahite, N. E., & Haun, J. (2012). *Sourcework: Academic Writing from Sources* (2nd ed). Boston/MA, USA: Heinle Cengage Learning.

Easterby-Smith, M., Thorpe, R., & Jackson, P. (2012). *Management Research* [Kindle edition] (4th ed.). London, England: Sage.

Hempel, C. G., & Oppenheim, P. (1948). Studies in the Logic of Explanation. *Philosophy of Science, 15*(2), 135–175. doi:10-1086/286983

Hogue, A., & Hogue, J. (2003). *The Essentials of English: A Writer's Handbook (with APA Style)*. Harlow, England: Longman.

Jaffe, S. (2003, March 10). No Pardon For Poor English in Science. *The Scientist*. Retrieved from http://www.the-scientist.com

Kumar, R. (2014): *Research Methodology: A step-by-step guide for beginners* [Kindle edition] (4th ed.). London: Sage.

Lapakko, D. (2014). *Argumentation: Critical Thinking in Action* (3rd ed.). New York City: iUniverse.

Macgilchrist, F. (2014). *Academic Writing*. Stuttgart: UTB.

Mallon, R. (2013), Naturalistic Approaches to Social Construction. In E. N. Zalta (Ed.), *The Stanford Encyclopedia of Philosophy*, (Winter 2014 ed.), Retrieved from http://plato.stanford.edu/

Negishi, M., & Dvorak, P. (2013, December 13). In Japan, Scented Fabric Softeners Wrinkle Some Noses. *The Wall Street Journal*. Retrieved from http://www.wsj.com

Okasha, S. (2002). *Philosophy of Science. A Very Short Introduction* [Kindle edition]. New York, NY: Oxford University Press.

Popper, K. (2005). *The Logic of Scientific Discovery* [Kindle edition] (2nd ed.). London, England: Routledge.

Priest, G. (2000). *Logic: A Very Short Introduction* [Kindle edition]. New York, NY: Oxford University Press.

Saunders, M. N. K., Lewis, P., & Thornhill, A. (2012). *Research Methods for Business Students* [Kindle edition] (6th ed.), Harlow, England: Pearson.

Skern, T. (2011). *Writing Scientific English: A Workbook* (2nd ed.). Wien: Facultas/UTB.

Siepmann, G., & Hannay, M. (2011). *Writing in English: A Guide für Advanced Learners* (2nd ed.). Tübingen: A. Francke/UTB.

Swales, J. M., & Feak, C. B. (2012). *Academic Writing for Graduate Students: Essential Tasks and Skills* (3rd ed.). Ann Arbor/Michigan: University of Michigan Press.

Turabian, K. L. (2007). *A Manual for Writers of Research Papers, Theses, and Dissertations. Chicago Style for Students and Researchers* [Kindle edition] (7th ed.). Chicago, Il: The University of Chicago Press.

Wallwork, A. (2011). *English for Writing Research Papers*. New York: Springer.

Weber-Wulff, D. (2014). *False Feathers: A Perspective on Academic Plagiarism*. Berlin Heidelberg: Springer.

Keyword index

abbreviation 146
absolute truth 10
abstract 141
abstract aims 92, 93
abstract analysis 166
academia 5
academic abbreviations 232
academic articles 108
academic journal 108
academic language 97, 239
academic misconduct 32
academic principles 4, 25
academic writing 239, 240, 241
accuracy 27, 242
addments 133
ad-hoc hypotheses 75
adjectives 244
advanced structuring technique 209
AILDMRaD 210
AILMRaD 210
AIMRaD 210
alphanumerical numbering system 143
American English 254

annex 134
anthology 109
APA style 225
appendix 155
Arabic numerals 134
Aristotle 48
article 108
author-date method 225, 226
author-page method 225, 228
author-title method 225, 228
back matter 134
bibliography 152
Bing 118
body 134
body matter 134
Boolean operations 125
British English 254
Carl Gustav Hempel 51
causal connection 169
causal hypothesis 62
causality 168
cause-effect hypothesis 75
citability 111

citation	220
citation index	115
clarity	33, 97
clear phrasing	247
clearness	33, 97
closed-ended questions	71
coherence theory of truth	11
cohesion	249, 276
collected work	109
collusion	155
combination	284
comma	256
comparability	35
comparison	172
compilation	284
comprehensibility	247
concise dictionary	108
concluding sentence	269, 273
conclusion	196
conference paper	110
consensus theory of truth	12
constructionism	12
constructive models	15
consultation paper	111
correlation hypothesis	75
correspondence theory of truth	11
course of investigation	193
cover page	140
credibility	112
critical acclaim	198
critical rationalism	48
cross reference	224
currentness	30
cynicism	246
dashes	258
data carrier	156
decadal numbering system	143
decision on an aim	164
declaration of originality	155
deductive reasoning	45, 187
deductive-nomological model	51
definitions	265, 266
description	167
descriptive objective	14
descriptors	122
developmental research	79
difference hypothesis	75
direct citation	220, 221
direct questions	71
directories	133, 145

Keyword index

discussion paper	109
distribution hypothesis	75
DN model	51
edited book	109
edited volume	109
edited work	108
empirical data	105
empirical research	80
empirical solution-driven style	84
epistemic objectives	13
exclamation marks	258
existential propositions	58
explanation	225
explanatory objective	14
factual tonality	246
falsifiability	30
falsification	57
falsificationism	48
figures	152, 259
flow of paragraphs	278
footnote referencing	153, 230, 231
formulas	147
front matter	134
functional relation	171
generalisations	242
g-index	115
glossary	154
Google	118
green paper	110
grey literature	117
Harvard referencing	225
Harvard style	225
Harvard system	225
headwords	120
Hempel's model	51
Hempel-Oppenheim model	51
h-index	115
HO-Scheme	51
hourglass model	211
humour	246
hyphens	258
hypotheses	74
hypothesis	74
hypothesis-driven style	85
i10-index	115
Ibid	230
IMRaD	209
indenting	277
index terms	122
indication	223

Keyword index

indicator hypothesis	60
indirect citation	220, 223
indirect questions	71
inductive reasoning	45
inductive-statistical model	53
information	224
information access	92
intention	169
intermediate text	151
Internet	117
interpretation	161
interpretation-based structuring	200
interrogative words	72
intersubjective comprehensibility	29
IS model	54
JEL classification system	142
joker	123
Journal Impact Factor	116
Journal of Economic Literature	142
journal ranking	116
keywords	120
legal documents	111
legal sources	111
libraries	117
linking repetition	252
links within sentences	250
list of algorithms	147
list of equations	147
list of figures	145
list of figures and tables	145
list of formulas	147
list of references	152
list of symbols	147
list of tables	145
lists of abbreviations	146
literature	105
literature-based research	79
logical reasoning	48
main body	134
manual	111
materiality	36
method	8, 9
methodology	9
mixed research approaches	80
MLA style	225
model	15
modus ponens	55
modus tollens	56
monograph	106
motivation	91

Keyword index

negative interpretation 162
nomological hypothesis 76
non-academic language 239
numbering 147
objective 28
objectivism 12
objectivity 28
ontology 10, 12
OPAC 119, 120
open-ended questions 71
outline 143, 193, 198
outlook 199
page numbering 134
paragraphs 268
paraphrase 220
parenthetical referencing 153, 225, 229
Paul Oppenheim 51
peer review 113
perceptibility 29
personal contribution 284
philosophical research 78
phrase search 126
plagiarism 155
Popper-Hempel model 51
positive interpretation 163

predictive objective 15
prescriptive objective 14
problem-based aims 92, 93
problem-based interpretation 174
proper composition 34, 97
punctuation 256
qualification 91
qualitative completeness 32
qualitative research 80
quantitative completeness 32
quantitative research 80
quasi-nomological hypothesis 76
question marks 258
quotation 220
reader 109
reality 10
reasoning 45
reference 219
referencing 281
relative truth 10
reliability 29
research method 195
research paper 109
Roman numerals 134
science 6

Keyword index

sciences	5
scientific hypotheses	75
scientific styles	81
sections	133
set of methods	9
signalling quality	283
social constructivism	12
social ontology	12
Social Science Citation Index	115
special characters	259
statistical hypothesis	76
structural elements	135
structure of the outline	192
structured bibliography	231
structured list of references	231
STW Thesaurus for Economics	122
subjectivism	12
summary	197
supporting sentences	269, 271
syllogism	48
symbols	147, 259
table of contents	143
tables	152
technical paper	111
textbook	107
theoretical solution-driven style	83
theories of truth	11
theory	7, 8
thesaurus	121, 122
theses	75
thesis	77
timeliness	30
title	96
topic	95
topic sentence	269, 270
traceability	29
true and fair representation	31
truncation	123, 124
truth	9, 10
universal propositions	58
validity	30
verification	57
white book	110
white paper	110
wildcard	123
working hypotheses	75
working paper	109

www.ingramcontent.com/pod-product-compliance
Lightning Source LLC
Chambersburg PA
CBHW081945230426
43669CB00019B/2927